Learning to Survive

LEARNING TO SURVIVE

Yurok Well-Being in High School

Mneesha Gellman

With a foreword by Jim McQuillen

PENN

UNIVERSITY OF PENNSYLVANIA PRESS

PHILADELPHIA

Published by
University of Pennsylvania Press
Philadelphia, Pennsylvania 19104–4112 USA
www.pennpress.org

EU Authorized Representative:
Easy Access System Europe - Mustamäe tee 50,
10621 Tallinn, Estonia, gpsr.requests@easproject.com

Printed in the United States of America on acid-free paper
10 9 8 7 6 5 4 3 2 1

A Cataloging-in-Publication record for this book
is available from the Library of Congress.

Paperback ISBN 978-1-5128-2851-1
Hardcover ISBN 978-1-5128-2852-8
Ebook ISBN 978-1-5128-2853-5

To students everywhere who have survived schools that do not reflect their cultures,
and to Victoria Carlson, for working to make it be different.

CONTENTS

FOREWORD

To the Yurok language teachers of today and those dear elders who had the profound vision to give us what we have today, we are grateful. We are grateful to those who have passed on (Aa-wok) and to those elders who maintained the fortitude, resilience, and vision to know that they represented the connection to maintain the Yurok language and well-being for future generations. This preservation work was done by Yurok elders despite a US government that attempted to exterminate Yurok people from the Northern California region in the pursuit of gold, timber, land, and other natural resources, and to remove the Native culture and language from the Yurok people through federally sponsored government boarding schools. Yes, there was a state-sponsored genocide in California.

Today Yurok people remain as California's most populous Indigenous Tribe in the state, and the Yurok language is now offered in the local public high schools in the Humboldt and Del Norte County region. The state now pays the expenses for these Yurok language classes. The classes meet the world language requirement for entry into California State University and the University of California (UC). This work continues and the prize seems obvious, yet there remains a fragility to the cause.

Yurok people realize, as the billboards read, that "culture is prevention." The Yurok language and cultural traditions can reclaim the youth and prevent social ills that young people face today, such as drug and alcohol abuse, lateral violence, self-destruction, and poor decision-making. There are many preventative formulas, healthy beliefs and customs, and ways of living well within the Yurok culture, and many of these are defined within the Yurok language. Yurok people believe their prayers are in their songs and the language of the Yurok people.

The work of supporting Indigenous language and culture in the public schools is up to all of us. It enriches us all to gain this knowledge, and to not allow the Yurok language to become extinct. It is up to us all to understand how important it is for Native students and other culturally diverse students to see themselves in the curriculum and on the school course menu in order to develop a strong sense of self-worth and a belief that their culture and history matters. This self-reflection needs to occur in the early years, and throughout the K–12 grades. We hope we have not taken this need for granted. Public schools are supposed to mirror the communities they serve, and the local control funding formula rules also respect the need for Indigenous languages, curricula, and courses on the school menus.

This book helps us to understand the role K–12 schools have in developing youth and the responsibility schools hold in shaping a healthy self-concept, positive mental health, and well-being. Schools continue to be central places that help shape and reinforce identity, as well as epicenters where students build lifelong skills for social interaction, self-esteem, and community building. Indigenous language classes can play a pivotal role in this development. Schools, though once used to strip language and culture, can also be a place of generational healing and a place to learn and practice restorative justice. Dr. Mneesha Gellman and the Yurok Language Program staff provide an eye-opening opportunity for the educational community to benefit and learn from on these issues.

Restorative justice is a response to wrongdoing that prioritizes repairing harm and recognizes that maintaining positive relationships with others is a core human need. This approach seeks to address the root causes of wrongdoing even to the point of transforming unjust systems and structures. The kind of educational interventions that Dr. Gellman documents, and that Yurok language teachers and students articulate, are a form of restorative justice. Curricular interventions through Yurok language courses are a means of enacting restorative practices in the classroom, with a focus on taking responsibility, building relationships, checking in on all those impacted, and allowing and facilitating healing and making amends. Student well-being is a responsibility for all to be a part of. To get there, we need more education that is culturally sustaining and interrupts the status quo.

Jim McQuillen, MFT, PPS, is a Yurok Tribal citizen, the Education Director for the Yurok Tribe, and a Member of the California State Board of Education.

PREFACE

We Are Made of Our Experiences

I bring my own life experiences and intergenerational legacies to these pages as you bring yours. Experiences are the filter through which we perceive and construct realities. I work as an outsider with Yurok Tribal members and other Native American communities in a region I also identify as home. When meeting for the first time or speaking at public events, Indigenous scholars and colleagues typically introduce themselves with their lineages to explain the context of who they are. Naming who our people are helps others situate us. To honor that relational way of situating the self, I follow that practice here, acknowledging that I do not claim Indigenous heritage in what is now California. My hope is that openness about who I am in relation to where and what I study can illustrate context in ways that make it more useful to others. Such personal narratives further an ethics of care in the social sciences (Montes and Paris Pombo 2019, Engster 2020), which at its root consists of demonstrating concern for the well-being of others. That is what I attempt to do here.

All four pairs of my great-grandparents fled their Eastern European *shtetls*[1] in the early 1900s, seeking respite from *pogroms*[2] against Jews and yearning for upward economic mobility. On my father's side, my great-grandparents came from somewhere near Kalvarija, Lithuania, near the Polish border. On my mother's side, my great-grandparents came from Poland, Russia, and the Galicia region of Eastern Europe. Though much of our family history has been lost, I know that my maternal great-grandmother, born in 1900 in what is now western Ukraine, lived with her half-brother in Vienna before transiting through France to the United States in 1920. In the summer of 2022, I visited the Vienna apartment building she lived in, reconstructed since its World War II bombing. I tried to imagine through her eyes the salvaged communal sinks in the hallway where multiple families would wash up, which are now decorative basins in a middle-class apartment block.

Both of my grandmothers repeatedly told me they knew we had extended family that died in pogroms and in the Holocaust, but I never took the time to get specifics, something I now deeply regret, as they have passed on and that family history is lost. I did, however, meet descendants of extended family who emigrated to Israel from Poland and Russia, and I have wrestled with the implications of that part of my identity in previous writings (Gellman and Vuinovich 2008). Human movement across and within borders is complicated, and I am committed to continuing to look at how I am implicated in it.

Nearly all my biological family in every direction is Ashkenazi Jewish, a group that went through the process of "becoming White" over time in the United States (Brodkin 1998). I see now that my own early grappling with an inherited religious minority status guided the interest in racial and ethnic minority politics that has shaped my academic career. At the same time, I recognize how different the challenges are that face disparate groups that broadly share minority labels.

I am also a product of settler colonialism in far Northern California. I grew up on the traditional lands of Wiyot, Karuk, Hupa, and Yurok people. When I was a child, in the Arcata-Eureka-Kneeland area of Humboldt County, we moved a lot in the early years. I attended Gateway School, Pacific Union Elementary School, Freshwater Elementary School, and Zane Junior High School, and graduated from Eureka High School in 1998. I had a range of educational experiences, but few included any mention of local Indigenous communities in the past or the present.

When I was in elementary school, my parents bought the cheapest piece of forested land they could find, located on land traditionally stewarded by the Wiyot people, in what is now named Greenwood Heights. My father, a carpenter and eventual electrician, built a cabin there and taught himself the necessary trades to make our family home. This included building a mound system to address the soil's poor percolation, the source of the land's lower price. My parents grew up in Detroit, Michigan, and their own parents moved the family farther and farther from the urban core during the White flight era of the 1960s and 70s. By the time my parents fled to the West Coast in the back-to-the-land hippie movement, they were fleeing the suburbs and a perfunctory Reform Judaism characterized by memorization and assimilation. But as Kaitlin Reed (Yurok/Hupa/Oneida) points out, whose land were they going back to (2023: 98–121)? That legacy is left for me to grapple with.

As a young person, I was thirsty for the world outside of what I knew. I eventually fled too. I went east to Bard College, to Latin America, Australia, and Southeast Asia for travels and an MA in peace and conflict studies (courtesy of the Rotary Foundation—thanks!), and then to the Midwest for a PhD at Northwestern University, where imposter syndrome weighed heavily. Pushing onward, I nursed my first child through doctoral fieldwork in Mexico and El Salvador, spending nearly a year doing interviews across multiple towns and cities with my portable family. Then I followed my husband's work to West Africa, writing my dissertation and raising a toddler in Côte d'Ivoire and Sierra Leone. I kept trying to understand, in this wide range of places, what allowed people to live together well and what undermined such efforts. Which conditions led to violence, and which to democratization?

My second child was born during a postdoctoral fellowship in Germany, a dreamy year where I had time to write, think, and grow another human. We then moved our family back to the United States when I got a tenure-track job in Boston at Emerson College. I have friends and colleagues scattered across the globe, alongside the stories of many people's pain and dreams that have been entrusted to me. The takeaway from years abroad is that unequal access to insufficient resources continues to produce conflict and inhibit coexistence, regardless of specific context. I keep trying to find ways to bring these underlying drivers of conflict to light. One could say I am relentless about it.

This wide range of international experience has been fruitful for a career in comparative politics, but I yearned to direct my research energy to places where I have long-standing connections. I was able to spend extended time back in the Humboldt area as a visiting researcher in the Department of Politics at California Polytechnic Institute, Humboldt, in both spring 2018 and spring 2022. That local affiliation was useful in explaining my role to school administrators and other stakeholders, who would otherwise wonder why they should spend time explaining to a random professor from Boston how things worked in their school and district.

A final reason it is important to explain my positionality here is to convey the depth of care that I have toward these schools. Though I usually live in Boston, I fiercely identify with far Northern California as home, even as I recognize the settler-colonialist implications of those feelings. This applies to my nascent feelings toward Boston as home as well. I put my political science tools to work investigating what the problems are and searching for their potential solutions in places that I care about.

At the end of the day, this work is not an abstract intellectual exercise. I have committed to working with the Yurok Tribe and others to share the findings long after this book is complete. I want schools to do a better job supporting student well-being, and I have made myself available to be part of that work. Experiences of acceptance or rejection at school form a large part of who young people are and grow to be in the world. Educational trauma, or affirmation, can carry forward into adult life. Constructing healthy Black, Indigenous, and People of Color (BIPOC) identity affirmation is within the reach of schools, with political will being the largest obstacle.

It is a very vulnerable feeling to put my analysis of communities that are so closely connected to my own growing up into print. While I iteratively consulted about the text with the Yurok people featured in the book, as well as with Yurok Tribal leaders, others from the communities discussed may disagree with me over representations of school and community experiences that do not match their own. Such concerns are perpetually a component of ethnographic work. I share the research framework in the appendices in order to provide the social science side of the intimate narratives presented in what follows. In bringing more visibility to the voices of Indigenous students and educators, I hope that my own identity and privilege can be leveraged for solutions rather than problems. Nobody is alone in their story.

PART I

Theorizing Well-Being

CHAPTER 1

The Impact of Stories

Some teachers here are teaching the wrong things. And then students go out in the world thinking they know what is right, but they have all this bad information, all these stereotypes. Some days I think, "What is the point of all this, anyway?"

—Meri, Focus Group 10.1 2022

I can't shake her story out of my head. Months after our conversation, the pain of a young woman I spoke with breaks through my routine, hovering over me. The discussion, which took place during fieldwork in a remote high school in far Northern California, churned up a slew of unanswered questions that come to me at unexpected moments: while washing the dishes, eating a meal, triaging my inbox. I can't turn away from her story because I refuse to believe nothing can be done to ease what she is living through.

As a researcher, I usually keep my emotions tightly locked up. But this young woman's testimony has squeezed in through the cracks, perhaps through the human exchange of giving voice and being heard. Meri[1] is a student in an upper-level Yurok language class at her local high school, located thirty minutes from her home on the Yurok Indian Reservation. Reluctant to start talking at first, she hid behind a sheaf of long black hair while the questions settled around her in the poorly lit conference room. We sat in the awkward pause, examining the aging carpet together until she claimed her space to speak: "I grew up with my sister and her kids, and we've done chores since we were able to reach the sink. There is always hard work for me to do at home, so it's hard to get schoolwork done. Now I live with [some other family members], and I'm expected to do all the cooking and cleaning. I do most of the shopping, too, and take care of my niece. I cook for my siblings who are in and out of the house and on drugs. I'm taking care of everyone, making sure there is shampoo, toilet paper, all the things for the house. It's not easy to find time or energy for school."

The intensity of Meri's responsibilities demonstrates what is called "parentalizing" in the academic literature, where children take on responsibilities usually associated with adults (Moore and Coyhis 2020: 81). Such parentalizing impacts Meri's well-being and her school success, as the expectations placed on her are more than she can sustain. This set-up-to-fail scenario only became worse when coupled with the COVID-19 pandemic, which had disproportionately fatal outcomes in Native communities (Foxworth et al. 2022). This was true in Meri's town of Klamath,[2] where many people died during the pandemic. "I'm not gonna lie, some days I just felt like I couldn't get out of bed. I just don't have the energy to do anything. I'm crying all the time. And then teachers try to understand by giving you more time to do the work, but I fell so far behind. It feels like I can't catch up. And then I almost have a panic attack when I come to school because it's all too much . . . I wish I could just have some freedom" (Focus Group 10.1 2022). The crushing weight of adult responsibility coupled with trauma is palpable in Meri's words. Her family burdens, exacerbated by the impact of the COVID-19 pandemic, were more than she could handle while keeping up with schoolwork.

Shortly after this interview, Meri fell off the map. I checked back at the school each time I returned for fieldwork, and I kept hearing that she hadn't been back to class in weeks. I could understand Meri's choice to skip school after hearing her describe how showing up to her classes just added another work shift to her day. All the domestic labor expected of her did not vanish just because she decided to try to get through high school. Plus, the learning environment itself did not make the effort seem worthwhile, as it was so far removed from the reality of her home life and culture. And the outcomes show the subpar results, with Native American school achievement much lower than that of White counterparts.[3] It does not have to be this way.

Meri appreciated the opportunity to study the Yurok language at school, and she identifies fully as a Yurok young woman.[4] She told me how much she enjoyed participating in Yurok ceremonies—she had carried medicine in dances and loved helping set up dance camps, cooking, and participating in community events. Regarding dances, she shared, "It's like I can feel the Creator watching over me there. You have your aunties and uncles around you . . . being up there in that country is so beautiful, that fresh air is so good" (Focus

Group 10.1 2022). But balancing her home responsibilities on the Yurok Indian Reservation with constant demands from school, in the context of a pandemic that disproportionately devastated Native communities, alongside ongoing structural challenges like family poverty and addiction, felt like too much.

When I returned to the area in 2024 and followed up with colleagues on this project, I heard through word of mouth that Meri was in an alternative high school completion program and working full-time. She was doing better, with a stable routine of work and some income to better support herself and her family. But it seemed like Meri's success happened in spite of her schooling, rather than because of the support she could have found there. The history of the formal educational sector in the United States in relation to Native Americans means this observation is no surprise to many readers. For me, Meri's story raises questions about what is needed in schools to make them sources of support for student well-being, especially for students like Meri, rather than stressful obstacles that undermine it.

My purpose in writing this book is to help identify solutions to the pressing problem of Native American marginalization within formal education. This means that while I mention major challenges within schools and communities, I do not address numerous variables—addiction, poverty, unemployment, illicit economies, domestic violence, mental health, homelessness, and many more—beyond engaging with them when they come up in interview and focus group data. That said, these variables shape students' lived experiences, as they did Meri's, in ways that can't be ignored.

In order to avoid a deficit approach, I deliberately look toward spaces of hope, where innovation and collaboration are possible, while also acknowledging the many hardships young people face today. In this context, I focus the book around two core themes—school climate and curricular representation—where educators and their school districts are capable of radical yet pragmatic interventions. In doing so, I attempt to call in, rather than call out, education sector colleagues, so that we may find ways to do the work that needs to be done to re-envision schooling as a contributor to youth wellness.

Schooling and Marginalization

Each day, students in schools around the world enter classrooms carrying emotional baggage from home. They carry scars from intergenerational trauma, their parents' debts and addictions, and the burdens of caring for siblings or working after-school jobs. These same students, along with others, also carry hopes for their next sports event, an upcoming date with a crush, or plans to fix up an old car that holds the promise of freedom. Yes, schools are expressions of power and nationalism (Paglayan 2022). There is a rich literature in education and adjacent fields that addresses BIPOC youth marginalization and success in educational spaces (Valenzuela 1999, Demmert and Towner 2003, Powers 2006, Pollock 2008, Au 2015). The unique circumstances of Native American students in predominantly White learning spaces have also been a topic of investigation (Adams 1995, Ongtooguk and Dybdahl 2008), as well as language survival for BIPOC students (Hornberger 2008, Faingold 2018).

Many teachers try to be trauma-informed educators ready to help connect young people with a range of services depending on their needs. Other teachers expect students to leave these multilayered, intersectional identities at the door. In a world where teacher evaluations are often connected to test scores, there is constant pressure to get students to focus on standardized lessons so that teachers and schools can fulfill state mandates and boost performance benchmarks. K–12 public education in the United States is defined by tropes that repeat across generations. Many educators teach similar material to what they themselves were taught. In the social sciences, textbooks frequently perpetuate manifest destiny narratives that uphold White exceptionalism (Gellman 2024b). Such approaches have short-term impacts—influencing the self-perception of different groups of students—as well as long-term impacts—reinforcing White supremacy as the bedrock structure of US society.

This book explores four schools in far Northern California that are dealing with extremely limited mental health resources, overburdened counselors, and the congruence of teachers and with their student bodies. I argue that marginalization in both school and curricula undermines healthy youth identity formation for many BIPOC students. Specifically, I make the case that for Native American students, such marginalization feeds the pernicious ongoing cycle of neocolonialism that permeates twenty-first-century schooling.

BIPOC marginalization is everybody's problem; it is not something that negatively affects only non-White-identifying people. Broadly, issues that inhibit BIPOC student well-being by extension impact the well-being of all students. While I narrowly concentrate on the experiences of high school–aged Native American youth and their educators, the themes addressed within these pages are broadly applicable to diverse K–12 and college populations. In my previous work (Gellman 2023), I address school climate and curricular representation in both the United States and Mexico in relation to civic, cultural, and political participation, arguing that access to Indigenous languages improves the agency of all students, regardless of background. In this book, I center the concept of well-being as something that schools can better contribute to by addressing the education politics that inform curricular choices, among other factors. Schooling has marginalized Native American youth for generations, but some communities are pushing back, redefining what school means through curricula, pedagogy, and more holistic means of evaluating student success.

Many Indigenous leaders, including those within the Yurok Tribe, want their youth to learn to live and succeed in both worlds—Indigenous and White. Success in public school-based education is important to the Yurok Tribe, even though the settler-colonial perspective is different from Yurok ones. "Success in both worlds" is a common slogan found on tribal hoodies given out to young people at summer camps and other educational events. By skipping out on the rest of the 2022 school year, Meri failed to meet a benchmark of school success in the White education system as she tried to balance culturally-based family responsibilities and her own internal struggles.

What can be done to support young people like Meri? As the statistics of Missing and Murdered Indigenous People (MMIP) show, the potential for harm to come to women, girls, two-spirit[5] people, and others who do not succeed in both worlds is entirely real. More than one hundred people from Native American communities in the United States were declared missing or murdered each year in 2020 and 2021 (Sovereign Bodies Institute 2021: 48). Such numbers show an ongoing pattern of power-based violence. In December 2021, during the same meeting where I sought permission to conduct the research project described in this book, the Yurok Tribal Council unanimously passed a resolution declaring a state of emergency regarding MMIP[6] in their community. The chairman made a powerful statement connecting MMIP to colonization: "The intergenerational impacts of 170 years of violence, trafficking, and murder through missions, massacres, forced relocation, state-sanctioned indentured servitude, boarding schools, widespread removal of children from their families through the child welfare system, disproportionate incarceration, police violence, and high rates of gender violence are still playing out to this day, and directly contribute to the crisis of Missing and Murdered Indigenous Women and Girls" (Casarez 2021).

I hope Meri and others like her find ways to create healthy lives rooted in cultural connection and free from violence. But we must acknowledge that her situation, like that of many BIPOC young women, is perilous. Meri is trapped in structurally derived circumstances that are mostly not of her own making. She is living out a story of colonization while searching for ways to be safe, caring for herself and others, and finding her place in the world.

Indigenous Languages and Culturecide

This book aims to convince readers that we need to do better for young people from marginalized communities. Based on painstakingly collected data from both theory-testing and interpretive social science methods, I share the results in the form of narratives to show what the human cost of ignoring youth well-being might be. To understand Meri's story, we must look at the history of settler colonialism, broken treaties, boarding school legacies, and intergenerational trauma. Specific to tribes of Northern California, such trauma is rooted in human rights abuses that included forced labor, legal enslavement, state-sanctioned murder, and genocide (Madley 2016; Madley 2019; Norton 1979). *Culturecide*, as defined in my previous work (Gellman 2023: 8), is the intentional killing of culture of a minority group by the majority. It does not imply physical destruction, as with genocide, and is a separate stage on the autonomy–assimilation spectrum as laid out by James Fenelon (Lakota/ Dakota, Gaelic Irish, and Norsk) (1998: 41).

To appreciate the way that Native American communities have survived and manifest contemporary presence despite such abuses, I look to spaces of *Native survivance*, or Native survival cojoined with resistance to assimilation (Vizenor 2009, Vizenor 2010, Sabzalian 2019). Survivance happens in many spaces, for example through cultural practices of Native tribes and nations themselves (Jacob 2013, Risling Baldy 2018, Lara-Cooper and Lara Sr. 2019) and in language practices (McCarty, Romero-Little et al. 2009, Wyman 2012, Yurok Tribe 2022, Overall 2022).

Of direct concern in this book, Native youth survivance and resistance to erasure in the formal education sector takes place through culturally responsive curriculum (Save California Salmon 2020, Casarez 2020, KTIEP n.d., Supahan n.d.) and pedagogy (hooks 1994, Paris and Alim 2014, Paris 2020). Cree scholar Stan Wilson summarizes in the conclusion of a book on Indigenous pedagogy, which he terms *Indigegogy*, "The educational experience for Indigenous peoples has been a disaster" (Wilson and Schellhammer 2021: 117). He goes on to explain that Indigenous people who have not assimilated or do not want to assimilate to English-only or settler-colonial education are further pushed out of the system (Wilson and Schellhammer 2021: 117). Such trauma has significant impacts on the wellness of Native American youth in mental health (Whitbeck, Walls et al. 2009, Gone 2013). And yet educational trauma is perpetuated generation after generation through White supremacist curricula in United States classrooms (Yacovone 2022, Gellman 2024b). How then, do we heal?

Defining Well-Being

Well-being is a slippery concept. Throughout this book, I look at definitions of well-being from both non-Indigenous and Indigenous perspectives and relate the definitions to the core objective of the study: how to support youth success and overall well-being in school. The target goal of well-being appears frequently in aspirational documents, including across multiple branches of United Nations (UN) organizations. For example, the UN's Sustainable Development Goals in its 2030 Agenda for Sustainable Development include well-being as a central concept. But what does it really consist of?

Traditionally, the term well-being has been assessed through both subjective and objective measures. For example, "Subjective constructs emphasize personal experiences and individual fulfillment, which include . . . finding meaning in life and experiencing a sense of personal growth . . . [and] feeling happy and being satisfied with one's own life" (Ross, Hinton et al. 2020). Such ephemeral feelings are also grounded in data with more objective definitions: "In contrast, objective approaches define well-being in terms of quality-of-life indicators such as material resources (income, food, and housing) and social attributes (education, health, political voice, social networks, and connections). Such objective indicators commonly reflect capabilities, which include both an individual's functioning and the opportunities provided in a given environment" (Ross, Hinton et al. 2020). In addition, relational well-being makes visible the fact that "the dynamic interplay of personal, societal, and environmental structures and processes" also contributes to well-being (Ross, Hinton et al. 2020).

Researchers have put forward the argument that well-being consists of five domains that each contain multiple requirements: "(1) Good health and optimum nutrition, (2) connectedness, positive values, and contribution to society, (3) safety and a supportive environment, (4) learning, competence, education, skills, and employability, and (5) agency and resilience" (Ross, Hinton et al. 2020). Finding ways to support access to these domains is the labor of states, local governments, school districts, civil society, and many more actors. I take these indicators as part of the complex package that constitutes well-being, recognizing the uniqueness of what each of these indicators looks like for individuals and communities.

Well-being can be fostered and supported throughout the pre-K and K–12 systems and across curricula. In this particular book, I narrow my focus to look at high school–level classes in order to understand how Yurok language courses operate as decolonizing spaces within colonizing institutions. I address themes of school climate and curricular representation from the teacher, student, and alumni perspectives.

Care in Research: Methodology and Methods

Indigenous researchers and allies have offered many important frameworks for enacting Indigenous ways of knowing and being in research by, with, and for Indigenous peoples (Wilson 2008, Brayboy, Gough et al. 2012, Tuhiwai Smith 2012, Berryman, SooHoo et al. 2013, Lee and Evans 2021). I have written repeatedly about the need to use some form of collaborative methodology when engaging in research pertaining to historically and contemporarily marginalized people, including Indigenous peoples (Gellman 2021, Gellman 2022a, Gellman 2023: 26–63, Gellman 2024a). In essence, collaborative methodology espouses a power-sharing model that lifts up stakeholder perspectives and participation rather than extracting knowledge for the researcher's benefit exclusively. This model of research with, not on, stakeholders has yet to be mainstreamed in many disciplines. Nevertheless, I am convinced it makes for not only more ethical research, but also better research, as the numerous community partnership aspects of collaboration also provide accountability and accuracy checkpoints.

Methodology refers to the philosophical framework of research, while methods are the data collection techniques used to gather information. I have been a mixed-methods researcher—predominantly qualitative—for many years, and this study is no exception. I used political ethnography, participant observation in classrooms and community spaces, interviews, focus groups, and surveys to triangulate information across multiple sources in numerous forms. I have justified this assemblage of methods in many of my previous works, but this book squarely centers testimony as core data. Why?

Though not uncomplicated, testimonial literature has a strong role in asserting political storytelling by Indigenous and other dispossessed peoples (Burgos-Debray 1983, Tula and Stephen 1994, Fujii 2010, Stephen 2013, Lara-Cooper, Everett Colegrove et al. 2022). Such testimonies and their academic midwives deliver narratives with emotional impact that would otherwise risk invisibility. In addition, "listening seriously" to narratives and testimonies is central to the tradition of critical race theory (CRT; Brayboy 2005: 428). Tribal critical race theory (TCRT), built as an extension of CRT to differentiate it from the Black–White binary and Civil Rights–era issues, places the existence of colonization at the core of society's issues (Brayboy 2005: 429; Brayboy 2013). In his seminal article laying out TCRT's core tenets, Bryan McKinley Jones Brayboy (Lumbee) shows how TCRT requires accounting for issues such as Tribal sovereignty, assimilatory education, and the reciprocal relationship between stories and theory, among others (Brayboy 2005: 429–430). TCRT undergirds this book, operating as a baseline starting assumption for the work that follows.

Since "colonization is endemic to society" and "educational policies toward Indigenous peoples are intimately linked around the problematic goal of assimilation" (Brayboy 2005: 429), Brayboy asserts that "stories are not separate from theory; they make up theory and are, therefore, real and legitimate sources of data and ways of being" (2005: 430). In this way, testimonies from students, teachers, and community members are not solely stories, but they contain ways of knowing and being within them. Such testimonies are therefore a methodologically culturally appropriate way to research concepts of, and challenges to, well-being for Native American youth in schools.

Brayboy's point about stories is worth highlighting from an additional angle. Readers will see aspects of more formal social science writing in this book, particularly so in this introduction and the appendices. Yet, I yearn to integrate the emotionality of testimony into social science without it diminishing the theoretical value of the arguments. I have found myself far more personally moved by books that make theoretical contributions but are presented in a narrative form, as opposed to the formulaic social science standard. For example, Kishan Lara-Cooper and Walter Lara Sr.'s edited volume *Ka'm-t'em* (2019), Timothy Pachirat's *Among Wolves* (2018), Diana Reay's *Miseducation* (2017), and Jeremy Slack's *Deported to Death* (2019) immerse and teach readers through emotionally engaged storytelling. Those are the types of books I look forward to reading, rather than the drier ones I force myself to read to keep up with my discipline. I write this book more in line with ones that I would want to read, in hopes that other researchers might do the same. In line with TCRT, stories need not be separate from theory, and such narratives can be powerful evidence of Indigenous voice.

Therefore, grounded in social scientific data, this book is crafted to invite readers to care and become invested through the use of a testimonial style. By feeling emotion, or even empathy, with the speakers as they testify about the conditions of their lives, I welcome readers to feel both intellectually and emotionally persuaded that the overall welfare of Native American high school students matters.

The invitation to care is foregrounded using extended excerpts of testimony from Yurok teachers, students, and community members who are involved in the work of language and cultural revitalization. Such lengthy excerpts are intentional. While I situate and analyze many quotes, it is important that the people featured in these pages get to speak for themselves. The issues brought to light through people's words are meant to jolt us out of complacency with the educational status quo. By stepping into classrooms and communities through the doorways of their own words, interviewees show us why we should care and what the consequences are if we fail to do so.

The many people who agreed to interviews with me make their own cases for why youth well-being is best served by culturally sustaining education. They convinced me—eloquently, passionately, and fervently. In turn, I hope to convince you, reader, that Native youth well-being is critical for educational systems to prioritize and support. Such well-being is connected more widely to the need to support other BIPOC groups within the confines of the formal education system. There is a role for allyship, or, in Dr. Bettina Love's conception, co-conspiratorship (2019: 117), in work opposing culturecide.

I do not know if I, or the social scientific research I engage in as my life's work, will effectively be part of genuine, viable solutions to situations like Meri's. But the pain she revealed to me in that windowless conference room is something I have thought about nearly every day since. This book is my attempt to convey young people's stories, and those of the educators who care for them, and to advocate for curricula and systems that support Native American well-being at school. I wonder who students like Meri will become in the world. After all, how can they achieve their dreams if they don't even get the opportunity to dream them?

Outline of the Book

The book proceeds as follows. In Chapter 2, I look closely at the concept of well-being and discuss how it can translate into cultural significance, especially for Native youth. Included are extended excerpts from an interview with clinical psychologist Dr. Virgil Moorehead Jr., a leader in advocating for culturally grounded mental health support that centers Native identity as a component of well-being.

Part II includes four chapters focusing on classroom dynamics and curricular impacts. Chapter 3 provides insights from multiple formal interviews and informal meetings from 2018 to 2022 with James Gensaw, the Yurok language teacher at Eureka High School (EHS), and some of his students. This chapter looks at the role of teachers as facilitators of decolonization, addressing the book's main themes of school climate and curricular representation from both teacher and student perspectives.

In Chapter 4, I unpack the case study of McKinleyville, California, a majority White town built on the Doctrine of Discovery. This colonizing framework of education is explored in detail, with excerpts from a talking circle with six upper-level Yurok language students, all of whom identify in some way as Native American. Participants expound on themes of discrimination and exclusion, and they offer specific examples of how their Native identities have been marginalized in their K–12 experiences. They also provide ideas for interventions to address harmful school-based behaviors.

Chapter 5 presents testimony from Barbara McQuillen, a Yurok elder, language-keeper, and teacher, who has spent decades working to pass on the Yurok language to others while increasing her own language knowledge. She is a culturally resonant adult for many Native American high school students, as she brings immense cultural knowledge, including Yurok language, history, customs, and artisan work, into her classrooms. She also brings a personal understanding of student circumstances to an otherwise predominantly White institution. By providing a safe space in her classes where Native American and non-Native students alike can learn from each other, she sees young people gaining more confidence in who they are. Supporting students who challenge the status quo enables language-keepers like Ms. McQuillen to impart cultural reclamation alongside grammar lessons.

Ms. Annie O'Rourke teaches Yurok at Hoopa Valley High School (HVHS), where a majority of the students are Native, and where school and community climates coupled with home life and resource limitations impact student well-being. In Chapter 6, I present youth, teacher, and administrator perspectives from the only public school included in this study that is located on a Native American reservation, and one that has a particularly heavy history in terms of education for Indigenous students. Whereas some schools offer only the Yurok language class and other small interventions in otherwise White-oriented curricula, the school district that HVHS resides in has been innovating for years and placing thoughtfully developed and age-appropriate Native American curricula throughout the K–12 system.

Part III shows multiple ways that Yurok people are engaged in language resurgence and survivance. In Chapter 7, Thayallen Gensaw reflects on what it means to grow up into Yurok manhood. Taking Yurok conceptions of gender norms into account, Thayallen sees his own development as a process of walking in two worlds. Thayallen also recounts the curricular spaces and experiences that have affected his own well-being.

Chapter 8 introduces Lozen Nez, an advocate for curricular change based on her personal experience enrolled in an Advanced Placement (AP) US History (APUSH) class as an eleventh grader. This chapter first provides context for the APUSH curriculum, then includes a discussion of a grievance letter Lozen submitted to her school board, along with some of the comments the letter received when it was posted online, and concludes with excerpts from an interview with Lozen and her younger brother.

In Chapter 9, I draw on interviews with the first two students to ever complete the California State Seal of Biliteracy in the Yurok language. Maurice Alvarado and Danielle Schunneman describe, in their own words, how teachers inspired them to show up to class and work toward standardized benchmarks of formal academic success. Within their stories are lessons about how schools make decisions that can increase student success by continuing to validate Native American identity and knowledge in formal curricular spaces.

Victoria Carlson has dedicated her life to keeping the Yurok language alive, and she shares the story of what drives her in Chapter 10. As the Yurok Language Program Manager for the Yurok Tribe's Education Department, Victoria creates both in-person and online language learning opportunities, teacher training programs, and curricula for numerous Yurok Tribal offices and projects, and also writes grants to support the program. In this chapter, Victoria articulates her story of cultural reclamation that spans generations and explains the importance of Yurok language revitalization and survivance of her people.

Part IV serves as the conclusion to the book, with a summary of how education can operate as a well-being tool. It is a call to action for stakeholders in a wide variety of roles connected to schools and BIPOC well-being. Taken together, the chapters tell a story about Indigenous invisibility and resistance, Native youth activism, and how addressing settler colonialism in the United States is deeply tied to addressing survivance in the schoolroom.

The book's epilogue holds my personal narrative of a road trip with my family at the conclusion of semester-long fieldwork in 2022. On this trip, we passed shrines dedicated to Missing and Murdered Indigenous Women (MMIW) on a remote highway in California. I then return to Meri's story to look at the risks that come with ignoring the role of well-being for Native American youth. In an intimate tone, I remind readers what is at stake if we turn away.

For those who want to see more of the social science research framework than what is provided in the chapters themselves, the appendices contain research protocol documents. These include the collaborative research design proposal approved by the Yurok Tribe, the informational letter and permission forms used by students and their guardians, and a table showing data sources. It is my hope that this book can appeal to both a general audience as well as fellow researchers through the combination of testimonials from Native youth and educators, alongside the research instruments provided in the appendices, and advocacy for collaborative methodology as a guiding framework.

CHAPTER 2

Thinking Outside the Box:
Youth Well-Being in the Face of Trauma

W ell-being is a goal that schools can help young people achieve and maintain. Although I recognize that schools cannot solve all the problems that young people encounter, public schools in the United States do serve as central spaces that connect people to state services. Schools promote health and nutrition through free meals, and when they are functioning well, schools can help young people feel supported in their development as they learn skills for both future careers and life. Subsequent chapters address how well-being for Native American students in particular can be better supported in public high schools. Before that, I first look at how Native American well-being is defined in relation to culture and mental health in far Northern California.

Native American Well-Being as Cultural Well-Being

There is an abundance of survey data and analyses that attempt to take youth experiences and translate them into indicators to evaluate youth well-being. Although the COVID-19 pandemic made such data collection extra challenging, and also somewhat distorted by pandemic realities, the 2019–2021 *Healthy Kids Survey* in California showed important general trends. Youth are exhibiting declining academic motivation and progress in school, as well as "the continuation of a long-term rise in chronic, debilitating sadness or hopelessness among secondary students in all grades and the high rate of suicidal ideation among high school students" (Austin, Hanson et al. 2023: i). Moreover, well-being as observed through mental health indicators "has clearly deteriorated for substantial numbers of youth, particularly for female students, who had almost twice the risk of chronic sadness as males" (Austin, Hanson et al. 2023: i).[1] These and other youth trends are documented—we know the kids are *not* alright—but intervening to fix them is a huge mandate.

Virgil Moorehead Jr., a member of the Big Lagoon Rancheria, a federally recognized Tribe of Yurok and Tolowa peoples, is the executive director of Two Feathers: Native American Family Services.[2] Two Feathers' mission is to "work with Native American children and families in a good way which includes using culturally based interventions that promote holistic health and developing respectful collaborations with both Native and non-Native agencies" (TF-NAFS 2022). Dr. Moorehead grew up in far Northern California—a McKinleyville High School (MHS) graduate—and then left for seventeen years to gain impressive credentials: college at UC Davis, a doctorate in psychology from the Wright Institute in Berkeley, and a postdoc at Stanford University. He also worked as a staff psychologist before moving back to his home region.

Trained as a clinical psychologist, Dr. Moorehead briefly taught at Humboldt State University (now California Polytechnic Institute, Humboldt, or Cal Poly Humboldt)[3] and then moved to Two Feathers, where he helps shape policies and programs on youth mental health. A highly regarded leader in Native American well-being, Dr. Moorehead and I met on a cold spring day in the bright Two Feathers conference room. Its walls are decorated with posters about culturally relevant wellness practices, assuring me that I had arrived in the right place.

Here, and throughout the book, I share extended quotes from Indigenous cultural leaders to facilitate a focus on the book's themes through their own voices and perspectives. I make my questions as concise as possible to maximize Dr. Moorehead's time to speak, which he does with a focused, serious gaze: "I think that in Native communities particularly, and others that have been oppressed currently and historically, the mental health system as is, which is very focused on an individualized biomedical model, isn't working. We have to think outside the box in how we do mental health, and that includes cultural programming that gets people to the services. For some Native families, that cultural part isn't important, but for others it is" (Moorehead Jr. 2022).

Dr. Moorehead describes how early in his time there, Two Feathers escalated integration of Native American culture into well-being support systems by obtaining a grant to use two local cultural practices to promote mental health and well-being for youth: the Flower Dance—the girl's coming of age ceremony—and the stick game. He notes that "those were our mental health strategies. From that grant, we put on the first program right here, and we had like ninety-five kids show up. And then we did about six more events, with different programming, and averaged about fifty to sixty Native youth each time" (Moorehead Jr. 2022). Given the rural context beleaguered by lack of public transportation in which Two Feathers works, getting this number of youth together for something that is optional is a significant accomplishment. Dr. Moorehead explains how such success came to be, most visibly through promoting programming on social media: "We raised awareness that Two Feathers was really infused with our local cultural traditions. That helped us build relationships, and since then we've formed an advisory board [with local respected elders]. We don't *just* do culture now, but that programming really helped to open the door in creating Two Feathers as it is today and started building trust. What we would like to do looking ahead is case study research, following some of the kids through the program to really under-stand them and their experiences of cultural programming put on by Two Feathers" (Moorehead Jr. 2022).

This kind of case study research is exciting to Dr. Moorehead, and his face lights up as he describes it. Such data would help his organization design the most impactful programming possible. In 2022, Dr. Moorehead notes that Two Feathers serves around 160 Native youth in one-on-one counseling, plus another fifty or more in programming.

I point to one of the wall posters, which lists terms like identity, self-esteem, and self-awareness and defines them, and ask Dr. Moorehead for his definition of well-being:

> We look at, how do you be a positive, contributing member of society? So, it's biological, but it's also existential. Purpose, meaning, being able to give and receive relationships, being able to provide empathy—there are existential things that I think the mental health system should help with. Now, you obviously help with anxiety and depression, that stuff. But also, how do we help kids feel good *in* themselves, feel like they have purpose and meaning? How do you define being more stable? Is well-being giving [the] shirt off your back when someone needs it? Is its opposite taking three burritos when others don't have any? Do Natives in high [Native status] families and with more cultural capital have more of it? (Moorehead Jr. 2022)

This philosophical approach to well-being complicates settler-colonial-derived definitions of well-being that focus on individual happiness. Dr. Moorehead's identification of well-being as something that includes existential needs, such as paths to make socially situated positive contributions to society, expands the vocabulary of what such work looks like by culturally situating it. The burrito example also points to the role of community well-being as integral to individual well-being: Even if someone can assuage hunger by eating three burritos, are they really fed, in the deeper sense of community-based well-being, if they have eaten so much while their neighbor is hungry?

Dr. Moorehead's reflection speaks to values held by many communities that prioritize collective over individual success. Well-being comes from serving a purpose within a community in a meaningful way. It is success situated in relationship. This is something that BIPOC students from a range of backgrounds articulated to me as missing during the COVID-19 pandemic. In the absence of community during the pandemic, young people were all the more vulnerable to anxiety and depression, as resources for maintaining their own well-being were not available.

Finally, Dr. Moorehead raises an interesting question about if high-status Native families and others with more cultural capital have more well-being. High-status families are usually those who help sponsor dances and other spaces for traditional ritual gatherings. They are generally perceived as being more culturally connected, and also as having more material resources. "I think the biggest influences in how culturally connected someone is are geography and relationships. If you are connected to a dance family, you are more likely to be connected to cultural traditions. I think the Rancheria families—like my family in Big Lagoon Rancheria—are less connected. I think the Yurok Tribe has done a good job recently with connecting people. If you are living in Klamath, you'll be more connected, if you are part of a dance family you will be more connected."

Cultural connection is a way of consolidating identity, demonstrating, through lived practices that may be public-facing or more personal, that someone is part of a set of traditions. My previous work examined the impact of access to Indigenous language classes in high school as an indicator of cultural connection (Gellman 2023), and I show there that being culturally connected has a number of protective factors for Indigenous youth. Dr. Moorehead's point that dance families and those in Klamath, for example, are more culturally connected opens up many questions that future researchers might pursue. For example, do those with more cultural capital in general have higher degrees of well-being? I don't address them here, but I note how cultural capital may be of relevance to a more complete understanding of factors contributing to well-being.

Dr. Moorehead cites the work of multiple researchers who inform his own thinking about well-being. Kishan Lara-Cooper, a professor of child development at Cal Poly Humboldt, has also written, along with colleagues, about practices of healing and resilience in Native American communities (Lara-Cooper and Lara Sr. 2019, Lara-Cooper, Everett Colegrove et al. 2022). In *Ka'm-t'em*, for example, the editors and numerous authors make the case for community-rooted cultural connection as central to Indigenous well-being (Lara-Cooper and Lara Sr. 2019).

Dr. Moorehead notes that Two Feathers' approach is in line with work such as that of Melissa Walls and colleagues, who investigate connections between youth mental health, intergenerational trauma, and self-harm behavior (Whitbeck, Walls et al. 2009, Walls and Whitbeck 2012, Walls, Hautala et al. 2014). Their work shows that culture plays a significant role in youth choices. By taking young people to local ceremonies, Dr. Moorehead explains, "They'll feel more confident about who they are, and then they'll feel more confident about learning more. That is the benefit of cultural connection."

He also cites Erica Prussing's work on "the empty circle" (Prussing 2007: 499–500), noting that "We never feel Indian *enough*—there is this 'empty circle,' with a lot of shame and imposter syndrome. For example, if you aren't from a dance family, if you are White, light skinned, if you've experienced a lot of trauma, then there are a lot of self-confidence issues. It is a postcolonial disorder" (Moorehead Jr. 2022). Crediting his mentor Joseph Gone for contributing to his thinking on how contemporary crises in Indian Country are in fact manifestations of "postcolonial distress," Dr. Moorehead notes that collective historical trauma undergoes intergenerational transfer without resolution (Kirmayer, Gone et al. 2014: 301).

In a conversation about well-being for local Native American communities, a local cultural leader of the Yurok Tribe told Dr. Moorehead, "What we're missing is that we're not developing people into elders." The role of elders is particularly vital in the wellness of Native American communities. "Elders are what I would describe as healthy people; elders are those that think of the whole community, and their decisions aren't self-serving or only for the benefits of status. They are truly committed to the overall well-being of the community. And how do our systems create those elders? What one of our local leaders would say is, 'We're kind of missing that.' We need to figure out how to do that [help people become elders]. When you take on leadership, do you take it on for power and status or because it's a responsibility to the community?"

The altruistic role of elders—to assume responsibility in a community because it is the right thing to do, and not for personal gain—is visible in Dr. Moorehead's description. But he rightfully queries how to support people to take that step, when such community-mindedness might run contrary to individual success. Luckily, Dr. Moorehead notes that there are some inspiring examples of people making the transition to elder status, with deep ethics of community care. He cites Judge Abbi Abinanti[4] as one such person, but states: "I think that we could do more. Yes, we need to work on the learning of language, the practices and cultures, the learning how to bead and weave baskets. But if you don't also learn what it means to be a good, positive, serving, healthy person, it doesn't matter. But you could learn about your own culture and then also benefit your own self. Mental health training teaches you to fix the anxiety, for example, but your role is to be neutral . . . but I think our role, the mental health that we're doing, is how to influence character, values, sensibilities" (Moorehead Jr. 2022). The call to action here is to embrace cultural practices as part of one's individual and community well-being, but to couple it with the formation of healthy mental and socioemotional practices. None of these things alone achieve well-being, but taken together, they offer a meaningful recipe.

Translating these theoretical ideas into specific plans of action for the local community is part of what Dr. Moorehead does at Two Feathers. He talks about a recent meeting where they discussed how to best serve the approximately seven hundred Yurok Tribe–enrolled kids in the region.[5] Finding a way for Two Feathers to identify those most in need of targeted interventions is Dr. Moorehead's goal, and it might include cultural programming, mental health services, employment opportunities, or other forms of support. Though 15 to 20 percent of Two Feathers clients are Yurok Tribal members, there still could be significantly improved coordination across multiple agencies, departments, and types of adults, including teachers.

For Dr. Moorehead, it makes sense to have people like the Yurok teachers featured in this book sitting in on mental health and well-being coordination meetings: "They could tell us, 'This kid has been through a lot,' and then we fill out profiles of the kids with demographics, like ACES [Adverse Childhood Experience Survey][6] kinds of stuff. Then you use the data and say, like,

'If you play with your odds, this child has seven adverse childhood experiences; we should probably get some wraparound programming for this kid.' We'd have to be really focused, deliberate, and coordinated to do that, right? And that's not what's happening."

Given that mental health experts like Dr. Moorehead identify that such coordinated support should be happening, why isn't it? Sadly, part of the reason is that people employed in the many roles that should be serving such kids may feel threatened or unsupported in their own work. Such challenges are not unique to youth well-being, but it is particularly devastating to see it undermined by adults unable to get over themselves. As Dr. Moorehead proclaims, "We have to get rid of egos and work together! Our theory of change is about relationships and engagement that is long-term and sustained. We need less time in meetings and more time knocking on doors, getting out there in the community" (Moorehead Jr. 2022). Such long-term, sustained relationships do require community engagement, and organizations like Two Feathers can fulfill crucial service provision in places that have very little of it.

In rural Humboldt and Del Norte counties, where the majority of the fieldwork for this project took place, free services to support well-being are extremely limited. There is basic health access for Native American people through United Indian Health Services,[7] but rural areas like this one lack the profusion of wraparound services available in more urban spaces where nonprofit organizations tend to cluster. The door knocking isn't metaphorical here. Dr. Moorehead and his team have to go house to house to identify needs and try to address them. No one else is providing that data, and much of Two Feathers' work still relies on word of mouth within communities.

The stakes are high. In the chapter he contributed to *Ka'm-t'em*, Dr. Moorehead cites the suicide cluster in 2015–2016, in which seven Yurok Tribal members died by suicide over the course of fifteen months, leading the Tribe to declare a state of emergency. There have been more suicides in the years since. Violence and its many associated ills continue to plague Indigenous communities, but these are not insular self-harms; they stem from the legacy of postcolonial trauma. Such trauma demands intervention, and cultural connection is one way to manifest it.

The weight of this responsibility hangs on Dr. Moorehead's frame, creasing his brow and tilting him forward in his chair. I ask, in what ways can schools help support well-being given the traumas Native youth face, and given the historical role of schools as cites of culturecide rather than cultural connection? He responds: "One thing I saw is that for my [younger] cousins at MHS, language was a door into interest in what it means to be Native. I don't think they were just trying to please me; I think they were being genuine. There are many variables, of course—other kids, poverty, intergenerational family patterns, dignity, self-respect, how society treats you, cultural capital or whatever you want to call it—but one of them was being part of MHS Yurok language for sure" (Moorehead Jr. 2022). The Yurok language is not a solution by itself, but by opening that door to cultural connection, it did something positive for his cousins. Sure, they might have initially signed up for Yurok language to score some points with their older cousin, or for any other reason. But once in the Yurok language classroom, young people had access to a means of cultural connection that they could take in multiple directions. Building well-being from cultural connection is easier than doing so without it.

The interview has come full circle. We started with cultural connection and how to increase it, walked through the many perils that Native youth face, and returned to increasing culturally meaningful activities as a way to construct a foundation for well-being. Yurok language classes, like dance family membership, are doorways into cultural connectedness. Such connection might shore up well-being for youth who can then carry culturally grounded identities into adulthood. At a minimum, when students are in culturally connected spaces, they are opening doorways of inquiry into the self and community. Learning how to *be* is a complicated process. When young people do this learning with access to culture, including in culturally sustaining education, alongside coordinated networks of providers of health and wellness services, they set trajectories for healthy lives. And those trajectories can carry them into becoming the next generation of elders that future generations will need.

Dr. Moorehead looks at his watch. I know my cues. He has spent time with me that he could have spent with a client, writing a grant, or implementing a program. I'm grateful for his time, and appreciative of the work. He is on the front lines of a mental health crisis caused by colonialism and intergenerational trauma, amplified by COVID-19. We push our chairs back and say goodbye.

Conclusion

Revitalizing rites of passage previously quashed by colonialism as part of cultural survivance is very much a part of well-being in far Northern California. Cutcha Risling Baldy (Hupa, Yurok, and Karuk), captures the notion of community and individual well-being as a culturally grounded process in the title of her book—*We Are Dancing for You*. While well-being includes many universal attributes, it also has particular cultural indicators. The Flower Dance, which Risling Baldy describes as a feminist and cultural revitalization process, serves as a ritual—a rite of passage—that strengthens community wellness in culturally rooted ways (Risling Baldy 2018). Rituals like this hold people in relationships with others that foster mutual accountability and responsibility for something much larger than any individual or family.

Cultural capital comes in a lot of forms. Serenity Bowen, a Miwuk-descendent therapist who focuses on Indigenous youth well-being in the Humboldt County area, notes that cultural connection has been a successful tool in her private practice. In a phone interview with me she explains, "Resilience is so complex because people have so many kinds of identities" (Bowen 2022). She is modest about her own impact, but echoes Dr. Moorehead in citing cultural connection as a vital element of Native youth well-being. Like Risling Baldy, she names the Flower Dance as one of the most powerful things for young Native women in the region. "Cultural connectivity, singing, language, dancing, participating in culture; it is so transformative," Bowen observes (2022).

Community support, including mental health practices that draw on shared cultural frameworks for Native American youth, both provides individual help in working toward overall health and wellness, and increases community resilience. It is a win-win to use decolonizing approaches that assist in cultural flourishing while also addressing the immediate needs of individuals. Moorehead, Bowen, and Risling Baldy all advocate for employing culturally centering practices to support well-being. This cultural revitalization provides a road map for the many different aspects of existence that can be served by linking well-being and relevant cultural knowledge. Investing in culturally grounded support practices that center Native identity as a component of well-being is smart policy. Finding the political will to prioritize such practices takes real leadership, and a hefty dose of determination.

PART II

Culturally Sustaining Teaching and Learning

CHAPTER 3

James Gensaw and His Students: "Gently Holding Space for Everyone"

Introduction: "Eureka: I Found It!"

Nestled against the coast of Humboldt Bay, Eureka, California, is still trying to reinvent itself.[1] From Indigenous homeland to gold rush outpost to logging center, this blue-collar town of 26,512 people is in a continual identity crisis. In the early 2000s, there was a debate about whether to build a liquid natural gas plant at the edge of Humboldt Bay (Easthouse 2003). The cannabis industry, synonymous with Humboldt County when it was illegal and booming, is now intensely regulated and wilting at the county level due to competitive pressure bottoming out wholesale prices. Growers have been trying to stay afloat in the face of big business that has moved into cultivation and distribution since marijuana's full legalization in California in 2016 (Greenson 2020). As of this writing, debate is ongoing over whether to allow a Norwegian company to build an enormous fish farm on the Samoa Spit, a strip of sand pushing against the Pacific Ocean (Alexander 2023; Savage 2022). Eureka continues to search for its economic foundation, bringing up questions of identity and economic stability for the town's residents.

Eureka High School (EHS) sits squarely in the center of town, a straight fourteen blocks up from the local courthouse and ominous salmon-pink jail. EHS is the school in this study that I am most familiar with since I am an alumna. It is also the closest school to the homes of family and friends I stay with when I return for fieldwork. My relationships with teachers there are in part based on long-standing connections and ease of access to the school—a twenty-five-minute drive from my childhood home, where my parents still live on their isolated mountaintop. In spring 2022, I was given a key to an empty office at the school, which made it possible to spontaneously drop into a class and invite a student to an interview. It also gave me cognitive dissonance, feeling like an adult at a place so intimately connected with my identity as a teenager.

With its logger mascot given pride of place on the front campus lawn, complete with a chewing-tobacco tin pressing through a rear pocket, EHS maintains a settler-colonial swagger amid a rapidly diversifying town (Gellman 2022b). The school and town were majority White during my time there as a student in the 1990s, but over the last several decades, increased Latinx,[2] Hmong, Vietnamese, Filipino, and Polynesian migration, among other groups, has changed the demographics (EdData 2022).

The numbers tell a story of their own. In a 2022 survey, Eureka's median family income was $51,979, a full $40,000 lower than the California average (United States Census Bureau 2024). In 2021–2022, of Eureka High School's 1,281 students, 785 were eligible for free lunch, and 150 were English learners (EdData 2022), but given a significant informal economic sector based around cannabis, as well as an undocumented population, this data is likely incomplete. The American Community 2022 survey showed 13.8 percent of the Eureka population speaks a language other than English at home, with more than 8 percent of that being Spanish (United States Census Bureau 2024). Fifty-five percent of the student body is racially diverse, with the remaining 45 percent White (EdData 2022). In 2021–2022, that meant 633 students were White, 69 were American Indian or Alaska Native, 297 were Hispanic or Latino, 118 were two or more races, 147 were Asian, 30 were Black or African American, and 18 were Native Hawaiian or Pacific Islander (EdData 2022).

School curricula have not caught up with the population change and still disseminate White-dominant content in many classes. But some educators have risen to the challenge of making what they teach more relevant to students of a wider range of backgrounds. These teachers innovate in a variety of ways, for example, by including units on local Native American history in US history classes (Anderson 2018) or teaching about migration in Spanish classes (Olson 2022). Other efforts are tokenistic and fall flat, like hallway and classroom decorations that reinforce stereotypes. For example, a "China hallway" theme during a week celebrating international cultures, complete with red lanterns, made one Chinese American student feel excluded and reduced to a Disney stereotype (Anonymous 2018). Such attempts, and their failures, are by no means unique to this school. The high levels of student-on-student harassment between classes, during lunch periods, and on school buses indicate a school climate plagued by toxic "joking" that demands intervention. Though students of all backgrounds generally report liking EHS, for BIPOC students from many backgrounds, this is mixed in with having to armor up emotionally to get through each day.

The Yurok Tribe is the largest Indigenous tribe in California, with 6,491 enrolled members in 2025, yet its language base consists of just sixteen advanced-level speakers. The Tribe's Education Department, through its Yurok Language Program, has been laboring to expand the speaker base by prioritizing language education for everyone. Yurok language is offered to everyone from Head Start–aged children (pre-K) through six schools in the K–12 system, and at the local community college. There are multiple types of adult classes, including some especially for Tribal employees as well as those open to everyone. As of 2025, there are approximately 750 beginning-level Yurok speakers and 45 intermediate speakers as well.

This chapter shows how culturally sustaining pedagogy can impact youth. This type of teaching is defined as when schools operate as "places where the cultural ways of being in communities of color are sustained, rather than eradicated" (CADOE 2024). How does culturally sustaining pedagogy incentivize students to both show up in school and work toward benchmarks such as the California State Seal of Biliteracy in Yurok? Such institutional credentialization is one way to increase student well-being by continuing to validate Native American knowledge in formal curricular spaces.

"In Yurok I feel human": Teaching as Decolonization

James Gensaw[3] is culturally grounded. A Yurok Tribal member of Yurok and Tolowa descent, he is one of the most advanced Yurok speakers alive today. Mr. Gensaw developed his language proficiency as an adult, learning from elders who instilled in him the importance of passing the language on to others. He also dances in ceremonies and gained local acclaim for his traditional eel-fishing skills. A former wrestler himself, he has been a dedicated youth wrestling coach for years.

Mr. Gensaw teaches in an Indigenous pedagogical style, relying on stories, games, talking circles, and other culturally resonant tools that may not always fit standard definitions of language teaching in settler-colonial educational frameworks. Instead of flash cards or vocabulary pages for learning animal names, for example, Mr. Gensaw tells the class Yurok origin stories about the animals, repeating their names in the language multiple times. As I observed his classes, it took me a while to set down my own expectations of what language learning should look like, having studied Spanish, French, Turkish, and German all in very standard Western classroom approaches.

Learning Yurok with Mr. Gensaw resonates with the concept of Indigegogy—teaching from a fundamentally Indigenous framework that shares language in connection with worldview (Wilson and Schellhammer 2021: 56). In doing so, he counters the forced adherence to a settler-colonial model of education that requires students to drop who they are and become who teachers need them to be (Wilson and Schellhammer 2021: 28–29). In addition to a wide range of computer and analog language-teaching tools, Mr. Gensaw uses a Yurok language grammar textbook created by UC Berkeley linguist Andrew Garrett in collaboration with the Yurok Tribe (Garrett 2014). He also teaches an acclaimed graphic novel about the role of Yurok soldiers in World War II, which includes Yurok language in the text (Lowry and Ekedal 2019). That textual adoption didn't come easy; in order to get the graphic novel approved, Mr. Gensaw had to educate a reluctant curriculum committee about why it was valid pedagogical material.

I worked with Mr. Gensaw and his students intermittently from 2018 to 2022 when he was the Yurok language teacher at Eureka High School and McKinleyville High School. In fall 2023, Mr. Gensaw left EHS and MHS to take over the Del Norte High School (DNHS) Yurok language courses, enabling the longtime Yurok teacher there to retire. The move also brought him—a single dad—closer to the Yurok Reservation, where he has family and where his three adolescent children are culturally rooted. As an alumnus of DNHS, he was excited about going back there as a teacher, but his EHS and MHS students cried when he told them he wouldn't be back next year.

Mr. Gensaw offers his students a tremendous gift—he treats them like adults and offers them a Yurok perspective on the local region, something that is far too frequently a rarity in public high schools. Mr. Gensaw does not define what he is doing as decolonizing curricula. Modestly, he says he just shows up and teaches language each day. But his impact is more than that. In the schools where he works, Mr. Gensaw has helped remake his classrooms into spaces that instill pride and confidence in Native students. He has also helped students from a range of backgrounds better understand the vibrant and contemporary Native culture that exists throughout what is now called the United States.

In 2022, after he received a teaching award, students reflected on Mr. Gensaw's teaching and his impact on their lives: "He cared about me in a way that I really needed, that I wasn't getting at home." "He was the safe adult I knew I could always talk to." "He treated me with respect when others didn't." "He was like a father figure to me." "His class was 40 percent of the reason I went to school each day." "He helped me understand that Native people still exist here, and that the stories I learned before about Columbus, about Native extinction, were wrong." And of course, "His classes were fun! We got to get up and move around." "His class wasn't stressful, and that is what I needed." These statements show the mark of an educator making an impact not only in his content expertise but holistically on student lives.

When I asked Mr. Gensaw where his approach to teaching comes from, he responded: "Training with the elders taught me about really being present, about gently holding space for everyone. I remember an essay from a student in one of my EHS classes years ago. They wrote, 'I feel like I'm a robot in all my other classes. In Yurok I feel human.' Students have so much pressure to get straight As, to do things right, or from some people to do the wrong thing. I try to make my classes a place where they can just be themselves" (Gensaw 2022).

Mr. Gensaw plays multiple roles for students in the classroom. He was the only Native American person on the faculty at both EHS and MHS, and one of very few at DNHS. He is also by nature a sympathetic adult, and by his own lived experience, one poised to be an ally to struggling BIPOC students. One consistent measure of Mr. Gensaw's impact in the classroom is the way students look to him as a positive role model. He represents what it means to be a Yurok person upholding his culture. His approach to teaching, though he himself does not label it so, is part of the movement to decolonize both curricula and the process by which it is implemented. At baseline, he hopes to expand the speaker base for the Yurok language.

Mr. Gensaw carries out this work quietly by showing up for his students day after day and being himself, all without apology. He brings culturally sustaining curricula to the schools where he teaches, and this work is ceaseless. Below, I share responses from Mr. Gensaw's students in focus groups and interviews; they reflect on their experiences of learning from him.

"To get more culture": Who Takes Yurok and Why

Across all four schools where Yurok is taught, Yurok I and II classes tend to be at maximum capacity. At EHS and MHS, there are up to thirty students from all backgrounds in Yurok I and II. The classes can feel boisterously out of control sometimes, with behavioral issues concentrated in freshman and sophomore students across demographics. They throw hats or food back and forth and lean over to look at each other's phones, which are supposed to be stowed away but frequently are in use.

Some students opt out of upper-level language classes after they fulfill the required two years for high school graduation. This thinning-out process means that even though Yurok classes frequently combine third- and fourth-year students, Yurok III and IV classes tend to have fewer than ten students. While students joke about getting sick of each other, there is an unspoken air of trust and intimacy in these classrooms that is not evident in the lower-level classes. These students have been taking Yurok together for years and know each other's backgrounds in ways that students in other classes may not, mainly because of the personal nature of Mr. Gensaw's talking circles.

In one focus group, two chatty young women, Kara and Heather (pseudonyms),[4] spoke to how they self-identify and why they are taking Yurok:

> *Kara:* I have enough percentage of Tolowa to qualify for that roll, but not Yurok. I took Yurok because the elders in my family are Yurok and it's nice to learn backstories about them that I never really knew. I just wanted to learn about Yurok history and language. And I also used to go to language camps when I was younger, where we would, like, stay with a bunch of our cousins and a bunch of random kids for the weekend and learn the language and stuff. I really liked it, so I thought this class would be similar.
>
> I feel like this class isn't just, like, learning a language. We're kinda learning about stuff that not everyone knows. Like, we're learning about different parts of history, so it's kinda history class too. We really never learned about Native stuff in our other classes. (Focus Group 1.1 2022)

For Kara, Yurok classes were an expression of her Yurok identity that she remembers from childhood, but that she doesn't qualify to claim officially through blood quantum. It is a doorway to Yurok-ness that reinforces things she had some exposure to in other spaces. Kara also notes the absence of Native content in her other classes, which makes its availability all the more special. She also observes that the language class is not solely about language, which Heather also articulates.

Heather: For me, I don't have enough blood quantum to be on the
Yurok roll or anything like that, but I still qualify for UIHS, so
I identify as Native. Plus, I had [family members] on the Yurok
Council and working at UIHS, so my family is very involved. We
go to dances and helped clean up the area when they first started
to bring back the Jump Dance around Orick, and my family has
a dance kitchen.[5] One of the main reasons I took Yurok was to
be able to get more culture, from not just my grandma. In this
class, we get a different aspect of the history that the teachers in
school—the actual history teachers—don't teach because that's
not what's written in the book. (Focus Group 1.1 2022)

For both of these young women, blood quantum requirements disqualify
them from official Yurok enrollment, but the language classes facilitate their
connection to their Yurok identities.

The idea that Mr. Gensaw is filling in the pieces of history that are not
written in the textbooks is highly significant. By adding the Yurok language
class to the curricula, he is able to conduct multiple types of interventions
with students in addition to helping to revitalize the language speaker base.
And it resonates with students.

Again, Kara and Heather comment about why Yurok language is
meaningful:

Kara: Not a lot of people speak it, and it's good learning on life skills.
Like, we learn a lot of empathy and stuff like that. And we're not
just learning language, we're learning community too.
Heather: It ties into culture. Plus, at least for me in freshman year,
which was hectic and crazy, Yurok was a safe space. We can talk
to the people in our class. We have [talking] circles.[6] We're able
to share and not feel like we're going to get judged or anything.
And it, like, spreads the culture to not just Native students. We
have White kids in there too. It's, like, weird to say but kids who
aren't Native descendants, they stuck it out for four years, and
they like the class and they like learning about it; that really
matters too. (Focus Group 1.1 2022)

Heather reflects the fact that the Yurok language class is a safe space amid a
hard first year of high school. In addition, the use of talking circles—something

available as a tool for all teachers but only taken up by some—created a non-judgmental space for students to share what was going on for them in a given moment. The point about the impact of having White students in the class is also significant for Heather. She notes her own appreciation of the non-Native students who made it all the way to level IV Yurok—their willing participation in something she feels culturally connected to was affirming for her. It speaks to the importance of making classes like this open to all students who want to take them.

Yet Heather and Kara note the vulnerability of Yurok at their school, since they know not everyone appreciates it. "If it [the Yurok class] were to be taken away, I feel like a lot of Native students would not have a place they could go. And then people who are interested in learning about the local cultures wouldn't have the chance to do that, because they don't teach it in our history classes" (Focus Group 1.1 2022). Both the safe space the class creates, as well as access to the content itself, are meaningful for these students. Kara and Heather go into more depth about the content about Native people they receive, or don't receive, in other classes:

> *Kara:* The books never really talked about, like, *Native* people. They talked about *Indian* people. So, it was kinda hard to understand, like, who they were talking about.
>
> *Heather:* And when they do talk about Natives, they don't talk about it enough or they, not to be rude, but they whitewash it to make it seem like, they're [White people] the good guys and this is how it went. "This is exactly how it happened, nothing bad," like, totally skipping over all the genocide and everything that happened!
>
> *Kara:* Yeah, I feel like the books are really old, and they just kinda summarize. Like, they'll say it [colonization happened] but in a really brief way. They'll say they [Whites] took over but they won't say what they did to the people. They just kinda say, "That's just what happened," and go on with it. They don't really explain the wrongness. (Focus Group 1.1 2022)

Through this research, I try to understand how that "wrongness" affects students. I asked young people from a variety of backgrounds about their memories of how they saw people with their own identities and backgrounds portrayed in the classroom. Answers ranged widely depending on demographics, but Native American students universally decried both the stereotypical depiction of the defeated Indian warrior and the lack of Native perspective on events such as the Gold Rush or the mission system. The young women explain:

> *Heather:* When we were younger, for Columbus Day, they would show us [glorifying] videos, and I was, like, "He didn't find the land!" There were already people that inhabited, like, everywhere! They were cooperating communities, they could talk to each other—in different languages, but still—they had trade systems. So, Columbus didn't discover anything, he just showed up and took his claim. And they didn't explain that!
>
> *Kara:* In my history class this year, the teacher kinda like went over Columbus Day and tried to explain the badness of Columbus Day too, like, both sides of it. But that's the first year they've ever done that! In Yurok, we talked about how people now are recognizing past wrongness and giving the rightful owners things back, like land. I've seen that happening in the present day. But people here are just now realizing what had been happening around here! (Focus Group 1.1 2022)

The students recount their numerous exposures to erroneous myths of settler colonialism, and also mention their own awareness that what was being taught was wrong. Kara also sees the possibility for change, with a history teacher who offered a critique of Columbus Day and mentioned land being returned to Indigenous people. But many challenges persist. Heather comments, "I didn't really pay attention in my history class because how they teach doesn't work for me. But there will be teachers or kids who say something that contradicts what actually happened. Like, they were talking about what happened at Indian Island, but they, like, don't say everything that happened" (Focus Group 1.1 2022).

Heather is referring to the island in Humboldt Bay that is the site of the Wiyot Tribe's World Renewal Ceremony. Labeled "Indian Island" by White people preceding the massacre of Wiyot people there in 1860, it has been renamed Duluwat Island since its return to the Wiyot Tribe in 2019. However, many high schoolers and others who were not particularly politically engaged tended to use the old name. While the return of the island to the

Wiyot people was heralded by some locally, there is generally little discussion of the massacre of Wiyot people that instituted its colonization.

Throughout our conversation, Kara and Heather describe how the absence of representation, or erroneous representation, leads to distorted views of local communities. And while both students are careful to say that their US history classes have mentioned some of these issues in more complex ways than they got in their previous K–10[7] schooling, they identify Yurok classes as unique spaces where real information and dialogue on Native American history and contemporary life are exchanged. These two young women shared their candid critiques with little expectation other than to be heard, and to set the record straight in a way they have available to them.

"I *knew*, but, like, I didn't *know*": Focus Group Reflections on Violence

Ideas from Heather and Kara's interview were reiterated in a Yurok III and IV student focus group at EHS. Tina and Jason identify as White, and Kevin identifies as Yurok and Hupa.[8] When asked why they had wanted to take Yurok language classes and if they knew about the genocide against Native American people locally before taking Yurok, students reflected as follows:

> *Jason:* I don't have any, like, Native American people in my family, but I just took the class because I thought it would be cool to learn since a lot of places didn't have it. Before, I knew that, like, it was their land, but I didn't know how bad it was until Gensaw would talk about it, and we would read stories or watch a movie on boarding schools and stuff like that.
>
> *Tina:* I don't have any [Native American] heritage either, but because it's an endangered language, I wanted to be part of helping to revive it. It would be really cool to see the language come back even though, like, that would be really tough. I didn't really know like anything about any of the massacres around here before. Mr. Gensaw gave us a bunch of articles on it. Since then, I've learned a lot more about it. I probably wouldn't have known that at all if I hadn't taken Yurok. What I really like is that you learn a lot of lessons too, with stories and stuff. Like, you don't just learn a language, you learn the culture too.

Both White students use the word "cool" to describe part of why they took Yurok, as it felt unique. They also both state that they want to be part of helping to bring back the language, with Tina more explicit than Jason about this goal. As non-heritage-speaking students, both Tina and Jason described how educative it was to learn about this reality of settler colonialism from Mr. Gensaw. Some of their sentiments are shared with, and some are different from, those of the heritage-speaking student in the focus group.

> *Kevin:* My dad's side all grew up in Hoopa and I decided to take
> it [Yurok] 'cause it's a language that my family speaks. I don't
> really think I knew what happened over the entire US and in
> Canada, with some of the boarding schools—I *knew*, but, like,
> I didn't *know* to the extent that I know now. If it wasn't for
> Gensaw, I wouldn't really know what happened. Like, he made
> us write papers on it! It's good to learn the history that has
> happened in this town and to learn more about the area that
> you are in. (Focus Group 3.3 2022)

As Heather and Kara did, Kevin makes visible the crucial link between language and history. The significance of one elective language class that essentially undoes the silence and misinformation perpetuated by years of previous schooling speaks to the importance of including Indigenous languages in curricula. It also points to the need to decolonize the curricula as a whole and to find ways to insert local truths into classes throughout the K–12 system. One class should not bear so much responsibility, but in the absence of alternatives, it is doing decolonizing work.

Culturally relevant curricula for BIPOC populations—the instructional use of information that shares BIPOC knowledge and perspectives—has mostly been in the national eye through the discourse on teaching critical race theory (Ladson-Billings 2021). The criminalization of CRT (Thomason 2023) is taking place as I write this book.[9] In response, some states and districts have tried to create culturally relevant curricula through ethnic studies courses, which have also been under attack by White politicians and administrators who are fearful of BIPOC empowerment (Cintli Rodriguez 2009). In stark contrast to states like Arizona and Florida, which have attempted to make teaching ethnic studies illegal (Cintli Rodriguez 2009, Prose 2023), California's state legislature passed Assembly Bill 101 in 2021. Expected to be implemented in 2025, the new law requires that all California high schools begin offering ethnic studies courses that highlight the overlooked experiences and contributions of Blacks, Latinxs, Native Americans, and Asian Americans (Fensterwald 2021). Through this requirement and a broader commitment to culturally sustaining pedagogy, California may be an example of how states can shift the heavy burden off Indigenous language classes to provide mainstreamed access to previously silenced information. California will also make ethnic studies a requirement for all students to graduate by 2030.

Changing the School Climate One Assembly at a Time

Several Novembers in a row in the 2010s, Mr. Gensaw would get the same request from a school administrator. Could he please bring students from the Native American Club (which he advises) to demonstrate Yurok dancing at lunchtime? Club members were directed to come in regalia to the quad, a central public space on the school grounds where students eat and socialize between classes. School administrators usually invited the local media to show off the dancing students, and footage was aired locally as part of demonstrating inclusion of Native American communities.

Such performative spectacle has been roundly criticized by Leilani Sabzalian (Alutiiq) in her analysis of how Native American Heritage Month plays out in schools (2019: 147–169). Performative spectacles happen when schools treat Native dances or other cultural displays as proof of their diversity, but do not invest in tangible inclusivity for Native students. Unfortunately, this has been the approach at EHS over many years.

Native American Club students take pride in sharing their regalia—which is painstakingly handmade with locally significant items such as feathers and shells—and their dancing, which is also laden with cultural significance. But given the lunchtime atmosphere, there was little behavior control beyond a few harried lunch monitors for the rowdy students surrounding the dancers. Mr. Gensaw describes how, on the one hand, it was nice that the school wanted the Native American students to share their culture, but on the other hand, "It wasn't always respectful. Some kids [in the audience] would make fun of the dancers, mimicking war cries and calling out 'chief!' The media would be invited to come cover the dancing as part of their Thanksgiving coverage, and it felt like we were a spectacle. Other cultural groups and issues would sometimes be presented in school assemblies in the gym, where teachers monitored student behavior. I thought, why didn't we get to have that? We needed more respect for sharing our culture" (Gensaw 2019).

One of the Yurok IV focus groups, composed of all seniors, reflected on the quad dancing, as they had attended when they were freshman and sophomores. They show different reactions, in line with their own identities (Kevin is Native; Tina and Jason are White):

> *Kevin:* Kids watching were yelling [demonstrates flapping hand over mouth in a mock war whoop]. They were saying the singers sound like dogs when they're jumping. They could've just been saying that to try and fit in with their friend group. 'Cause if they say it once and saw that people laughed, they just keep going, but it could also be deeper than that.
>
> *Jason:* I feel like the [Native] singers just, like, make noises like that.
>
> *Tina:* Well, I think when people see something they don't understand or don't have background on it, it's very easy for them to say stuff like that.
>
> *Jason:* People will joke about that stuff, but they're saying it even if they don't mean it. Even if they do laugh in the moment, they might be covering up because they don't want to butt heads about it. I think you gotta go to every new person nonjudgmental. (Focus Group 3.3 2022).

While the Native student identified the problematic behavior, all three students note that student ridicule of the dancers might be coming from a place of ignorance or social complacency, as seen in kids who try to fit in with others who are laughing.

Both Tina and Kevin responded that they tried to not care about the ridiculing behavior and would walk away from it if they could. But Tina also notes, "I guess also it is kind of a privilege for me 'cause, like, I'm not Native American or of any other ethnicity, so I can just block it out" (Focus Group 3.3 2022). The strategy of blocking it out is echoed by the Native student:

> *Kevin:* I kind of learned not to take offense from it 'cause it's been said so many times that it's, like, you just learn to ignore it, kind of. I mean, if it doesn't make you feel the right way then you should speak up about it . . .

Tina: But once you've spoken up about it, and stand up for yourself
so many times and it still keeps happening or nothing really
changes, then it's, like, "Okay, what is left for me to do?"
Everybody's just used to it. (Focus Group 3.3 2022)

The accumulated micro- and macroaggressions against Native students can
be debilitating, especially when, as Tina points out, nothing really changes
even if people speak out against it. One might wonder, where are the adults
while all this is happening? Kevin and Tina note the complacency of the
adults; even if teachers lay ground rules for respectful language and speaking,
they don't necessarily enforce them:

Kevin: Yeah, I don't think nobody's trying to put a stop to it. Teachers
say like, "no bullying," that I guess would be the broad thing to
cover or "no racial slurs." But other than that, they don't really
say nothing else.

Tina: Most of the teachers will say [no bullying] to us, but they
don't really reinforce it. Some teachers definitely will, but the
majority of them don't, and they just let kids get away with
whatever. So, a lot of kids then don't take them seriously. They
tell me "Don't use racial slurs" or "don't bully," but they've
never stopped me before, so I'm not taking that seriously.
(Focus Group 3.3 2022)

Tina, Jason, and Kevin were all in their final spring semester of high school,
and their disillusionment is telling. They have watched for years as teachers
and staff have ineffectively repeated the mantra of no bullying without actually shutting down discriminatory behavior happening around them. The
impunity this instills in people who discriminate, and the hopelessness of
other students that things will change, is concerning as students transition to
become the next adult members of the community.

Each of these students had a fairly different stance on the issue of the
dance example. Jason, a White, sporty male, brushes off the discrimination
and is mostly quiet as his classmates talk; Tina, an empathetic White female,
tries to see it both ways, and the Native student, Kevin, mentions that he has
learned to just ignore the toxicity around him in order to get through his
days. In many ways, this focus group was a painful but insightful glimpse into

how student positionality is deterministic in how young people process and manage school climate.

As for Mr. Gensaw, when he described the dancing on the quad situation, I asked if he could request to bring the students to dance at a school assembly space instead, where student behavior could be monitored. The next time he got the annual request he did just that, and it was granted. Students danced without being demeaned by their peers, and the audience perhaps received the dancing differently, since it took place in a mandatory assembly. There were no behavioral issues that time.

Conclusion

Mr. Gensaw faces the impact of colonization at every turn within his classroom, school, and district. His presence, by supporting student well-being individually as well as collectively, is deeply rooted in decolonizing educational spaces. For Native American students at EHS, the school climate is quite toxic, and Yurok classes are a place of reprieve (Gellman 2023: 196–215). White students show various degrees of awareness of these school and community climate issues. By and large, the most aware White students are the ones in the Yurok classes, where issues of discrimination are discussed overtly. By contrast, when I spoke with White students in US history or civics classes, which served as controls for the theory-testing portion of the study, their awareness of school climate issues, or of much of anything related to Native American history, culture, or discrimination, was generally much lower. Teachers from those classes are likely well-meaning educators who want to do right by their students. But they don't have the personal background or professional training that allows them to facilitate as Mr. Gensaw is doing.

This chapter showed that Yurok classes are more than just language instruction. The student focus groups directly spoke to the impacts of discrimination and misrepresentation on Native American students from the wider school community. Yurok language classes are safe spaces of affirmation for Native American students, and they are spaces for learning to undo past misconceptions for White students. The classes are also microcosms of learning and model how to be together in diverse communities, where practices of vulnerability and appreciation across difference are modeled by the teacher and mimicked by the students.

Eureka as a town continues to grapple with its economic and cultural foundations. The verdict is still out as to how the community will sustain itself. Whatever path the town takes economically will surely impact its demographic composition and character. In the meantime, the school district and schools themselves have opportunities to engage in best practices that support Native American well-being.

CHAPTER 4

"To Not Think of Native Identity as a Sin": Learning as Affirmation

Introduction: "Where the Horses Have the Right of Way"

Sixteen miles north of Eureka along the coast, McKinleyville, California, is an outdoor recreation–focused town.[1] Based on the 2020 Census, McKinleyville's population is 16,262 and the median family income is $68,239 (United States Census Bureau 2024). In 2022, there was 53.9 percent employment and 4.4 percent of people were without health coverage (United States Census Bureau 2024). McKinleyville hosts the Arcata–Eureka area airport, the region's link to the world beyond the Redwood Curtain. The town was renamed from Minorville to McKinleyville in 1901 in commemoration of the assassination of William McKinley, the twenty-fifth President of the United States, whose racism and refusal to challenge the status quo are prevalent throughout White Humboldt County.[2]

In an homage to the Doctrine of Discovery, the town's Chamber of Commerce website advertises upcoming Pony Express Days, "A McKinleyville Tradition Since 1968," but lacks any historical context for either the event or the town itself (McKinleyville Chamber of Commerce 2022). There is no explanation of what the Pony Express Days are commemorating on their website. In fact, it is a celebration of the horseback-rider-based Pony Express postal service that stretched from Missouri to California from 1860–1861. Perhaps it is assumed that locals already know. In 2022, a local Indigenous food vendor was among those listed to sell refreshments at Pony Express Days. What does it mean to have an Indigenous food booth at an annual celebration that commemorates settler colonialism? This tension, a fusion of capitalism and colonialism, runs through the community and its education system.

The town motto makes it clear that outdoor lifestyles come first, and these days horseback riding is for pleasure rather than for the ranching labor that was common during colonization. There are significant disparities in McKinleyville, which has long been perceived as a local racist stronghold and extremely White, with Native Americans the least advantaged (Race Counts 2024). As a smaller town with less industrial and service sector base, McKinleyville has diversified much more slowly than Eureka, but its demographics are changing. An expanding BIPOC population is perceptible in the town and schools. Native American and Latinx families who want to move out of Eureka are frequently priced out of university town Arcata and end up relocating farther north to McKinleyville.

McKinleyville High School is located in the Northern Humboldt Union High School District (NHUHSD). Located near feeder elementary and middle schools, MHS's classrooms are set off outdoor hallways in an open campus model that feels airy and spacious. The majority of students enroll at MHS after completing eighth grade at one of several elementary or middle schools, including McKinleyville Middle School, Big Lagoon Elementary School, Fieldbrook Elementary School, Orick Elementary School, and Trinidad Middle School. Students rarely transfer from Arcata into McKinleyville—instead the reverse often occurs.

In 2021–2022, MHS had 583 enrolled students, with the following racial and ethnic breakdown: 343 White, 52 American Indian or Alaska Native, 67 Hispanic or Latino, 78 two or more races, and 29 not reported (EdData 2022). The American Community 2022 survey showed just over 8 percent of people in McKinleyville speaking a language other than English at home, with 5 percent of that speaking Spanish and 0.4 percent speaking "other languages" (United States Census Bureau 2024). In 2021–2022, 246 MHS students were eligible for free lunch. The NHUHSD leadership is open to ideas about increasing inclusivity, as a local newspaper article on the necessity of Indigenous curriculum points out (Wipf 2022). At the same time, BIPOC students in this district expressed a litany of complaints about the microaggressions and overt misrepresentation they experienced both at MHS and at neighboring elementary and middle schools during their K–8 education.

The Politics of Yurok in McKinleyville High School

MHS has offered Yurok language classes as part of the standard language elective curriculum since 2008.[3] Prior to the 2020–2021 academic year at MHS, the Yurok language was available in only one class period per day, with levels I through IV all together. There were as many as thirty-six students in the classroom at one time, with a priority for Native students to enroll. Any language pedagogue will say that teaching four levels of language in one class is not a good approach, as it undermines the progress of students in the higher levels or leaves beginner students frustrated. Combining classes is a tactic used by schools when budget constraints require courses to be filled to maximum capacity.

Yurok language classes at all four schools included in this book relied on combining Yurok language levels to some degree. In 2021–2022, the four levels at MHS were split into two classes, with I–II combined and III–IV combined. This was an improvement over the all-in-one model, but still problematic for language growth because it generally results in teaching to the lowest level of language learner.

James Gensaw taught Yurok at MHS from 2019 to 2022, during which time he was also the Yurok language teacher at EHS. Even though it was logistically stressful for his family, he took over the Yurok language levels I–II and III–IV classes at MHS so that his cousin, former Yurok teacher Awok[4] Kathleen Vigil, could retire in 2020.[5] Had he not stepped in, the classes would have been cancelled because there was no other teacher available.

Being split between two schools is problematic for teachers. Neither school was able to offer Mr. Gensaw a full-time position, so he would teach in the mornings at EHS, drive some twenty minutes north during his lunch break, and teach at MHS in the afternoons. This dual part-time appointment meant he was never able to participate in afternoon faculty meetings at EHS, nor was he available for morning faculty meetings at MHS. As such, he was unable to be fully integrated with either school team. It also meant a lot of lunches eaten in his truck speeding up the highway.

One goal of the Yurok Language Program is to have Yurok language teachers not only be certified to teach Yurok but obtain their California teacher's certification as well. This can help place language teachers in full-time positions. Mr. Gensaw's move to Del Norte High School in the fall of 2022 allows him to make exactly that change by adding Native American Studies and study halls to his teaching load. In the sections that follow, Mr. Gensaw and his students unpack the legacy of colonization in relation to their own identities and education.

"To be more connected to my roots": Colonization's Legacy

Twenty froggies went to school
Down beside a rushing pool
Twenty little coats of green,
Twenty vests all white and clean . . .

Master Bullfrog, brave and stern,
Called the classes in their turn;
Taught them how to nobly strive,
Also how to leap and dive . . .

Polished in a high degree,
As each froggie ought to be,
Now they sit on other logs
Teaching other little frogs
    —George Cooper, traditional children's poem (1876)

At MHS, there are thirty-two students in Yurok I–II, and only seven students in Yurok III–IV. I pull students out of the large class for smaller focus groups in whatever conference room or empty office the kindly administrative assistants will let me squat in. For the tiny Yurok III–IV class, Mr. Gensaw and I agree one day that we could use a talking circle format to basically cover the same ground as a focus group, but with the whole class in the classroom.

Mr. Gensaw likes to open student talking circles with a song or ritual to help students bring their attention into the space. On a brisk March afternoon in 2022, Mr. Gensaw prefaces his song by talking about how a Yurok elder, who had been enrolled in a boarding school, taught him the lyrics of the twenty froggies song, but set to Yurok singing patterns. As Mr. Gensaw starts to sing, students settle into a moment of calm and respectful quiet. One student joins in, matching Mr. Gensaw's vocal patterns. Mr. Gensaw then passes a talking feather around and starts by asking students how they are. Each student takes the feather and responds; many of them say they are tired, and they pass the feather along (Focus Group 4.1 2022).

Six students participate in the talking circle, and all six identify as Native American in some way—with Wiyot, Yurok, Karuk, and Tolowa identities represented. Multiple students self-identify as being from mixed White and Native American backgrounds. They all name family identity as their motivation for taking Yurok, with several preceded by siblings who had already taken it. Here is an excerpt, with pseudonyms for participants, in their own voices:

> *Mark:* I know other languages would be more useful if I traveled, but my grandpa is a fluent Karuk speaker, so I wanted to take something closer to me. Plus, everyone should be living more in the Native way. It's good to try to have the best understanding you can about Native culture, and we do that here.
>
> *Jorge:* I'm taking this class so I can personally get more connected to my Yurok background. And all my siblings did Yurok. It's always cool to learn all the little things behind what we see, like in ceremony or just outside around us.
>
> *Ella:* I want to be more connected to my roots and appreciate what the ancestors passed down to us. At family gatherings we'd speak Yurok sometimes, and I want to learn Wiyot someday. My [half-] siblings have a White dad, and they are basically White. I want them to learn to not think of Native identity as a sin, and to prove to my White grandma that it isn't a sin. To do that, I need to learn more myself. I'm trying to hold on to the part of our family history that isn't White.

Each of the three students makes direct connections between language and identity and wanting to connect more with their Native heritage. For Mark, since Karuk isn't a language elective option, Yurok language classes still allow him to get closer to his Karuk and Yurok identity. Jorge, as a younger sibling, is following the curricular pathway of his siblings. And Ella recognizes that in order to support her White family members to stop seeing Native identity as something that is sinful, she needs to better educate herself about it. Even though, like Mark, she'd prefer a different local Native language that is more predominant in her family heritage, she takes Yurok because she can still get

some benefits of Native identity consolidation from it. Mr. Gensaw also comments on these language trade-offs.

> *Mr. Gensaw:* When I was in high school [at DNHS] they only offered
> Tolowa, so I took it, 'cause I'm also Tolowa. But I wanted to learn
> *my* language—Yurok. Because elders spoke it, I thought everyone
> spoke Yurok! I thought I needed to catch up! I never thought I'd
> be a teacher, but elders told me I needed to be. They told me that
> if the language was lost, it would be my fault for not passing it on.
> I don't want them to lose the class here, so even though it is less
> convenient for my family, I stepped up to keep the class when the
> previous teacher retired. (Focus Group 4.1 2022)

The sense of responsibility that Mr. Gensaw feels, to not be the one responsible
for more language loss, is one that is resonant of Dr. Moorehead's discussion in
Chapter 2 of needing more elders who put the community first. Mr. Gensaw is
doing just that. By shouldering the responsibility of language transmission, he
is sacrificing his own personal convenience for the greater good.

When the talking feather comes to me, I offer that I'm interested in studying language revitalization spaces because they seem like concrete steps in
addressing previous language theft. I then seed another question about experiences of Native American representation in K–12 curricula:

> *Joe:* Well, something I remember is I've always been taught about
> Christopher Columbus, and how he was, like, good—he did
> everything right. And then I took Yurok and I started to learn
> a lot more. I started seeing, like, a bunch of bad stuff. Finally, in
> my government class the teacher started teaching us about, like,
> all the genocides and everything that was happening. That was
> just one experience where I was taught wrong and not given the
> true history.
>
> *Allen:* I think about, like, Christopher Columbus stuff and
> Thanksgiving, like, how your whole life through school, you're
> kinda just taught that it was this nice meal between the Indians
> and pilgrims, and it really wasn't at all. I think that's something
> that the education system really likes to put on kids, that there
> was this super great thing, when it just wasn't.

Greg: Yeah, my [elementary school] teacher was pretty good at explaining, like, the whole Christopher Columbus thing. She didn't just, like, say how good he was. She would talk about how, like, he was bad to people and he wasn't good. She wouldn't just, you know, lie to us and go with what normal schools do. (Focus Group 4.1 2022)

The glorification of Columbus and Thanksgiving were the two most common examples of problematic curricula that students pointed out time and again across multiple schools (Gellman 2024). A handful of students had experiences like those of Joe and Greg, who had educators willing to disrupt those myths, but it was uncommon.

The California mission unit was another example of problematic curriculum that came up in the talking circle. One student—a senior, a leader in the Native American Club and the one who joined Mr. Gensaw in the opening song of the circle—shared a powerful experience of trying to change a problematic curricular norm, which I quote at length.

Mark: I've had a lot of bad experiences in the schooling system coming up.[6] But the one thing that I remember most of all was in fourth grade, we were learning about the missions.[7] And well, me and my mom helped kinda change the whole way they taught it 'cause it was all wrong, but the one thing that stood out to me the most was we were building these dioramas of missions, and you know, I refused.

One of the questions was like, "Say five bad things about the missions and five good things." I did the bad things perfectly, you know, and the teacher was like, "Well you gotta put good things about the missions too," and I'm like, "Well, as a Native person, like, missions were a terrible thing! They were ridding us of our culture and our language and trying to change us as a people." My teacher tried to make me put down at least one good thing about the missions and in my eyes, as a ten-year-old kid, I'm like, I don't have much education about this, but I know enough to know that it [mission philosophy] was trying to colonize and dehumanize our Native peoples all up and down the California coast.

> And at the end of that unit, they told us we could dress up
> for school, and one of the things they told us we could dress up
> was an Indian, you know, no matter if you were White, Brown,
> whatever. You could come to school dressed as a little Injun kid,
> and I was like—I lost it! I went home to my mom like, "Mom,
> they're trying to say it's okay for us to, like, battle against the
> colonists at school!" I forget what the objective was, but it was
> going to be basically, like, colonists versus Native Americans.
> (Focus Group 4.1 2022)

After identifying multiple highly problematic aspects of his fourth-grade mission unit curriculum, Mark conveyed the situation to his mother, who then engaged in a direct intervention with the teacher. In the intervention, it becomes clear that the teacher did not previously recognize the mission unit, or the colonists-versus-Native Americans role play, as offensive. But in Mark's perception, the intervention had long-term positive impact on how this portion of the curriculum was taught.

> Me and my mom went down there to the school, to my teacher's
> room after school, and my mom was like, "This is not okay. This is not
> something that should be taught as a good thing and this is not the
> truth of how these missions shaped Native peoples." The teachers were
> coming to a realization, you know, like, "Oh I've never known this, I
> thought this was an okay thing." It felt like they were saying, "Yeah, we
> dehumanized Natives a little bit, it isn't the worst thing ever."
>   Now [teachers] completely changed how they teach it because of
> me and my mom stepping up. Just me as a ten-year-old kid being like,
> this is wrong. This is not how you should teach this. I'm not opposed
> to the whole mission unit, it's just about the proper teaching of it. It
> could be "This is what it stood for, and this is what the reasoning was
> behind it." History like that shouldn't be walked around just because
> it's controversial. It should be shown in a way that people can under-
> stand the true meaning behind it. Like "Alright, we built our mission,
> and what went on in it?" They could talk about colonizing Natives
> and taking their language away. (Focus Group 4.1 2022)

Mark shows the way that formal educational spaces continue to harm identity for Native students like him, and also pass on colonizing stereotypes to everyone. The demand that Mark and his mother made was to more accurately reflect history, something that positively affects Native and non-Native well-being alike.

In his description of recognizing the unacceptability of the mission unit, Mark demonstrates the integral role of family-based learning in identity affirmation. Without his mother's willingness to take the time to visit the school and speak with the teacher, Mark's experience of the fourth grade would have been a significantly different one. By interrupting a toxic narrative, Mark's mother changed not only her own child's educational experience, but hopefully those of subsequent classes of fourth graders.

Other focus group participants also testify to the significance of family members who intervened in the mission units:

Ella: I can definitely add to what [Mark] said, because that same exact year a few classrooms down I was in one of those classes. When I told my aunt that they were trying to get me to try to actually build a mission, she turned to me with shock on her face, and she's like, "No! You are not!" So, we went to the school and said, "Can we do a presentation and wear regalia and have everyone sit, and she can come in and show them what really was going on?" So, my family dressed me, I went in, and I sang and danced in front of two classes. I was really young at the time, so I had stage fright, but it was pretty amazing to see the look on the kids' faces when they saw the regalia! I even had one of my cousins out in the audience! He came up and started to, you know, jump center and sing some of his songs too!

My teachers were super surprised and had no idea that's what it [Native culture] was like. My aunties stood beside me in their regalia too and gave a presentation on why missions aren't okay, and all these things really helped structure how it was taught for future classes. The next year, instead of talking about missions, my old teacher actually had me and my cousin go and do a presentation on our culture and our tribe, and we both sang and danced for our class, so it was pretty amazing, actually. I'm proud to have strong Native women in my family to stand up to that kind of stuff. (Focus Group 4.1 2022)

Ella, like Mark, had family willing to go to her teachers and explain why the mission unit approach was wrong, and offer a culturally grounded corrective instead. In Ella's case, dancing in regalia exposed her teachers and fellow students to actual Native culture, rather than replicating the cardboard and sugar-cube stereotype of happy Indians working at magnanimous missions. But Ella's family is of mixed identity, and the grandma on the White side of her family strongly supports mainstream educational approaches. When Ella told her what happened regarding the mission unit, her White grandmother "was livid."

> That's my—"Your own Yurok language is sin!"—grandma. She
> freaked out and was like, "Why wouldn't [you] build a mission, and
> why won't you learn about them?" And I'm like, "Dude, really?" Her
> husband was Native! He was Yurok, but with my grandma, he just
> didn't really bring culture to them because he was so scared of her.
> She was raised solely on the happy life picture life of [White] Amer-
> ica. It took me having a Flower Dance[8] for her to be able to, like, kind
> of accept it more. Now I'm happy to see that some teachers are trying
> to do it right. In seventh grade, my teacher had us do research on
> Indigenous peoples. That was better. (Focus Group 4.1 2022)

Like Mark, Ella's experience of family intervention into misrepresentation of the California missions resulted in a positive interruption of the silence of Native perspectives in the curriculum. Ella's aunties helped shift her fourth-grade education experience from one of absence of information to a celebration of contemporary Native presence.

Another focus group participant, Jorge, reflects on his own educational experiences, realizing that in his whole childhood, through elementary, middle, and high school, Native peoples were not talked about or taught.

> *Jorge:* I got all my teachings of, like, Native culture and whatnot
> from my parents. It really wasn't until I was older that I realized
> how much the school did not teach us about Native culture
> at all. Like sometimes at school I'd be talking to people, and
> they didn't even know there are multiple Native languages.
> They think that all Native people speak one language! That
> was, like, such a shock to me because I knew that my whole
> life, that there's so many tribes around here that speak different

languages! It kinda made me realize that people are not really educated on even just the local tribes.

But I say that one of the good things, I guess, in elementary school was we actually had a project where they made us research tribes all over the United States. We didn't really do a good job at it, but they did a good job getting us to think about it. I really didn't have a negative experience of Native things, but now that I'm looking back at it, like, during my time at elementary school, I guess they haven't really taught me about anything Native. (Focus Group 4.1 2022)

Jorge's reflection shows a mixed experience of Native recognition, mostly centered in an absence of information. In the safe space of Mr. Gensaw's talking circle, Jorge is able to reflect on just how little information about Native people ever came from school, and also how much ignorance there was about Nativeness among his peers and teachers.

Optimistically, Mr. Gensaw noted that by the time his son was in fourth grade, just a few years younger than this group of students, the teachers presented choices: "Either you make a mission or you can make a local tribal house" (Focus Group 4.1 2022). Greg chimed in that their dad had helped them make a plank house for that assignment. On the one hand, such options are better than forcing all children to make mission models. On the other hand, it is still a settler-colonial curricular framework to think that the option of glorifying the missions is acceptable. As Deborah Miranda satirizes in her postcolonial thought experiment on schooling in relation to California Indigenous identity, we would not accept an assignment asking children to construct plantations of enslaved Africans or African Americans, nor would we accept tooth-picked representations of German concentration camps (Miranda 2012: 186–191). Why then, do we allow it with missions? Mr. Gensaw critiques the whole idea of mission-building: "Should I put a Barbie doll or something inside the walls, you know, since that's what they did if Indians died in there sometimes, just buried them in the walls?" (Focus Group 4.1 2022).

Norms communicated in the schoolroom are expected to be internalized, upheld, and reproduced by students. Student experiences of lessons that were either silencing or harmful leave many Native American students feeling like they have to wear multiple identities to survive. This feeling of living in two worlds can be overwhelming and frustrating for young people.

Living in Two Different Worlds

The term "culture" is used by most Native American people I speak with as a shorthand for Native American culture. This is in contrast to White culture, which is never defined by Native students with that same word and instead is modified with words like "dominant," "colonizer," or "White." When the talking stick feather comes back to me, I ask the group about how they see links between culture and resilience:

> *Joe:* I just think of everything my family's been through. We just learned a lot from my family since we did our family tree project.[9] And I found out that my grandparents, well, a lot of them went to boarding schools, and I just think of everything they went through. Whenever I'm in a hard spot in my life, I think of that, and it helps me push through difficult situations.
> *Allen:* Kinda just what he [Joe] said, like, going back to my ancestors and just thinking—I'm sure they went through the same thing, probably harder stuff, so that gives me strength.
> *Greg:* Yeah . . . it could be a lot worse. (Focus Group 4.1 2022)

Joe, Allen, and Greg all describe different ways to access resilience, which can strengthen well-being. Reflecting on the hardship of one's ancestors helps these young people recognize what is manageable in their own lives. When the talking stick comes to Mark, he expounds on how this functions in his own perspective:

> *Mark:* You know, those people that went through colonization went through the worst of it. And one thing I tell myself that helps me get by is that each generation should be better than the last. I look at some of the generations that are still with me, that have struggled with addiction and whatnot. What I can do—my part—is try to not have those issues and be better than the last. Because it's not only making myself proud and making people that are still with me proud, it's the people that died for their land, that died for this place they take care of and call home. They look down on us [after death] and know what we fought for wasn't for nothing. The cause we fought for, to keep our peoples alive and make sure they have a voice wasn't for nothing.

> We all have hard days, I have hard days, and that's just one of the things that helps me get by. There are people that have come before me that have seen harder things, and I can always do my best to be the best version of myself for not only myself but for them. (Focus Group 4.1 2022)

Here, Mark is able to compare his own suffering to the experiences of ancestors under colonization. Not only does it motivate him to be his best self, but it also helps him place himself in social context, where he is the continuation of ancestral hope and survival.

When these students reflect on the experiences of their ancestors, it makes their own hardship more possible to withstand. They know they physically exist because previous family members fought to survive and won. The students nod along to each other's statements, affirming each other in the focused hush of the classroom talking circle.

As ancestral survival is in the lineage of their existence, so too is culture in the lineage of their identity as Yurok, Hupa, Karuk, Tolowa, or Wiyot young people. They know that cultural meaning is part of keeping themselves and their communities well. Jorge describes how Brush Dances, or other religion and culture practices, can help people:

> *Jorge:* You can kinda tell how people act, if they're kinda cultured or not cultured. If they grew up, like, around their own stuff, 'cause Brush Dances from my experiences, do help people make them less angry or mad. The whole presence when you go to a Brush Dance is so . . . like, I can't explain it but if you go there, everyone is so respectful. So, people who have kids who grew up going to a Brush Dance, they kinda learn that respect compared to people who don't go to ceremonies or anything like that. It's just one of the good things about the ceremonies in general. (Focus Group 4.1 2022)

The impact of cultural connectedness on behavior is visible for Jorge. Mr. Gensaw agrees with and affirms what the students have said thus far. He then adds:

> Also, I think being able to be on our land has a lot of power and energy. Going down to the mouth [of the Klamath River] to go fishing, or being next to the river, or doing healing and knowing

that my people have been doing this since the beginning of time, and that rivers have always been there, or going up into the mountains and getting deer, elk . . . that's also a tool, that's medicine. I know some of you are doing these things, and that's also part of resilience.

Like this land, this river, those mountains, those trees, those deer, those elk, those ducks, all those salmon—those are medicine. I think all those help build identity and resilience for me. You know, it's like, "Hey I'm having a hard time, I'm going to go down and go fishing, go down by the water, clear my brain, clear my mind." So, don't forget about that. Culture's not all about dances, ceremonies, things like that. Sometimes it's not those tangible things. It could be some of those things that are not so black and white. The places are very powerful. (Focus Group 4.1 2022)

The notion of land as medicine, rather than as a commodity that can be bought and sold, is part of Mr. Gensaw's worldview, and one he explains to his students and me. His description of relying on traditional engagement with the land and place as healing exemplifies the gulf between Native and White worldviews. In addition to the calming sensation of being at the river, Mr. Gensaw articulates the sense of temporal connection to ancestors when he does any sort of ritual on the river. In these ways, culture is the bedrock on which well-being can be built.

As the talking feather circulates, the Yurok students continue to express the divide between Native people who grow up connected to their culture and those who do not. Jorge, softly at first, but getting more animated as he speaks, shares his impressions that the worldviews of people who don't learn about their history are different from those who are culturally engaged:

> *Jorge:* Like, just the whole world, it kinda expands if you do cultural stuff; you see how it is not just you. It's a bunch of other people, rivers, nature, animals, etcetera. Everything around you kinda teaches you that, it connects you. Learning about culture makes you more aware of things. (Focus Group 4.1 2022)

Mark, who identifies as culturally connected, continues Jorge's theme, using the "we" voice to talk about himself and others currently practicing Native traditions:

Mark: The people who are active practitioners of their culture, you know, we have this feeling of connection to this place we live, who we are as people. Like, we're people that live in two different worlds. The feelings we feel are much greater than just a person that walks around on the street. Like, it's so hard to explain, but the people that are disconnected from their culture and don't have that understanding, those people struggle the most, because they still have those feelings but don't necessarily know how to deal with them.

Some of us are lucky. We have culture and community, we can go down by the river and understand that's a place of healing. There's a lot of Indian kids, Native kids on this campus that aren't connected to their culture. I see them struggling more than me because they don't have those healthy outlets.

Jorge: You pretty much put my thoughts into words. Like, I have family members who were very disconnected from their culture until recently. Once my family showed them [how to connect], they just, like, had less anger in them, less hate. Connecting totally changes your view. (Focus Group 4.1 2022)

Mark and Jorge's exchange shows how they both perceive the benefits of cultural connections. Having healthy outlets, less anger, allows for flourishing, which can happen in both Native and White spaces. The theme of "success in both worlds" is a prominent slogan of the Yurok Tribe, with local Native youth program sweatshirts printed with that sentiment across the back. The reality of it, however, may be easier to print than to perform.

Living in both worlds successfully means managing the societal expectations of Native culture—home, family, and associated cultural and spiritual participation—and of White culture, encountered in school, sports, and other out-of-community extracurriculars or jobs. Succeeding in both worlds means surviving two different sets of competing expectations and managing them well enough to achieve the benchmarks needed to define success. This might look like completing homework to a high standard while also performing childcare or helping with preparations for a ceremony. It means living with two different sets of criteria and trying to ace both. Success is possible, but it isn't guaranteed.

A lot of times, young people who may have more contact with White culture than Native culture end up sliding into behaviors that distance themselves even further from the Native part of their identities. I ask the group for their suggestions of how to better connect young people to culture. They admit what they don't know, and they also identify addressable issues within their own school:

> *Jorge:* I have no clue really, but more resources to help people find
>   who they are, not just Native people, but all different types
>   of backgrounds. I also want more representation around the
>   school because our classroom is on the far side [of campus],
>   where no one ever sees it, and there's nothing else Native
>   around. If there were resources, I'd want people to know more
>   about the local tribes around here.
>
>   And I think a lot of people at this school, from my experience,
>   think only Native people can take this class! Or "it would be like
>   disrespectful if I just go in there and take the class," or something
>   like that, 'cause there's no knowledge of what the Yurok language
>   class does. No one knows nothing about it.

Allen concurs that more representation of Native people and Native culture would help raise awareness. Joe echoes Allen and Jorge's points, adding that he's had friends who didn't even know that the Yurok class existed, which he partially attributes to their classroom being on the farthest end of the school, where fewer people go. He also points out a discrepancy in the way Yurok counts toward grade point average, which is lower than classes that have an AP test, like Spanish.[10] Joe tells us that some of his friends would have taken Yurok III and IV, but because there wasn't an extra grade point attached, they took Spanish instead.

The point about classroom location in relation to Native marginalization is not trivial. Mr. Gensaw describes how some people at MHS don't even know he is a teacher there. The Yurok classroom is at the very end of a long hallway bordering one of the parking lots. Its doorway faces no other classroom, and it is about as far as one can get from the main administrative office within the school. I admit, some days when I am running late to Mr. Gensaw's classes, I don't always make the long walk to the office to sign in as a visitor first. My own visibility as a researcher is limited because of the basic geography of the classroom. Mr. Gensaw similarly is invisible since he goes from the parking lot to his classroom after hustling up from EHS. He rarely interacts with school staff or fellow teachers given his peripheral classroom.

In contrast, the Yurok classroom at EHS is near the top of a main staircase and in a hall with many other classrooms. Since his door at EHS is almost always open, anyone passing through most of the second floor sees Mr. Gensaw or is seen by him, and he frequently stands at the door to greet students and chat. At MHS, something as basic as classroom location can diminish Native representation in the school. Being peripheral geographically bleeds into being peripheral socially as well. Though the classroom has signs up in the window expressing Native pride, the only people who would see them are those walking on the far edge of campus. There is little representation of Native presence elsewhere at MHS.[11]

Finally, Mr. Gensaw, tasked with advocating for the language classes as well as teaching them, wonders, "If there were more Yurok language classes here, would more non-Native kids take them? Having Yurok I–II and III–IV levels all combined gives it a small presence at school and makes it harder to teach! Plus, non-Native American people *should* learn the language. That's what my auntie Kathleen, who started this class, always said" (Focus Group 4.1 2022). As he carries out the responsibility of making the Yurok language available to all those at MHS who want to learn, Mr. Gensaw faces obstacles, but he is gifted with an engaged Yurok III–IV class composed of students curious about themselves, their cultures, and how they can succeed in both worlds.

"If you can pray in Yurok, the ancestors can hear you"

While the first focus group at MHS was a mix of juniors and seniors, the second group was mostly sophomores, fifteen to sixteen years old, and from the large, combined Yurok I–II class. Four students who returned signed permission forms to do focus groups, Daria, Paula, Sonya, and Kyle,[12] trailed me down the long hallway to the conference room in the central school office, where we spread out along a wide oblong table under a skylight. The students in this group all self-identified as Native American across four different local tribes—Karuk, Tolowa, Trinidad Rancheria (composed of Yurok, Wiyot, and Tolowa people), and Yurok. Three of the four participants said they were enrolled tribal members and one was a descendant.

Like the Yurok III–IV focus group participants, this group articulated various degrees of family trauma and resilience that led them to sign up for Yurok language class.

Daria: My great-grandma was put into boarding school. After that, we lost a lot of language. Out of fear of it happening [being targeted] again, our family dropped everything related to our culture. Being able to take Yurok, to get some of it back, is very important to me.

Paula: I am very fortunate and blessed to be so involved in my culture. Even before taking the class, I knew this was an opportunity to be part of another step in language revitalization. We definitely have had a huge loss, but I also like to think of it in a positive light; I get to use it [language] to better the next generations, to bring that back in the world.

The third student, Sonya, shares a similar response as her classmates, with elders impacted by boarding schools, and her appreciation of the chance to bring Yurok back. She particularly appreciates Mr. Gensaw for the way he brings up things that happened in the past and connects them to the present. Kyle, the descendant who is not tribally enrolled, shyly offered, "Since my family isn't active in the Native community, I felt it was important to learn Yurok" (Focus Group 6.2 2022). For him, like Heather and Kara in Chapter 3, the language class was a doorway into Nativeness that was otherwise somewhat closed to him.

One interesting rhetorical pattern worth confronting in studies of language revitalization is the use of the term "loss." The notion that Native American languages were "lost" is, in my analysis, a regurgitation of White supremacist justification for Native subjugation. In fact, the languages were stolen and oppressed through deliberate processes of culturecide.

Cutcha Risling Baldy, in her book on revitalization of Native American practices in California, points out that Native people are frequently portrayed as being "in the last stages of existence. This is to solidify the settler-colonial desire for an eventual inheriting of the land, a rightful, uninhabited, ahistorical passing of ownership from the poor, dying Indigenous to the stronger, healthier, more vibrant settler-colonial society" (Risling Baldy 2018: 5). Because the use of words like "loss" tend to play into this trope of inevitable extinction, I frequently offer gentle interventions when it comes up, as I did with this focus group. Native American students tend to vigorously nod when I explain my own preference for terms like "stolen" for land, or "oppressed" for Indigenous languages. Students sometimes then try out using different terms for colonizing dynamics that change the shape of the discussion. Such interventions are ones that could also be happening in classrooms and are part of larger movements for grammatical justice (Mack and Palfrey 2020) that demand more accuracy and accountability in the language that we use.

Language translation across academic and community spaces happens with other terms as well. Neither the students nor adults I speak with, including those doing language reclamation work, use academic language like "cultural rights activism" to define what they are doing. And yet, the actions many people describe doing in the process of working for cultural survivance—survival and presence (Vizenor 2010)—are indicators of activism. Daily practices of resistance to the status quo are often potent components of social movements precisely because they may not be recognized as such (Scott 1990).

The Yurok I–II focus group describes how they do rights work as a daily practice:

> *Paula:* I know that when I've done ceremony in the past, my aunt
> told me, "If you can pray in Yurok, the ancestors can hear you.
> They can give you what you need; it goes straight to them." To
> get to use our language in medicine and ceremony, it is also
> a slap in the face to all the colonizers. Even to our parents,
> because they're a product of the sterilization era.
> *Daria:* For me personally, being able to take it [language] home
> and tell my grandma things, teach her words in Yurok, I can
> tell it makes her feel more connected to her background.
> And we walk around on our land and can name things in the
> language—that feels like a way to show we are strong. (Focus
> Group 6.2 2022)

Paula and Daria describe small acts—praying in Yurok, naming the landscape in Yurok—that may not seem revolutionary. Yet in the face of attempted culturecide, such actions assert Indigenous presence in ways that constitute a rejection of erasure.

Erasure is not only of the past, but of ongoing discrimination and cultural misrepresentation of Native peoples. Students explain how they have lived through and challenged such erasure. Kyle shares that he didn't know much about how Native people were treated, and wasn't taught it before the Yurok class. Sonya agrees, mentioning that even though she identifies as Native, she didn't know as much as she should have. She first learned about boarding schools from Mr. Gensaw, who, in her words, "has taught me a lot about what's brought us here" (Focus Group 6.2 2022).

Like many other Native students I spoke with, some in this group commented on certain aspects of the curriculum, and popular culture, that were highly problematic in their elementary-age years. I quote them at length, as their exchange demonstrates solidarity for each other as they respond to each other's educational trauma:

Daria: In the fourth grade, we had to do the missions project, and it was so backwards! My dad pulled me out of it and told the teacher, "My daughter will not be participating in that." It was so wrong, what they would say in school and in history books. I knew from my family it was wrong, but most of my classmates didn't and just went along with it.

Paula: For me it goes as far back as Disney movies. I've never seen *Pocahontas* all the way through because mom told me the real truth about it, and we turned it off. I was so mad about it that I was wanting to teach my teachers. I was fighting that whole time to try to get the truth out. Teachers would point at the history books and tell me, "But it doesn't say that in the book."

Daria: It shouldn't be your job to educate people!

Paula: I know. My mom said, "It's the school system failing you guys. It is not your job to educate people."

Sonya: It's crazy how many lies are in the history books. My dad was shocked when he saw what I was bringing home.

Paula: The stories are so recycled. There are so many lies.

Kyle: For me, in elementary and middle school, we weren't taught what our people were put through. We were told someone else's story.

Daria: I remember one time in my eighth-grade history class, we all got to pick a tribe and write a paper about it. I did my own tribe and was proud of it. But my teacher tried to tell me that what I was saying was wrong, because I didn't look it up on a website or in a book. I talked to my family and got the information from them. But the teacher said that didn't count. The history books make Native people sound barbaric; they dehumanize them. Why were the books saying this stuff? I didn't want to use them! (Focus Group 6.2 2022)

As this conversation showcases, the undermining of Native youth wellness through the sabotage of healthy identity construction is happening in schools every day. Well-being, the holistic concept that includes physical, mental, and emotional health and the ability to feel content even while navigating obstacles, includes identity affirmation as an aspect of socioemotional health, as Dr. Moorehead described in Chapter 2. Yet this affirmation is sorely lacking in so many schools and across many curricula.

Being told "someone else's story" in formal education is not a benign act. When that story includes the domination and destruction of one's own social group, it can be downright harmful. The dominant story of how missions helped "civilize Indians" is one that students mentioned over and over as being offensive and in opposition to what they learned from their families. Some students and their family members spoke up about this misrepresentation, while others did not. The absence of curricula about boarding schools, despite plenty of time being spent on units including missions and the Gold Rush, was corrected only in the Yurok language classes. In at least three of the schools where I did fieldwork, students who did not take those classes could graduate high school and never learn about boarding schools. Only in Hoopa, at the school located on a reservation and in the footprint of a former boarding school, is that history more discussed in US history classes. Given the ongoing misinformation, how are Native youth participating in the world around them, and constructing their futures? The following section lifts up student voices as they describe their burdens and dreams.

"We *still* have to fight"

Past misrepresentation is connected to ongoing injustice. MHS Yurok I-II students are able to draw these lines of interconnection for themselves:

> *Paula:* It isn't just the past that had bad things happen. We *still* have
> to fight for things like water rights and treaty rights. The biggest
> thing around here is the Klamath thing, trying to get rid of the
> dams to help the fish. We are *still* being colonized! My political
> flame was lit in fifth grade when DAPL [protests about the
> Dakota Access Pipeline] was happening. To see people who
> look like me not having basic human rights like clean drinking
> water, it hit home. Since then, water rights have been a huge

thing in my mind. Water also translates into food, and our
people are dealing with that from repercussions of the Klamath
fish kill. Even now in later years, we don't have enough fish in
the rivers. (Focus Group 6.2 2022)

This environmental concern over food and traditional rights was mirrored
by all students in this focus group, but in different ways and with a range of
results depending on their circumstances:

Daria: I have a big issue when it comes to hunting and agricultural
rights. Kids at school will brag about killing more animals than
the legal limits or wasting meat. Or kids will argue with me
about how big corporations process meat. I say, "You're killing
family farms, with companies building crazy buildings [for the
meat industry], it's not okay!" My family, we're big hunters, but
we respect all life. People come poach on our property all the
time. I saw a doe that was pregnant killed on our land. That's not
okay. Because someone thought it was fun to come kill a doe out
of season—that gets me worked up! (Focus Group 6.2 2022)

For Daria, the connection between her Native identity and her care for
the land and animals is so obvious to her that she takes it as a given. She
knows what is okay and not okay without ambiguity. Sonya mirrors this care
embedded in her own worldview, noting her concerns over environmental
destruction and climate change, and her anger that people ignore these problems. Daria jumps in again to locally situate the uniqueness of Humboldt
County environmental issues: "There are so many big [marijuana] grows, it
is destroying the land.[13] The water district on our part of [the mountain] is
being stretched. They just had to kick out a big grow because it was using too
much water. The grow they're trying to put in, not only would it look terrible,
it would also use all the water.[14] They have to have respect for the land, like
people who grow [food] crops and know they need to rotate their fields. But
they [marijuana growers] don't!" (Focus Group 6.2 2022).

In rural far Northern California, hunting, agriculture, and water usage
in marijuana cultivation will continue to be environmental issues facing the
next generation. As the region sorts out what the regulation of the marijuana
industry will look like in the years to come, there are no easy answers on the

horizon, but youth awareness of the issues contributes to the construction of their own identities.

Daria, Paula, Sonya, and Kyle also have regular lives as young people in their area. They play sports and help their families with chores at home and on their land—one of them described "vaccinating cows" as regular familial labor. Their resilience comes from the usual sources—friends and family— as well as feeling connected to their tribes. Daria comments, "I get strength from knowing that I come from a long line of fighters." Others describe going camping, attending ceremonies, or going to "places where I can go to be by myself, to let off steam" as important to keeping themselves well.

Education and educational access are included in many definitions of well-being because they are keys that can unlock so many other types of wellness. Because family and community play such an important role for these students, the idea of moving away for college, something that several juniors in the group are already thinking about, comes up in relation to the role of family as support network:

Sonya: I know for me, I want to move away for college, but it is scary to move away and have family not as close as I want them to be. Not having my friends who I've grown up with around me is scary too. I'm excited about college, but also nervous not having the support system that I've had since I was a kid.

Kyle: I'm not leaving. I want to go to college at CR [College of the Redwoods, the local community college] and play football for them. I've been playing for eight years now. After that, I want to do something in construction.

Sonya: My big goal has always been Hawaii [points to Hawaii college sweatshirt]. I want to major in psychology and marine biology because I want to help the environment, and especially help marine animals. After college, I hope to do something having to do with the ocean.

Paula: After high school, I really want to get some work experience and get me some money for college, maybe pursuing social work. I personally have seen the effects of what a not-so-great counselor can have on schoolchildren. It's my dream to give kids a positive person they can go to. Ideally, I will not stay in Humboldt [County] for college. But I'll probably have to go to a two-year program first. If I go to CR, it is close enough to home that it is just a drive away.

Daria: After high school, I'll go to CR for a year and do the dental assistant program, then after a few years go into the dental hygienist program. (Focus Group 6.2 2022)

Across construction, marine biology, school counseling, and dental assistant work, these young people have a range of dreams and plans, and they will meet plenty of obstacles on their paths ahead. But one obstacle is something they already confront daily—a school climate marred by hostility toward Native American students, as the next section shows.

School Climate: "They say it to fit in with friends"

In this all Native American MHS focus group, students were universally frustrated by the kinds of racial and ethnic slurs they heard directed toward themselves and others. While Daria—a more White-passing and very outgoing student—describes the school as a welcoming place, in the same breath she identifies closed-mindedness as one of the bigger problems at the school:

Daria: Me and [a fellow student] did a presentation of the Brush Dance in full regalia, and then they showed a video of it in other classes for Native American Heritage Month. One kid was making fun of it when it was being shown in a study hall. And then another kid yelled a racial slur at that kid. The teacher kinda heard what was being said, and I told her about it afterwards. She said, "That's not okay," but she didn't intervene then or later. When we danced [live], it was just in front of Yurok class and people were respectful. (Focus Group 6.2 2022)

Daria's classmates chime in with their own impressions of this event. Sonya cites ignorance: "Those kids in the study hall, they don't even understand what is hurtful about it," while Daria exclaims, "Just cause your parents say it [slurs], doesn't mean it's okay!" (Focus Group 6.2 2022).

Paula identifies path-dependent behavior as a problem at school, but also appreciates how things have changed even in her lifetime:

Paula: A lot of people don't want to unlearn what they've been
  taught. When I was in elementary school, I heard some bad
  stuff about racism here. But in the last two years, I think they've
  really tried to make more safe space. Like, they still had BIPOC
  meetings[15] during the pandemic, where only people of color
  were invited. Or people who are connected to BIPOC people.
  My dad is White, but because he's my dad he would be eligible
  to go. Being able to sit in on those meetings was eye-opening
  for me about what people have experienced here. It was really
  nice to see that our administration was there and listening. The
  principal facilitated the meetings and seeing that happen was
  really helpful.

Responsive school leadership was meaningful to Paula in feeling like there
was a space to be heard. She also feels like the school has gotten better over
time, but other students identify the complex ways that problems persist.

Kyle: On the one hand, our school is pretty inclusive and tries to
  teach about racism and discrimination. On the other hand, kids
  here are really arrogant and think it's a joke.
Daria: A lot of them will say things to fit in with friends. Sometimes
  it doesn't have anything to do with racial background; they'll
  say things to everyone. Honestly, a lot of it comes from middle
  school. Remember what happened there? At McKinleyville
  Middle School, Mr. X said the n-word like eight times! And I
  was the one kicked out for standing up and saying something!

This example, which Daria shares in a matter-of-fact way, is deeply disturbing. For a middle school teacher to say the "n-word," even, giving the benefit
of the doubt, if it was in reference to a historical or literary lesson, gives students permission to also say the word. Such verbal patterns then continue
into high school, where they can also be encouraged by similarly problematic
teachers.

Kyle: One of our teachers here, Mrs. Y, has been known to use racial
  slurs and slurs in general. I don't know if the administration
  knows about it. But students and faculty both say stuff. I

> remember Mr. X looked straight at me and said the n-word over
> and over, "Because [n-word] is going to be said in the movie." So,
> he acted like he was preparing us, but I was like, "Shut the hell
> up, you don't need to keep saying it!" (Focus Group 6.2 2022)

The harm in saying certain slurs out loud has become widely acknowledged in collegiate circles, where the use of asterisks and other ways of indicating language without using it is fairly commonplace. While saying things to fit in with friends may be quintessential youth behavior, it is not something everyone outgrows. Further, in addition to students, sometimes teachers are the problem too. In such a context, it is hard to support youth well-being.

Bystander intervention has been taught before at MHS. Yurok II students received these trainings earlier this year. Students completed a mandatory training unit on intervention in discriminatory behavior, but it was via prerecorded videos, not live or in-person sessions. Some of the focus group students were skeptical of the impact of this type of training. Sonya astutely noted that to really change school climate, the school would need to make such training more regular and in person and "continually reinforce it! Even just redoing the training after some time could help. If people aren't learning and applying the actions, it isn't working!" (Focus Group 6.2 2022).

> *Daria:* People were saying, "It's so dumb!" They [training creators]
> could have made it more with like, things that a high school
> student might say. Because it felt so different from how we
> would talk. People were laughing about it and not taking it
> seriously. I think at least in part because of the way it was
> worded.
> *Paula:* I think a lot of stuff that is a problem at this school is tiptoed
> around. The administration doesn't really apply the kind of stuff
> the training talked about. They might do something about one
> example of bad behavior, but they are not addressing the real
> issues that everyone sees on a day-to-day basis.

The complaint that not enough is done to intervene in bad behavior was shared across respondents in most of the schools. At MHS, Kyle reiterates the toll this takes on him: "A lot of kids are so disrespectful! For some people, they will make jokes and interfere with other people's learning all day long" (Focus Group 6.2 2022).

Bystander intervention trainings are a potentially useful tool for schools to interrupt harmful behavior.[16] But being open to such content can also make students vulnerable to further heckling from peers and teachers. Inherently, intervention is about standing up in the face of wrongdoing and trying to reset interactions. This is not easy work for anyone, including adolescents.

Yet it has never been clearer that intervention is needed. For example, the 2015 lawsuit brought by the American Civil Liberties Union (ACLU) against Eureka City Schools showed regular discriminatory behavior by staff and a lack of intervention to protect students from other students as well as district personnel (ACLUNorCal 2015). Several similar lawsuits in the 2010s and 2020s against far Northern California schools show comparable issues of discrimination against BIPOC and other minority-identity students. In many interviews with students across a range of schools and contexts in the region, it is evident that teachers and staff may potentially both help and hinder school climates. Equipping schools, their teachers, staff, and students to chart new behavior patterns is part of a slow but necessary process of reshaping school interactions to increase student well-being.

Conclusion

School climate exists in context. Humboldt County's long history of White supremacist education elevates White stories at the expense of Native American ones. The long-standing practice of teaching victors' histories undermines identity affirmation for Native youth and perpetuates misinformation for everyone. These issues were further exacerbated by the isolation of the pandemic. Students around the world missed out on a year or two of in-person instruction and socialization. One of the many results was more immature middle school behavior spilling into high school. In addition, heightened levels of social anxiety have carried into the post-lockdown phase. Students themselves know this was part of what they were experiencing (Focus Group 6.2 2022), but it doesn't change the reality that they have to live with these challenges.

In fact, the students I spoke with were highly aware of the numerous variables compounding to adversely affect their own success. They named them: family violence, housing insecurity, food insecurity, addiction, mental health issues, lack of employment, and on and on. Adult-level responsibilities are the reality for many young people who step in to take care of themselves and their families. Daria, a tired expression on her face, voiced her concern for her classmates. "A lot of the kids here don't have a great home life. Some kids are couch surfing to get away from their families, and I wish they could have a normal childhood. I wish they wouldn't have to be the parents to their siblings, that it wouldn't have to be so hard for them growing up" (Focus Group 6.2 2022). The objective elements of well-being—basics like material resources sufficient to meet bodily needs, plus physical security—are still elusive for many people. What can schools do to intervene when these problems are so much bigger than education?

Yurok language classes are not a panacea to solve the myriad problems young people face. Rather, Yurok language classes exemplify culturally sustaining curricula that foster positive intervention in identity formation, something that young people do every day. White supremacist education does not lead to Native flourishing. Accurate local history, safe adults who share cultural backgrounds with heritage speakers, and classroom environments where people support each other all serve to bolster young people's welfare against the onslaught of discrimination that school environments, and the curricula, keep on dishing out.

CHAPTER 5

Barbara McQuillen: Yurok Elder, Language-Keeper, and Teacher

Introduction: Not the End of the Trail

Del Norte High School (DNHS) is extremely remote, ninety minutes due north of McKinleyville along the coast. The high school is located in Crescent City, a small town that many people drive straight through on Highway 101 without stopping. Lined with one-story wooden buildings faded by coastal weather, Crescent City is one of the last stops for services before crossing into Oregon, a half an hour north.

Based on the 2020 Census, Crescent City's population was 22,819, and the median family income was $60,702 (United States Census Bureau 2024). There was 44.7 percent employment and 5.6 percent without health coverage (United States Census Bureau 2024). However, this town, like many rural communities with prisons, counts the incarcerated people within its population, so the data profile remains somewhat opaque. Del Norte County hosts the state's only super-maximum-security prison, Pelican Bay State Prison, with just over 2,100 people incarcerated there.[1] Crescent City is the seat of Del Norte County, the most northern and western county in California. A large slice of the population is connected to prison industries, whether as correctional officers, administrators, or contractors, among others. Local Indigenous people tend to work as fishing guides, in logging and other local industries, or for tribes and tribal businesses.

Like McKinleyville, Crescent City is a politically conservative town that bills itself as an outdoor recreation destination, with an oceanside harbor pressed against world-renowned redwoods. As with Humboldt and Trinity

Counties, Del Norte County shares the settler-colonial history of Indigenous displacement, enslavement, and murder by early settlers. The region was also a hotbed of gold mining and logging during the nineteenth and twentieth centuries. It is infamous as the site of the largest tsunami to ever hit the United States, in 1964.

The American Community 2022 survey showed 13 percent of people in Crescent City speak a language other than English at home, with more than 9.2 percent of that Spanish-speaking and 0.2 percent "other languages," which could include Native languages (United States Census Bureau 2024). The one high school in town includes students from a broad range of backgrounds. Like EHS, DNHS has a nearly equal split between White and BIPOC students. In 2021–2022, that meant 567 students were White, 135 were American Indian or Alaska Native, 262 were Hispanic or Latino, 57 were two or more races, 57 were Asian, and 12 were Black or African American (EdData 2022). In 2021–2022, 606 of DNHS's 1,104 students were eligible for free lunch (EdData 2024).

DNHS has the Warriors as its mascot, and until the late 1990s included a Plains-style Native American headdress as its mascot image. Unlike Indian reservation–based Hoopa Valley High School, which also claims the Warriors as its mascot—which seems empowering for its majority-Native student body—Del Norte's engagement with Warrior imagery is problematic. In a majority-White school, such imagery feeds into the narrative of Native conquest that characterizes White regional narratives. Warriors in Del Norte are a symbol of something conquered, much like the "End of the Trail" image of the defeated Native American on horseback that greets visitors at the Trees of Mystery tourist attraction on Highway 101, just before Crescent City. These settler-colonial symbols permeate the town and the region.

The Craft and Challenges of Teaching Yurok Language

Barbara McQuillen's classroom, off a tiled hallway at DNHS, is cheerfully decorated in bright posters with Yurok greetings and phrases. To spend time in her classes, I would rise in the dark to drive the two hours from my childhood home to the school, catching the sunlight filtering through the redwoods and reflecting off the ocean out of the corner of my eye as I steered the hairpin turns. Ms. McQuillen's language class ran first period, a combined

Yurok II–III–IV class, which put students from three years of language study in one class. As with Mr. Gensaw, this was done to fill the seats in the class, but it has made both the teaching and the learning challenging, as students are at multiple levels of language study.

A Yurok elder, language-keeper, and language teacher, Ms. McQuillen has spent decades working to pass on the Yurok language to others while increasing her own language knowledge. She is a culturally resonant adult for many Native American students at DNHS, where she brings a personal understanding of their circumstances to an otherwise predominantly White institution. Several of her students relate to her like a grandmother figure and an honored elder, though not all the students—especially first- and second-year students and those coming from non-Native or less traditional homes—understand that she deserves respect based on her elder status.

As one of the sixteen advanced-level Yurok speakers living today, Ms. McQuillen holds the dual gift and burden of working for language reclamation in a context riddled with challenges for language continuity. In addition to teaching high school Yurok, Ms. McQuillen has been a staff member in the Yurok Language Program for twenty-seven years. Her brother is the director of the Tribe's Education Department. Ms. McQuillen brings immense cultural knowledge, including Yurok language, history, customs, and artisan work like beading, into her classrooms. Yurok language classes are special interdisciplinary spaces that function in multiple educational ways. As with other Yurok teachers, Ms. McQuillen brings storytelling and cultural context to the vocabulary she imparts. Sometimes students can be rude, disruptive, or sleep through class. Others try to learn, but the combined levels of students can make it slow going.

One cloudy day in spring 2022, after observing her Yurok class, I stayed in the room as the students filtered out.[2] Ms. McQuillen and I sat down across the table for a formal interview, building on one we had first done in 2017 (McQuillen 2017, McQuillen 2022).[3] Ms. McQuillen switches between teaching sometimes-unruly high schoolers and eager tribal employees, the latter of whom have the option of getting paid to take Yurok language classes as part of their jobs.[4]

Some things work and others don't when it comes to teaching Yurok at DNHS. Ms. McQuillen explains the positives—kids are interested in Yurok words—and the negatives—that it is hard to get them to show up on time in the classroom.

Well, I think what is working is participation. Kids seem pretty interested in participation *if* the topic is something that they connect to.
A lot of times they don't want to learn the background things. They
just want to know words for this and that, not the background of
how to form sentences, maybe not necessarily the grammar.

Things that aren't working: attendance is really spotty this year.
It's really unusual to have a full class, to have everybody here. Tardiness is a big thing. Students come in late every day because they have
to drop somebody off, and do this or that, wait for a ride or whatever. They say, "There's nothing I can do about it, I can't *not* take my
brother to school. I can't *not* wait for them to drop so-and-so off!"
So yeah, that makes it hard to start the lesson when you know that
three students are going to come, but come late, and then they have a
hard time participating because they didn't get the instruction in the
beginning.

While to some extent punctuality and regular attendance are issues in schools
around the world, the rural, isolated location of DNHS makes these particularly challenging. In such remote locations, young people are dependent on
adults having functional vehicles and the gas money to get them where they
need to go. There is a school bus that shuttles students between Klamath and
Crescent City public schools, but sometimes student schedules are at the
whim of other family members or their own time management.

Ms. McQuillen recognizes the fragility of students' lives: "I get in the
[school computer] system every day and I mark tardy, tardy, tardy, or absent,
but there's never any follow-up to that. Or maybe they did their detention
time or whatever for being tardy. But I really don't want them to be disci-
plined. Certain students, there's no way they can get here on time. Other ones
I know, I see them in the hall, they could be here on time, but it just doesn't
seem that important to them to be in here by the eight o'clock bell. That makes
it a little difficult."

Attendance and tardiness are major issues for Ms. McQuillen and many
other teachers in maintaining classroom organization and schedules. But they
are connected to even larger structural problems having to do with access to
resources, education, and other aspects of public infrastructure. Despite these
structural obstacles, there continues to be student interest in Yurok language
learning: "Every year, the class starts out huge; everybody wants to take Yurok
language! And then they switch out when they figure out it's kind of serious,

you know, that they're gonna *learn*. But I have a few students that genuinely are really interested in learning."

As in any high school population, some students just show up in Yurok because they need to meet their world language requirement. Ms. McQuillen acknowledges that "there's not really much I can do to engage them in learning. They can probably use simple Yurok and select a verb, but as far as speaking, they're not really interested." It is not uncommon for some portion of any group of students to lack intrinsic motivation, and not respond to extrinsic motivation. Teachers recognize their own limitations in reaching students who don't want to be reached.

But there are also a good number of students—at DNHS they tend to be more culturally connected heritage-speakers—who want to be there for their own growth. They, of course, are more interested in learning Yurok: "The ones that are serious or have some kind of Yurok or Native background at home or something are really wanting to know a lot of specific stuff around ceremony, making things, gathering, those type of things. Because I think they have that at home, or they go to tribal programs, well-being groups or something like that, so they're more interested." Student motivation is a major issue in high schools generally. Given the variables of precariousness that are at play in the lives of many Native American youth, motivation is a serious one that impacts the Yurok classroom as well. But Ms. McQuillen perseveres, teaching Yurok to all who are open to it.

Technology and Slippery Metrics of Yurok Reclamation

What success looks like in language reclamation for tribes with tiny speaker bases can be different in each community. For the Yurok Language Program, the pandemic, though a curse in so many ways, actually facilitated instructional pivots that have expanded access to the language. In short, the pandemic required a digital turn, and that meant that Yurok language access online removed physical travel—a massive barrier for people in this remote corner of California—as a requirement to learn. Ms. McQuillen describes the Yurok Language Program efforts, which her coworker Brittany Vigil has innovated with technology, games, and increased availability: "Some people have access to a lot more than just what we were doing in the past, trying to teach in-person classes with a handful of people there. Language is really way more out there now and classes are virtual—that's one good thing about the pandemic! I mean, in-person stuff is nice, but I think it's more accessible for people, that you're not driving to Weitchpec, Crescent City, or Klamath[5] for a language class."

As much as in-person classes bring a host of intangible social benefits to well-being, the driving distances really can be a deterrent to attendance. Ms. McQuillen explains how the new approach tries to meet multiple needs: "We do both live language classes and a lot of recorded classes. We take one of the daily classes that I teach and we record it, and then Brittany does this whole thing with the learning pathway: a review with audio of what we did, reinforcement games, a video of the actual class. So yeah, it's pretty good."

The logistics of language accessibility through the digital turn have expanded who Yurok language teachers can reach, and increased the number of language learning techniques they can offer online. Ms. McQuillen adds that the increased availability of Yurok language classes has also made it more credible. "There isn't as much stigma as say, ten years ago, when there were negative comments, like, 'Oh you guys are making this up.'" When I ask what has changed to facilitate greater interest in and acceptance of the language, Ms. McQuillen responds:

> I think it's just the more people that we have in the program, and each person's outreach. Their group of people that they hang with or whatever, they talk about language and how it's progressed and how people are learning. Also, I think it's just a lot more younger people that are giving that momentum and wanting to speak, young mothers that have babies and children, that want their children to know some language. At my age, I've heard speakers—fluent elder speakers—but younger people have never grown up with language in their household, and they want that for their children—something that they missed or that generation missed.

With Yurok accessible in so many formats and mediums, there are more and more people connected to learning the language. The increased interest in Yurok language across generations is part of the deep rebuilding of a speaker base. Among Ms. McQuillen's colleagues in the Yurok Language Program are several mothers raising their children as first-language Yurok speakers. That level of language reclamation is part of generational repair from culturecide, and its impact and legacy remain to be seen.

Language Reclamation in Action

Success in language reclamation, especially with a language as endangered as Yurok, can be hard to quantify. Adding a few new advanced-level speakers each year can be a victory, even when the speaker numbers for other languages may be dramatically higher. Ms. McQuillen defines what success means for her as a language teacher:

> Success looks like having students that have come through here
> [DNHS] and go on to do something with language after high school,
> to still be very much involved in language. For instance, Nicole
> Peters[6]—she came through DNHS language classes and then she
> went to college. Then she applied for the *Kee Laa-yo-lue-mehl* [They
> Will Teach] Scholarship and continued her language study and even
> now is still very interested in speaking and taking the classes, doing a
> lot of focus on Yurok language. She works at the Chah-pekw Visitor's
> Center[7] and has incorporated a lot of language into their signage
> and panels and whatnot. It's pretty cool to see a former student still
> working with language.

In this example, a former student took her language foundation from high school and kept pursuing it. She is thus able to bring language into spaces where it previously wasn't as common, including using it to make signage in Yurok, something that can visually reach many people.

Sometimes Ms. McQuillen feels like Yurok language-keepers are making an impact with transmissions, like with examples of former students who utilize language post-high school. Other times the results are mixed: "Every year you have exceptional students that work hard. But a lot of times I don't really know what happens to them, and a lot of times your exceptional student may be non-Native. They go off and they have all this language, but I don't think they ever have an opportunity to use it again. Whereas I think high school-age students who are local [Native], you know who their family is and you know what they're up to. I guess a lot of 'em go to work for the Yurok Tribe as summer interns or even later on professionally there's some that go to work and they know language and have the opportunity to speak."

The issue of non-Native students being strong Yurok language students in the classroom but then not maintaining it afterward is frustrating, but part of the compromise the Yurok Tribe has made to make the language accessible to as many people as possible. Non-Natives have also played a major role in Yurok language preservation. Andrew Garrett, a White linguistics professor at UC Berkeley, wrote the main Yurok language textbook that many schools use, and he regularly participates in workshops to share knowledge back to Yurok language learners.

In fact, research shows the importance of expanding access to minority languages for their own survival in as many ways as possible to as many people as possible, from Yiddish theater to Gaelic cooking classes in Canada (Margolis 2023) to Kaska (Yukon territory of Alaska; Meek 2010) and Sami language workshops in Finland (Olthuis, Kivelä et al. 2013). These can be policy interventions by states, with financial support to community groups willing to enact language transmission in a variety of creative ways. It is harder to maintain transmission activities beyond what there is financing to support. Notably, the Yurok Tribe was expected to initially partially fund the Yurok language teacher positions at the high schools, with districts eventually stepping in to cover the costs at MHS in the 1980s, HVHS in 1997, DNHS in 2005, and EHS in 2010.

Creating sufficient incentives and supports for new Yurok language teachers can be challenging. Ms. McQuillen also astutely identifies space for language continuity as a barrier to language revitalization: "I think just providing opportunities for these students to use language after they're out of school, when they're not here, would help. Usually that's the homework in here: 'Go home and speak to somebody, teach somebody something that you've learned in here, that's your homework every day.' And maybe once a week we'll discuss what they did outside of class, for language. 'What'd you share? What'd you teach?'"

Asking "What did you share or teach?" as part of classwork is a tool for intergenerational language transmission. It facilitates language dissemination from students back into their families and communities. This example of students being asked what they shared about language also shows why having Yurok in the public high schools is such a powerful intervention. It is a consistent medium for language access that reinforces social dissemination. The school format brings regular accountability for young people, as well as reinforcement for language-learning techniques. The formal space of the school classroom fosters the widest language access possible to grow more speakers.

Whiteness and Identity Conflicts

I ask research questions about identity and culture, so it isn't surprising that many conversations with Native American students ended up centering on skin. Insecurity and confusion for White-passing students was a constant part of their own identity experiences. Ms. McQuillen reflects, "I have a lot of students in here that, *I* know who they are, I know who their family is, but their skin tone doesn't reflect the deep connections that their ancestors had here, to Yurok or Tolowa, or whichever one they come from. A lot of them are very disconnected from anything as far as Native culture. Even though their families in the past were really connected, they are disconnected."

Even though skin color in principle has nothing to do with degree of cultural connection, social forces operate such that students who are lighter have to work to prove their Nativeness, whereas students with darker coloring may instead have to contend with racist discrimination if they are not White-passing. Part of what Ms. McQuillen provides is a safe environment to help all students, regardless of their appearance, to connect to their culture, if they are open to it. Sometimes this happens because she knows the student's family and can seed their interest. She explains:

> I think it means a lot to go home and ask a parent something like, "My teacher said that I come from the village of Wehl-kwew, and that there's dances held there. I don't know this; can you tell me more? Where do my people come from?" And they come back and say, "My dad asked his aunt, who told him that this happened," or whatever. I think that a lot of them get a real connection from that.
>
> I had one girl quite a few years ago that came from a Yurok family but really didn't know anything about her history or her past; her culture. She actually wrote me this nice card that said, "Thank you for teaching me and helping me with my identity and who I am. I've looked into this, I talked to my dad's brother or something about this." So, they really do get a sense of connection.

The benefits of well-being in terms of cultural grounding can supersede the specific goal of Yurok language learning. Even though this can feel contradictory for language teachers, it is part of a larger goal of helping Native students better connect to their culture. "Even if they don't ever go out and really use Yurok language, I think the cultural part is really internalized for them. I'd like to think they have that for life, you know. It helps them in some way—not just, 'I'm Yurok but I don't know anything about that.'"

There is no question that White-passing young people experience the duality of White privilege and identity erasure at the same time. Lighter-skinned students over the years have quipped to me about getting let off with a warning by White police officers when pulled over for speeding on local roads, while their darker-skinned friends ended up with a ticket. But in social spaces like a new school classroom, students with more identifiably Native features benefit from having their identity recognized, whereas it can be socially difficult for Whiter-appearing Native students to assert their Native presence.

Ms. McQuillen notes how she sees youth identity in relation to Whiteness within her own family: "My son is very fair-skinned, and you wouldn't know he's Yurok if you didn't know who he was. But being raised by a strong cultural family [laughs], he grew up [knowing] everything about being a dance family, culture bearers, language people. He spent a lot of time with non-Native people at DNHS. Coming from a cultural family, he was self-confident as a Yurok man. Now that he's grown, he is comfortable with Native people and non-Native people." Such repertoires of moving between identities are fairly typical in youth who are raised in minority homes but attend school or other activities in ethnic majority settings. Although this can lead to identity-based frustration or clashes, young people with a strongly consolidated sense of self, like Ms. McQuillen's son, can move more easily in both worlds.

Support for students dealing with these types of identity issues as they come of age is crucial. Educators like Ms. McQuillen have developed curricula and assignments over the years to prompt students to explore their own backgrounds:

> Knowing who they are matters. I do a family tree project here in the
> first semester, where they have to get up and share who their family
> is. And I can reiterate, "Wow, your great-great-grandpa was *Poy
> 'we-son* [translation: boss] for that village!" And the class is all going,
> "Oh yeah," and maybe becoming more accepting of those students.
> We don't make a big deal about people in here about what they look
> like. Everybody in here is treated equal, everybody has the same

opportunity to speak, and to learn, no matter their complexion. But I think there's always gonna be some people who judge people by their appearance.

The family tree project is one that Yurok language teachers in other schools do too. James Gensaw's students at EHS and MHS also described learning from it and feeling more connected to their roots after researching it. The utility of this kind of culturally engaged pedagogy is meaningful for students across a range of backgrounds, as Ms. McQuillen describes: "Even if they're non-Indian, they [students] have something in their family that they can highlight or be proud of or go back and take a look at. Or they can even say, 'You know, my great-grandpa wasn't such a good guy, he did this and I'm not gonna be like that,' or whatever."

The jump from identity to well-being is not a large one. A solid sense of one's own identity facilitates well-being. The opposite is also true, Ms. McQuillen notes: "A big part of the whole well-being thing is language and worldview. We are learning exactly what these words and phrases mean and how we see things. I think it's part of making a whole human, to have that part of the puzzle fulfilled. And then maybe learning a lot of cultural knowledge helps mental well-being."

Ms. McQuillen sees the impact of appearance on student well-being, and does her best to mitigate it in the classroom: "How you fit in, the darkness or lightness of a child's skin, and how they identify culturally, it's not just in school, but how they thrive or not for their whole life. Some of them fit in really well because they're confident in who they are, and others are just learning about themselves. The light-skinned students don't have to deal with the same things as darker-skinned students. I had a visibly Native student saying, 'Shut the f—up, White girl!' And it's a Native girl sitting there, from a well-known Yurok family, but she is visibly White and didn't know much about herself."

This anecdote highlights the intragroup discrimination—colorism—that plagues Native American communities just as it does Latinx or African American communities. For each of these groups, BIPOC youth must then defend themselves on two fronts: from White people who insult them, but also from co-ethnics. The impact of the slurs may be interpreted differently depending on who such insults come from, but the bottom line is that both darker- and lighter-skinned students experience identity-based targeting, and the characteristics prized by one group may be the subject of taunts for the other. By helping students learn more about themselves, Yurok language classes are a place to move away from stereotypes, but it is hard work.

Insults can have detrimental impacts on student well-being: "I think that the whole mental health thing is connected to being confident in who you are, and understanding who you are, learning about your ancestors, and things maybe they did. When I know students' families, I can say, 'I knew them, I knew your grandpa, I knew your great-grandpa, I actually spoke to them, I saw them.' So that kinda connects them, to know that 'Oh yeah, these people were Yurok people and I'm Yurok.' I think language is part of that whole self-confidence and being who you are."

Ms. McQuillen intuitively knows what the empirical data proves. When students feel affirmed in their identities, and when those identities are welcomed and honored in educational spaces, it can increase well-being and success in school. Moreover, when students identify with and feel personally connected to their teachers, it motivates them to attend and participate in class.

Throughout her teaching career, Ms. McQuillen has played this role for students, acting in line with her own cultural framework of relating to Yurok youth. In addition to my own research, student-teacher congruence studies confirm that this approach brings protective benefits to young people (Lindsay and Hart 2017, Joshi, Doan et al. 2018, Redding 2019). Finding ways to recognize this additional labor that some teachers do is important to prevent educator burnout and remunerate the often invisible labor performed by BIPOC faculty.

Undoing Ignorance Among Staff and Teachers

This book shares numerous examples of the toxic school climate for Native American youth. In addition, language teachers described how administrators, fellow teachers, and staff also committed acts of insensitivity. Sometimes discrimination was intentional, but often it came from ignorance. Regardless, it contributes to a hostile school climate for adults and youth alike, through furthering systemic racism, White supremacy, and Native erasure.

Ms. McQuillen clears her throat and gently describes:

Right towards the end of spring break, the job announcements came out and they were advertising for a Tolowa language teacher at Del

Norte. So, when I got back on Monday, I emailed human resources:
"I see you're advertising for a Tolowa language teacher. Do you know
when you're going to advertise for a Yurok language teacher?" And
the person responds, "Oh, my mistake, I'm sorry, I thought it was
Tolowa and it's Yurok. We're advertising for a Yurok teacher," so
we had to change that. It was, like, [laughs bitterly] Tolowa, Yurok,
different. Right. That sort of thing has happened for years. I think
maybe there's some awareness [from school and district administra-
tors] when they're meeting with Tribal representatives in education
or whatever. If there's some issue they think, "Well, we have Yurok
language and we have Tolowa language."

There is a weighty unspoken critique here. Reading between the lines of Ms.
McQuillen's diplomatic retelling, the dynamic at DNHS points toward super-
ficial tokenism of Native American curricula by the school district. To some
staff, they can't tell the languages apart, and though she is too polite to say it,
Ms. McQuillen's story also illustrates the school district's approach of feeling
they have done enough just by adding the language classes to the curriculum.
This could be interpreted as: "Native Americans have their languages in the
schools—what more do they want?" As with any incremental form of racial
awareness and reparation, White administrators tend to see language classes
as the fulfillment of the mandate of culturally inclusive education, rather than
a beginning step.

Certainly, there are actions that do try to go deeper. As Ms. McQuillen
said of the school principal, who has added Tolowa and Yurok greetings to
her morning addresses on the school loudspeaker, "I think her heart is really
in the right place." Using Native greetings over the school loudspeaker in the
morning is symbolically powerful. Such actions not only reinforce the acceptability of Native languages in schools, but also push non-Native people to be
exposed to the validation of Native presence. The principal herself admit-
ted in a conversation with me that she has made missteps in working with
Native American colleagues in the region and that she is trying to learn from
her mistakes. This degree of cultural humility connotes an authentic starting
place from which real learning across cultures can begin.

For many tribal members working for cultural flourishing, language
classes are just the starting point for much larger goals. There is much more
work to be done to support Native American students who continue to deal
with assimilationist pressures in school, and in the communities off the

reservations. Meanwhile, White-derived indicators of school success may not capture the unique cultural labor Native American students and teachers undertake to assert Native presence in schools.

Ms. McQuillen has plenty of reasons to feel pessimistic. She has taught in public schools and in the community long enough to encounter all the threats to cultural reclamation that happen to her students, from food and housing insecurity to family violence to English dominance as a legacy of culturecide. But she has also seen significant change in Del Norte School District over the years, and this helps her remain optimistic. Albeit with many setbacks, she feels things are moving in the right direction, toward increased cultural awareness and respect. She notes, "At least our history is acknowledged now, and what happened to our people is more understood."

Such infusion of knowledge is a direct result of the dedication and educative efforts of people like Ms. McQuillen. Non-Native teachers play a very minimal role in sharing this kind of locally relevant history, and in fact, in many cases, they need to be learners themselves. In describing a past district-wide training she participated in for teachers, staff, and administrators at DNHS, Ms. McQuillen reflected:

> I do a lot of teaching about language loss and boarding schools and what happened to Native children here. One year I was shocked; I was at an in-service here for Del Norte High and they brought in a speaker that talked about boarding schools and the impact on Native people. There were people there at that training that said, "We didn't know this happened." These were adults! My colleagues! They responded to the speaker: "We didn't know that there was a boarding school era, or that this happened [forced boarding school internment] to children here in the United States." I couldn't believe that people in this county, that were working in our schools, didn't even know that history! They didn't understand the historical trauma that was placed on these students, so how would they be able to teach them? They just identify behavioral issues instead!

This final point—teachers who do not understand this historical trauma are then poised to identify Native American students as simply students with behavioral problems, rather than work with them through trauma—has major implications for student success. The over disciplining of BIPOC students has gotten more attention in recent years (Nance 2015) but remains unresolved.

The telling moment at the in-service Ms. McQuillen described was an admission that the school lacks not only trauma-informed expertise, but even the most basic facts about the contours of trauma shaping their students' lives. Ms. McQuillen's question: "How would such teachers be able to teach them?" is one that everyone involved in education should ask. Do we have enough grounding in the sociocultural histories of the communities we serve to be versatile educators who meet the needs of learners? Does our institution practice an ethic of trauma-informed care that supports students in distress rather than punishing them for physical, social, or emotional dysregulation that is shaped from intergenerational wounds, what Eduardo Duran has labeled the "soul wound" (2006)? If not, what interventions need to be made to bring this information to educators and to the staff and administrators who make our institutions run?

As that institutional change is slow, Ms. McQuillen has made it her practice to provide a safe space in her classes where Native American and non-Native students alike can learn from each other. She gestures around the empty classroom where we are sitting during her prep period: "I've had a lot of kids come through here and I let them speak their minds. It gives them a little more confidence in who they are or the world around them, to be able to say, 'I don't think so.'" By supporting students who challenge the status quo, language-keepers like Ms. McQuillen impart well-being through cultural learning under the guise of grammar lessons.

Conclusion

Ms. McQuillen loves working with high school students, but her commute from Klamath got to be too much. From the Yurok reservation to Crescent City, it is a difficult, thirty-minute commute with the highway crumbling into the ocean. And it can often take much longer because of ongoing construction and washout cycles at Last Chance Grade that seem never-ending.[8] When James Gensaw, a DNHS alum and the EHS and MHS Yurok teacher, shared that he was willing to move back north to teach at DNHS, Ms. McQuillen was able to retire knowing that the classes would keep going. She taught the Yurok language at DNHS for twelve years, retiring in 2022, just as I was finishing up the research for this book. When I saw her a few months into retirement, she was enjoying teaching the language to adult learners in the community part-time through the Yurok Language Program. She was also able to teach from the Yurok Language Program's Klamath office, saving her the commute. In addition to the work on language revitalization she has done with so many DNHS students, she has also planted the seeds of self-confidence in young people. Her approach to well-being is multilayered, and she is playing the long game.

CHAPTER 6

Annie O'Rourke and Her Students: Redefining "How to Be Civilized"

Introduction: From Boarding School to Culturally Sustaining Curricula Leader

Driving into the Hoopa Valley, the Trinity River, a tributary of the Klamath River that feeds into the Pacific Ocean, winds like a blue ribbon through rock and mountains.[1] The Hoopa Valley Indian Reservation encompasses a high school and elementary school campus across the street from the river. Salmon sculptures jumping out of implied water decorate the school fence. The Yurok language has been an elective course for decades alongside the Hupa language at Hoopa Valley High School (HVHS). The two tribes, plus the Karuk, live alongside each other and do ceremonies together. Intermarriage and children who identify with multiple tribes are common.

In 1893, the Hoopa Indian Boarding School was established on what is now the reservation as part of a broad agenda of culturecide by the Bureau of Indian Affairs (BIA). As in many Indigenous communities, the BIA agenda revolved around the mission of teaching *Na:tinixwe* (the word for Hupa in the Hupa language) children "how to be 'civilized'—to kill off all that made them Hupa" (Tracy 2019). From a population of roughly 1,000 Hupa people, more than half were killed from various impacts of early White colonization, including murder, enslavement, and disease exposure (Cahill 2011).

The boarding school transitioned to a day school in 1932 and from there it eventually fell under the purview of the Klamath Trinity Joint Unified School District (KTJUSD), named for the confluence of the Klamath and Trinity Rivers in Weitchpec (*Wetchpues* in Yurok). *Wetchpues* is on the Yurok Indian Reservation and has an elementary school that is also part of KTJUSD, a public school district of Humboldt County. KTJUSD also manages Hoopa Elementary School and Captain John's Continuation School, both on the same campus as HVHS. Some current HVHS students' great-grandparents or other family elders were interned in the boarding school when they were children. Intergenerational trauma from that time still impacts the Valley community.

In 2021, the Hoopa Valley population was 3,348, with a median household income of $42,361, and 23.2 percent of the population lives within an economic definition of poverty (Cubit 2022). The school offered free and reduced-price breakfast and lunch to 180 students, out of a total enrolled population of 263 in the 2020–2021 school year (EdData 2022). In 2020–2021, HVHS was roughly 78.3 percent Native American and 11 percent White, and the remaining 11.7 percent was a combination of Latinx (7.6 percent), two or more races (1.9 percent) and Black (0.8 percent; EdData 2022).

Native American reservations are frequently discussed from a deficit perspective. After introducing the Yurok language teacher, this chapter documents threats to youth well-being, namely community climates and structural constraints such as home life and resource limitations. While accounting for student testimonials to the effects of poverty and addiction, I weave in discussion of how the KTJUSD is leading the way in decolonizing school curricula. The necessity, rooted in trauma, to innovate in student support rests on a foundation of remarkable, locally relevant curricula. This is in line with the Community Cultural Wealth model of lifting culture as valuable in struggles for social justice (Yosso 2005). Not ignoring the problems, I instead focus on the cultural resources available to young people.

Though the buildings of HVHS sit in nearly the same footprint as the previous boarding school, the current guiding mission of the school is considerably different. Featuring an Indigenous-infused curriculum, including Yurok and Hupa languages, a cultural connections class, and the Indian Land Tenure Curriculum, HVHS has important lessons to offer other schools in the area. This chapter looks at well-being challenges, as well as how the district is a regional leader in decolonizing school curricula.

Ms. Annie: Language-Keeping as Family Responsibility

Morek[2]Annie O'Rourke is a vivacious local-girl-made-good. She graduated from HVHS in 2012, went to college and got credentialed as an English teacher, eventually made her way back to work at HVHS to teach English as well as the Yurok language, and briefly served as the school librarian. As with James Gensaw's move to DNHS, Annie's arrival enabled her Auntie Carole Lewis, the long-serving Yurok language teacher, to retire. She continues to split her teaching time between English and Yurok courses.

Dark-haired and full of energy, Ms. Annie, as the students call her, comes from a lineage of language-keepers. Her father grew up in a multigenerational household with a grandmother, Minnie Reed, who spoke to her grandchildren—including language-keepers and cultural educators Kay Inong, Carole Lewis, and Margo Robbins—in Yurok. Minnie Reed's daughter, Ms. Annie's paternal grandmother, attended a Southern California boarding school along with her sisters, and did not teach her children the Yurok language, even though Minnie continued to speak it at home. Thus, there were multiple approaches to languages under one roof. Minnie Reed was quite active in her efforts to pass down the language, and she made many hours of language recordings and is a featured language-keeper in the "Basic Yurok" textbook (Garrett 2014) that is used today in high school and community Yurok language classrooms.

Ms. Annie's father didn't get to take Yurok in school because it wasn't offered then, so "it is a pretty big deal for him that his daughter is a language teacher in the school. He's talked to me about the generation before him, and their time in boarding schools, away from land and community. That had great effect on his ability to learn language" (O'Rourke 2022). When Ms. Annie talks about the boarding schools with her students, she tries to balance out the heavy, serious topics with days that are more lighthearted. But, as she says, "There are times when these discussions have to be had" (O'Rourke 2022).

Ms. Annie joined the HVHS faculty in the fall of 2020, in the midst of the COVID-19 pandemic, so when we spoke in 2022, she had yet to experience a fully normal year of in-person teaching. She notes that attendance was one of the hardest issues in 2021–2022: "The top reasons students are absent is home security. A lot of them are moving, or some of them have to make alternative arrangements to have safe places to stay. I ask them why is it that they have to be gone, and what I can do to support them. And I remind them, 'Hey, we miss you when you're not here! We're thinking of you, and we can't wait to have you back. We want you to be here!'" (O'Rourke 2022).

While housing insecurity is the leading reason students aren't in school, it isn't the only one. "Busing has been unreliable for downriver[3] kids. We don't have any spare bus drivers right now. Whenever the downriver bus driver can't make it to work, the kids just can't get to school. I think we are at an all-time low in providing bus service. I don't remember it ever being this bad. For others, it is waking up on time. Or for classes held later in the day, it is always our sports teams needing to leave for games. And since the Yurok III–IV class is so small, when we miss our athletes, we are down to three students! It makes it a lot of pressure on those students who are here" (O'Rourke 2022).

A competitive person, Ms. Annie liked to challenge herself in language classes to learn as much as she could as a student. She sees language-keeping as "a family responsibility, something you have to pass on because a lot of people have put in the work to keep it going. It definitely *is* a big responsibility. I try not to put too much of the weight of that responsibility onto my students, because sometimes it can be too much pressure for them" (O'Rourke 2022). A role model for many young people who clearly look up to and adore her, Ms. Annie is part of the Native cultural reclamation process, and she also demonstrates a strong ethics of care toward her students.

In connecting with students, Ms. Annie brings in her personal life as a teaching tool. She shares that in class "I talk about my baby—she's one and a half—and I explain how I talk to her in the language. She is going to be part of keeping the language alive. I try to model keeping it alive in my own life, talking to her and to others in Yurok" (O'Rourke 2022). By setting this example of language revitalization within her own family structure and then sharing it with her students, Ms. Annie is norming Yurok language engagement. She is also showing that Yurok isn't only spoken by elders, but that a new generation of Yurok first language-speakers is being made.

> It is really encouraging that other people are doing the same thing. Brittany [Vigil, who works for the Yurok Language Program] has talked about how her son's first language is Yurok, and there are others. It really gives me hope, that my baby is going to have a peer group of all these other babies who are growing up with Yurok as their first language. When we get to do in-person language meetings, she'll be able to feel like it is more normal and it will be a bonding experience. I'd like to see more babies growing up like that, so we'll have more people closer to fluency. That is my distant dream, and in the more immediate, it starts with my students! (O'Rourke 2022)

The goal that today's babies are tomorrow's fluent Yurok speakers shows the timeline Ms. Annie is working on, but as she says, in the near future, her students are the next speakers.

Ms. Annie's full-time teaching load at HVHS includes English during the periods when she is not teaching Yurok. She comments:

Things are really different between those two classes. The English classes are fine—I love reading and books and worked as a librarian here before. But the Yurok classes are really special. You get to put the Yurok values first in the Yurok classes. With decolonization, you get to learn the values of the people, because it is built into the language itself. When students ask about something, we can go on tangents about values and culture. For example, when we learn the two ways to say "thank you" in Yurok, we can talk about practices of generosity in our culture. Just by learning the language, we learn about things that we didn't realize were colonized, and then we get to unlearn them. (O'Rourke 2022)

The juxtaposition between "fine" English classes and deeply decolonizing Yurok language classes highlights the importance of culturally sustaining curricula. Most of the students in Ms. Annie's Yurok II and III–IV classes are Yurok-identified, whether enrolled or descendants. There is also a non-Native student as well as a few Karuk students enrolled. The Yurok courses are open to everyone willing to take them.

Ms. Annie can relate to students coming to the language as learners, since she herself is still expanding her language abilities. Her personal goal is to pass the Yurok III assessment for teachers, which confers a lifetime language teaching credential from the Yurok Language Program. She quips, "Maybe by the time I retire, I'll be able to consider myself fluent!" Adults like Ms. Annie model gracefully that messing up can be essential for learning. Making mistakes is appreciated in language classes that require constant verbal risk-taking. Ms. Annie describes how "in my classes, there has been such comfort and support among students; they don't have to worry about making mistakes. The classroom community is a source of resiliency for them" (O'Rourke 2022).

Resilience and Culturally Sustaining Curricula in Far Northern California

Students at EHS, MHS, and DNHS frequently did not know the definition of the word "resilience," and I often discussed it with students before the interview began, going over the concept with them as we walked to the room where interviews or focus groups would take place. Once the audio recorder clicked on, I often resorted to terms like "inner strength" to maintain conceptual clarity for those who were unfamiliar with the term. In marked contrast, students at HVHS were quite familiar with the idea of resilience. Through a trauma-informed care approach that the school has tried to implement for years, multiple teachers and administrators have spoken to HVHS students about the significance of resilience in relation to intergenerational trauma and their own lives.

I don't delve into the Adverse Childhood Experience Survey (ACES) data in a systematic way in this book. But every time I go to Hoopa, someone reminds me about the extremely high ACES scores across students, faculty, and staff. Anecdotally, high ACES scores in the Valley make the familiarity with the word resilience a testament to the school's efforts to address them through trauma-informed care. Such a care approach has persisted through the dedication of educators and administrators amid nearly constant administrative leadership churn,[4] which is a significant cause of instability at HVHS.

During the five years spent intermittently collecting data at HVHS for two different phases of research with the Yurok Tribe's Education Department, I sought permission from four different school principals[5] and two district superintendents.[6] This instability is itself traumatic for some students who crave stability at school when they aren't getting it at home. Teachers reported more fights and negative student behavior in the immediate aftermath of each principal turnover, and teachers expressed anxiety about having to renegotiate their own work plans with each transition. In contrast, EHS, MHS, and DNHS did not have such instability. Though there were occasional changes to leadership at those schools, they maintained a degree of consistency distinct from HVHS.

KTJUSD hosts the Indian Education Program, which is partially funded by the Federal Title VII Indian Education Act in order to "meet the special educational and culturally-related academic needs of Indian children" (KTJUSD 2022). Additional government funders and the Indian Land Tenure Foundation have supported Native American educators in the creation and implementation of curricula based on Hoopa, Yurok, and Karuk history and culture (KTJUSD 2022). Culturally sustaining curricula have been adopted by KTJUSD schools and have also been shared out to other educators through the Humboldt County Office of Education (HCOE).

For example, in spring 2022, educators versed in the Indian Land Tenure Curriculum—including Native-grounded conflict resolution practices and Indigenous educational media production (Lowry 2014, Lowry and Ekedal 2019)—helped facilitate a five-part series on diversity in education through the HCOE, which I attended. HCOE offered the workshops on Zoom and took roll for participants from local schools who were then compensated for their time. Such professional development reached dozens of people at each workshop, and the conversations in the chats showed dynamically engaged participants. Making such innovations stick after the workshops is often the hard part for time-strapped educators. Nonetheless, the HCOE series showed a growing awareness in the region that the KTJUSD curricula is a local example of culturally relevant work that others could learn from. HCOE was then able to expand this interest into an expansive Native American Studies Model Curriculum plan (HCOE 2024), an important future area of exploration and implementation for scholars and teachers alike.

It is empowering for KTJUSD, a school often pointed to as an example of what isn't working, to be recognized for something so positive. The curricular innovation on culturally relevant topics is derived from the unique situation of having a public school situated on a reservation. Ms. Annie comments:

> Teachers have a little more freedom to guide and shape our curriculum. Our departments are smaller than other schools, so we have more space and choice in what and how we represent things. We have some teachers who are really passionate about learning more so that they can teach more, while others shy away from it. In most instances, if misrepresentation happens in class, students are comfortable enough that they will talk to a teacher themselves and come to me if it doesn't go well. Students for the most part feel comfortable voicing concerns or bring it to a teacher to be brought up later. (O'Rourke 2022)

Student empowerment is significant in creating a sense of agency for young people. Ms. Annie's assertion that "if a conversation doesn't go the way they want it, students will sit down with us and talk about it" shows that students are engaged in their own lives, and in the life of their community, and are willing to take time to be involved. These indicators of participation in school life reinforce well-being, as they are part of meaning-making and connection between students, teachers, and staff.

Ms. Annie also mentions the unique space of HVHS, where teachers may practice more humility about what they know as compared to other schools. "Teachers recognize they can get it wrong and are generally humble about it. I think a lot of it has to do with being on a reservation. Teachers, every single day on their drive to work, recognize that, sure, they are a teacher, but they are a guest on the reservation. I think one danger that is present in this school is if teachers forget that guest status. No matter how long you are here, always be willing to decenter yourself in the classroom" (O'Rourke 2022).

While there are a small number of teachers from Hoopa who also live on or near the reservation, many commute from coastal towns and are clear outsiders. The more teachers are willing to decenter themselves in learning spaces, the more likely young people can see school as a place where their own stories are recognized, and greater opportunities to support well-being can take place. Students agree.

Tai's Testimony: Culture in the Face of Multiple Insecurities

Insecurity in the Hoopa Valley is visible across housing, food, medical care, and many other fields. Digital connectedness is just one of many areas in which resource scarcity highlights the impacts of colonization compounded by rural isolation. The COVID-19 pandemic put the digital divide in stark relief around the world. Because of its highly rural location surrounded by mountains, internet connection is limited in the Hoopa Valley. Many students and some school staff did not have internet at home before the COVID-19 pandemic. KTJUSD tried valiantly to address this digital divide by distributing internet hotspots and Chromebooks to anyone who needed them. It also opened Wi-Fi networks so that people could come to the school parking lot and use the internet from their cars. Even with these measures, the internet signal strength was not sufficient, and the schedule of connectivity availability was too challenging to hold synchronous classes.

For the year (March 2020 to March 2021) many children in the United States, including my own, lived on Zoom for school. At HVHS, teachers sent paper packets to students for asynchronous work, and also made internet-based asynchronous work available. Because of fear around COVID-19 exposure, given its disproportionate toll on Native American populations, the school also allowed students to continue with independent studies via packets for the 2021–2022 school year. Some teachers mentioned that this was a significant burden for them because they had to prepare additional lesson plans for the packets. There was an understanding that independent study would not be generally available in the 2022–2023 school year, but instead reserved for extraordinary cases, since all the schools in the district were back in person and planned to stay that way.

For students, the social isolation during the lost year of COVID-19 had deep reverberations, and this is true across all four schools. In this section, I share the perspective of an HVHS student who was enrolled in Yurok IV in spring 2022. Quiet and hardworking, with an inner steely strength evident in my classroom observations, Tai[7] reflected, "Personally, after being on independent study for so long and social distancing, it's really hard for me to integrate back into being able to be social with people, just like, interacting. I noticed that my anxiety spiked a lot from not being social with people, and I usually have a hard time with classes like language where I know that I have to interact. After COVID, it's kinda hard to be able to do that. I forgot how, you know? Just because I haven't been around anybody for a really long time" (Anonymous 2022a).

The rural setting of HVHS and its population make for particularly extreme experiences of COVID-19 isolation. Whereas in cities and towns, lockdown might still mean seeing people in neighboring buildings or outside, in Hoopa, it could mean not seeing people outside one's household for days at a time. In the return to in-person instruction, teachers were part of breaking up this isolation. Tai spoke warmly about being comfortable with the Yurok language teacher because they were connected to each other through Yurok ceremony outside of class: "In all honesty, it's easier to be in this class than most of my other classes because of the personal connection I have with Ms. Annie. I used to be a purity dancer in the mountain dances, and the camp that I stayed in was with her relations, so I know her family and all the connections in it that way. Whereas in some other classes it's a little bit harder because I don't know the teacher as well" (Anonymous 2022a). By having a cultural connection to Ms. Annie outside of class, Tai was able to overcome some of their social anxiety to learn from her in the Yurok classes.

Moreover, the impact of culturally sustaining curricula in helping Tai feel welcome at school underscores the core argument I make in this book: "Yurok class makes school kinda feel like home, you know? Being raised with a cultural perspective on life, it just feels more like home when we get to talk about that stuff in class or when I'm learning my language. With my grandma, we always used to sing Yurok songs, and when I got here they were singing those songs. I was like, 'Oh, I know those!' So it was like a feeling of connection and just, home" (Anonymous 2022a).

I ask Tai if they can comment on the connection to that feeling of home in relation to their own resilience: "Traditions are what we evolve around, and we base who we are as a people off of certain things that we see within our wildlife around here. One of the things that most of the tribes in this area really take after is their sense of family. We take after the woodpecker because woodpeckers mate for life. We as a people, once you choose to be with a certain group of people, you stay with them, you grow with them, and you learn how to be with them" (Anonymous 2022a).

This identification of human characteristics with those of the animal world is an attribute of Tai's cultural connectedness. Woodpeckers—a common bird in far Northern California whose feathers are used in regalia—exhibit a lifelong companionship that Tai sees take place in people. To "stay together, grow together, and learn how to be together" is as poetic a description of resilience as any I have encountered.

Tai also talks about the way their rural and Indigenously grounded upbringing is intertwined. "I think that on a very personal level, growing up in such a remote area with culture, it has taught me a lot and most of it is how to survive. If I ever went to a city and asked somebody if they knew how to run a chainsaw, or if they knew how to track a deer and you know, just skin it and process it so that you have food for winter, they would be clueless. Whereas I, as a descendant, I've learned how to do all that. I do it regularly with my family. We also learn about that kind of stuff in cultural connections with Ms. Scott"[8] (Anonymous 2022a).

Tai radiates a solitary energy, and I could see, observing them in class many times, that they were not one of the popular kids. In some ways, Tai seemed like a grown-up miscast in a child role, and Tai talked about how they preferred the company of elders to those their own age, especially because Tai could learn from them. This sense of elder appreciation was particularly resonant with being able to learn the Yurok language. "I like to be involved, and it makes me feel more connected to my elders. Being able to sit around a campfire or in a house where you have elders speaking a different language than you; when you're younger you feel a little left out because you don't know what they're saying. But when you're older and you put in that effort to learn, that need to want to know that kind of stuff drives you, motivates you to want to be like them. I know the elders in my family, they're amazing people, and 100 percent, they're my role models. I think that they've set a good example for me" (Anonymous 2022a). The self-reflection that being motivated and putting in effort drives Tai to learn the Yurok language is hopeful for the language revitalization process. And Tai's comment that they want to emulate their elders shows the way those elders offer a guide to well-being for Tai.

The role of their elders is in contrast to what Tai sees in some of their peers their own age: "I do wish that some of the kids around here were more cultural-based. Because you'll see kids who say that they participate in dances and stuff, but when you get to know them, it's just not there. I wish that kids were more in tune with that and in tune with their natural resources and how their ancestors used to do stuff because that really does affect your daily life" (Anonymous 2022a).

Tai's testimony sounds wise beyond their years, more like an elder than a teenager. This can be a very lonely way to be when one actually *is* a teenager. Such separation from peers is perhaps exacerbated by their approach to cell phones versus the majority of their classmates: "Personally, I love technology, but sometimes I think it gets in the way because when you think about my culture, I don't think about phones or computers or anything modern. I think about being outside and learning the land and learning how to read the river and read tracks. I think about being connected as a people. I think the reason why I'm so connected with my culture is because I didn't have a phone until I was fifteen. I never had that, and it really drove me to want to learn more about nature and about how we can use our resources. Because I didn't have a phone, I wasn't on my phone!" (Anonymous 2022a).

Tai sees delayed phone access as contributing to their connection to nature—since a phone wasn't available, they spent more time outside being in touch with the land and culture. Now, even though they have a phone, the value of cultural connectedness stays with them. Tai laments the role of phones at school, stating, "I think that schools are not as strict as they should be on the technology that kids bring to school because it really is a distraction" (Anonymous 2022a). And even though Tai reports that a lot of kids will say that the phone is not a distraction, "I'll be walking through the halls and I'll see kids on their phone and I just feel out of place" (Anonymous 2022a). Phone users might not recognize that they are distracted, but Tai recognizes the alienated feeling of being different, of preferring to pay attention to nature than to a screen. On this social issue, they are able to readily diagnose the problem of disrupted cultural connection in addition to critiquing it.

Tai expands to describe other barriers to their own success that they or their classmates are dealing with: "Every kid learns in a different way, so sometimes I wish that teachers had multiple ways to explain one thing, because if I don't understand something, I'll have to figure out something online, like, from a different professor from another school. When I don't understand what Ms. Annie is talking about, I'll usually go onto the Yurok dictionary online. It's the Berkeley edition and they have audio readings, so I'll sit there and I'll listen to them. It's not always easy to learn about language when somebody's only teaching it one way, or if the student isn't Yurok and hasn't heard it" (Anonymous 2022a). Figuring out how to access other means to learn that better fit their learning style shows a resourcefulness on Tai's part. Using the online Yurok dictionary, with both visual and audio components, is a useful supplement to classes that are also managing many different stages of language learning.

The openness of Yurok courses to all who want to be there is important for expanding the speaker base, but also brings challenges. "Yurok is for anybody who wants to learn about the language. So sometimes, if a student wasn't brought up with the language in their life, they have to start from the very beginning. But sometimes the teacher doesn't want to start from the very beginning, and it's kinda hard and sometimes they'll just expect you to be where the rest of class is. But then you're like, 'Oh no, what am I doing? I wasn't brought up with this!'" (Anonymous 2022a).

Tai notes that though they grew up mostly without the language, every now and then they will recognize something they heard an elder say, and it makes it easier to learn. In addition, Tai goes on to say, in a manner of speaking, that they wish there was differentiated instruction, even though they don't use that term: "Sometimes I wish that they would identify a student as who they are rather than a whole group, because it's different for every student when you have to learn about a culture or a type of language" (Anonymous 2022a). This issue was present in all the Yurok language classes across the four high schools, and, indeed, in many other kinds of classrooms around the world. Teachers have to balance reaching beginners while also holding the interest of those with more context, and it is a delicate balance, unsolved here as elsewhere.

When asked about post–high school plans, Tai articulates a feasible one. They want to leave the area to study nursing in order to help people. They also astutely point out some of the ways their education has been lacking.

I feel that, like, in such a small community I haven't been exposed to how the world works as much as other people have. I wish they [HVHS] had a junior seminar and not just a senior seminar, because at this age I should be learning about credit and debit and how to set up a bank account and how to put a car seat in a car because a lot of times people don't know how to do that. We should be learning this by now, but we're not. It's because we have such a small school and are so low on funds and stuff, but it's not anything that can't be fixed. It's just not gonna be fixed by the time I leave! (Anonymous 2022a)

This request for basic life skill instruction was echoed by Tai's counterparts in the Yurok III–IV class at EHS. Young folks want help learning how to adult, and schools seem like a realistic place to obtain those skills. And yet high schools continue to produce graduates who don't understand the difference between credit or debit or how to read a pay stub.

Another similarity across HVHS and EHS is Yurok-descendant student sadness around being shut out of official tribal enrollment. Questions about Native American identity are particularly fraught in ways that are distinct from other ethno-racial classifications in the United States because of the role of blood quantum, used to determine who is eligible for official tribal status. Tai identifies as a Yurok tribal descendant. Their blood quantum is too low (meaning previous generations had children with non-Yurok people—one-eighth blood quantum is the cutoff), so Tai does not qualify to enroll in the Yurok Tribe. This means that, though they can get health care through UIHS, which is open to any Native American descendant, they are ineligible for benefits that the Tribe offers only to enrolled members, such as college scholarships or traditional hunting and fishing rights.

In a snapshot of contemporary life, Tai mentions that they have half-siblings on the Yurok roll because the siblings have a Yurok-enrolled dad, whereas Tai's biological dad is White. Tai's non-enrolled status does not impede their Yurok identity, and they are self-reflective about how such status pushes them to be more independent: "From my point of view, I love my culture and I love learning about it! But because I would never get any help from the Tribe, I know that I'm gonna have to like, toughen up a lot more than other kids out here because I don't have that backup money that kids use.[9] So I'm gonna have to find a way to go off on my own, figure out my own stuff. I also don't really have parents, so I don't have that guidance that other people do. So, I'll have to figure out on my own how to do things" (Anonymous 2022a). Tai has overcome numerous challenges already to get to this stage in their schooling. At one point homeless, they speak warmly about the guardian they live with now, and focus on care for their siblings as their personal mission.

Echoing students from a range of demographic backgrounds who have gone through difficult family circumstances, Tai talks about one of their goals for themselves as supporting others. They hope to eventually have financial and housing stability so that they can take care of themselves as well as their younger siblings: "I would personally become their guardian or foster them. I would even become a foster parent for Native families so that at least the kids will still be in a Native descendant's home. I want to be able to take care of any of my siblings or relations if I ever need to. Because no one should ever have to go through the things that I have witnessed or been through. So, that's my personal motivation" (Anonymous 2022a).

Pausing to scan around us, making sure they won't be overheard from our perch in the open-air hallway outside the classroom, Tai connects toxic households in the Valley to conflicts at school. "A lot of time there's conflicts between families, or they have an argument and then kids bring that to school. People think that they can get away with having a higher-up family, or a certain position in the Tribe, and they get benefits that are unequal to others. There's a lot of conflicts on the reservation" (Anonymous 2022). That conflict within the reservation community is in turn exacerbated by the stresses of conflict off the reservation, where Native American students and community members still find themselves the targets of identity-based discrimination. I turn to this issue in the following section.

Delia's Determination: "I'll never give up"

Delia[10] is a dynamic high school senior and an enrolled member of the Yurok Tribe. She flips a glossy black ponytail over her shoulder as we talk and clicks fancy painted nails over her phone screen while narrating her life:

> We are pretty culturally connected at the high school. Yurok and Native Literature are two of my favorite classes. Ms. Moore [Hupa language and Native American literature teacher] is a really good teacher. It feels better when you have a Native teacher. She tells us what we need to know and makes it enjoyable, and also from a Native perspective. I wish we had that for civics too. I'm not too into the whole politics and government thing, and I definitely don't enjoy general education. Mr. Anderson [civics teacher] is teaching what

happened decades ago. He does talk about Indigenous people, and he is respectful. He could be teaching civics based more on our kind of civics, but they don't test us on that. (Anonymous 2022b)

Delia acknowledges that since Indigenous civics is not part of the testing rubric, there is less incentive to teach it, even with a teacher who is well-intentioned and respectful of the community he teaches and lives in. She knows her strengths, and appreciates the cultural content of her education. "I'm a good writer, and I enjoy the cultural classes. I was a teaching assistant in Cultural Connections for a while. When I was in there, they were making regalia for dolls and traditional houses. She [the teacher, Ms. Scott] tells a lot of stories, gives us the knowledge that all of us should know. Honestly, taking Yurok is all about staying true to who you are. It is an honor to learn it. I want to learn more, and it is very important to me. I wish we had Karuk here too along with Yurok and Hupa. We have to keep our languages alive, keep our traditions alive" (Anonymous 2022b).

Delia's identity as a Yurok woman is deeply important to her, but it hasn't been an easy journey: "We are a very culturally connected family. My sister is having her Flower Dance soon. I didn't get to have one. I've been in foster care on and off throughout my whole life. My parents have mostly been on unemployment, though my mom worked for the Tribe for a while. She had to go to rehab, and that meant quitting her job in order to get us [me and siblings] back. She's had a bunch of hoops to jump through to bring us back together. I'm really close with my mom and dad now, and my parents are so proud of me" (Anonymous 2022b).

Like Tai, Delia shares the impact of family trauma in her life, and how she is holding fast to her dreams as she navigates it. "I'm one of [many] siblings and the first in my family to go to college. I want to inspire my young siblings to go too. They can do anything they can set their minds to. I just toured the college I'm going to go to over spring break. I got a big scholarship, so I won't have to pay for tuition or anything. My grandma worries about me being so far from my support system, but I feel like I need to go. There is such a lack of resources around here. I need to go far away, especially in the profession I want, to be a Native actor" (Anonymous 2022b). Her self-determination has already gained her a scholarship to a four-year school out of the county, but she knows that she has academic ground to make up in order to succeed there.

I feel like we are far behind academically at HVHS. Other schools are further ahead knowledge-wise. I didn't do too good a job starting high school. I got caught up in the wrong crowd and skipped a lot of school, but I figured it out. I'm telling my brothers and sisters to take school seriously. You gotta always look ahead. Not just where you are now, but what do you love to do, you have to pursue it. I wish I had learned that earlier and gotten better grades in my early years here. There is so much raw talent here on the reservation, but people get caught up in drugs or alcohol. We need more resources in the Valley, things that people could do. This is always where my roots are going to be rooted, but I want to go out and try to do something! (Anonymous 2022)

As in earlier chapters, Delia echoes the "success in both worlds" approach, leaving her home community to pursue her goals, but feeling deeply rooted in herself at the same time.

In reflecting on well-being, Delia talks about how hard the COVID-19 pandemic was, when she missed out on a year of school, staying home, being on independent study, and not seeing anybody—in her words, "That sucked!" But she also notes that the pandemic gave her a lot of time with her family, which was a positive thing as her parents were in a good way then, and it gave them time to bond and heal.

Being in foster care off and on my whole life definitely made me strong and independent. I had to do a lot for my younger siblings. I want to be that inspiration, to help them believe in themselves, because they have such potential! My mom and dad are so encouraging. I know it may sound bad that I've been in foster care, but they are so supportive now. And I learned so much from them in how to be strong. They are such good people, such good parents. Everyone has their struggles, and for them it is substance abuse, but that don't define who they are.

When I move [for college] it is going to be hard because I am such a family person. It'll make me sad, but it'll also make me happy too because I'm doing what I love. It is an amazing feeling. That's what my resilience is—I may struggle a bit, but I know what I need to do and what I don't need to be doing, and I'll never give up. (Anonymous 2022b)

As Delia names the trauma she has accumulated in her life, she also names the inner resources to be strong in the face of hardship. Knowing what she needs to do, and what she needs to stay away from, is part of defining and fueling her own resilience. This is part of how Delia tends her own well-being, even in the face of what others might identify as a hard childhood.

Extracurricular Racism: Being Native in Sports

I admit, I am not that interested in organized sports. I was never particularly good at them, though I did play years of softball. Maybe that is why my questions as a researcher stayed close to places I liked to frequent, such as classrooms, or places I had to pass through, like hallways and buses. I didn't ask that much about discrimination in extracurricular activities like football or soccer. But a focus group with some boisterous Yurok II students in a windowless conference room in the administrative wing of HVHS changed that. With sheetrock walls blocking out the sunny spring day, we begin with their reflections on their personal identities.

Vicky is a young woman on the Karuk roll, and Tim is enrolled in the Yurok Tribe. They are both involved in their respective Native communities, participating in dances and doing traditional activities like hunting, gathering, basket weaving, and fishing. Tim introduces himself: "My dad teaches me about my culture, and so does my mom and grandma. I take a lot of pride in being Yurok. Being Native doesn't really affect me as much as someone else because I have light skin, so I look like a White person. That can be hard too. When I try to leave Hoopa, I try to wear a Yurok shirt or a sweatshirt with a Native design or something to show that I'm Native" (Focus Group 11.1 2022).

Like many other White-passing students, Tim finds other ways to indicate his Native identity through clothing so that he isn't written off as White. At the same time, his minority identity prompts him to connect more with other minorities. Tim continues: "I grew up from the time I was a baby until [a number of] years ago in Eureka, and there I had more African American friends than anyone else. I think being Native made me feel like they could connect with me more. Everyone I've been around people-wise have always been nice to me. My African American friends always took an interest in my culture, like how I would play stick games and go fishing. But when I came to Hoopa, that is when it backfired. I had to prove myself as Native" (Focus

Group 11.1 2022). Vicky joined in to share that "The way he'd wear Native designs when he'd travel out-town,[11] I relate to that. I would always wear my hair in braids when I'd travel for wrestling. I say on my [online] profile that I'm Native" (Focus Group 11.1 2022). Both Tim and Vicky find ways to signal their Native identities to others because they are proud of it.

HVHS is by no stretch of the imagination a perfect school climate. There is internal colorism and associated discrimination among Native American students, who judge each other based on internally held criteria of acceptability rather than external othering. There is also social drama that comes about from a combination of typical youth boredom and the complex and lasting impacts of intergenerational trauma. Fights frequently get physical. Rates of Native youth self-harm through drugs, alcohol, suicide, and other risky behaviors like driving under the influence are all high, and HVHS's dedicated team of wellness staff are both devoted and busy.

Nevertheless, there is also a strong internal identity solidarity among the majority-Native HVHS students that was evident whenever I went back to HVHS.[12] That solidarity shows up in mutually supporting each other in hard social situations off the reservation. When student-athletes ventured to play sports in nearby coastal towns, those were what they described as their worst discriminatory moments.

> *Tim:* I've played football for years. With the reffing,[13] they were always letting dirty plays go by the other team, including by students who were being super terrible, like calling me a "dirty little Native." In Ferndale, it was really bad. The refs let it all go when the other team fouled. It did not feel fair.
> *Vicky:* Yeah, when it comes to reffing, it seems like they are racially motivated. Definitely the out-town refs are not on our side. It has been like that for so long. I've wrestled for many years and the refs have always behaved the same. (Focus Group 11.1 2022)

These students didn't accept that such behavior was okay, but they also weren't sure how to intervene in it.

> *Tim:* I tried to get it to change. When there was that one situation where the [Native] kid got slammed on his head, I tried to spread the word. I got ahold of someone [White] who has a lot

of followers, and I explained how the refs are being racist. He just wrote back "I don't understand." I was expecting him to spread the word, but he didn't. I tried to talk to the principal at that school, but it just led to prohibiting fans from attending events to try to make it less crazy. It has been happening for so long around here that everyone here just expects it. We all know what we are getting into before we play the game. We are just numb to it. Especially going against Ferndale.

Vicky: I don't think it is as bad in wrestling as in football, but that stuff is still happening.

Tim: Kids on the teams for Ferndale are playing right along with the coaches—they are both saying horrible things to us, but mostly the students. The coaches just don't intervene. It's not like I say, "Yay, I get to go play Ferndale and experience racism!" I just want to play the sport and go out there and have fun. I try to focus on the game and do what is best for my team. If the other team is going to be negative, I don't mind—it is just something I have to deal with. (Focus Group 11.1 2022)

The sense of futility in intervention, that it didn't get better when Tim tried, even reaching out to a White influencer, is defeating. In fact, the scale of the culture change necessary to address racism can be debilitating for people of all walks of life and contexts. Vicky and Tim push back against the reality of such incessant discrimination.

Vicky: I am tired of it! We shouldn't have to be resilient all the time! It is mentally draining to have to deal with this constantly.

Tim: Agreed, it is tiring to have to have such a thick skin all the time. It would be one thing if all of the Valley was united and nice to each other and we only had to deal with stuff from outsiders. But we are so divided here in the Valley too! (Focus Group 11.1 2022)

Vicky's comment that "We shouldn't have to be resilient all the time" has stuck with me for months after she made it. Why should we expect students to be strong enough to take all the abuse that comes their way? The resilience required for these young people to get through their days is simply too much to ask. It is incumbent on school and district administrators to address the toxic school climates that extend to their extracurriculars. For HVHS, this means addressing racist behavior among students at other schools, an even harder task than addressing it within one's own school.

This challenge spurred some spontaneous brainstorming together. I asked Tim and Vicky if they wanted my assistance to design a letter to employ anytime there was overt racism during one of their sporting events. They said yes, and I shared a rough draft with them the following week—they gave input, and I incorporated it. The idea was that school leaders could name the behaviors and build a track record, rather than perpetually letting such behavior go. Then the HVHS principal or athletics coach could send a customized letter to the principal and coach of the opposing team they had played. I sent a working draft of the letter to the principal. But since he was leaving the job at the end of the school year, I don't believe it was ever used. Administrative turnover makes it hard to build systems.

Both Tim and Vicky are committed to sports, with each hoping to play professionally in their respective activities of football and wrestling. They also each have backup plans—counseling for Tim and nursing for Vicky—that make sense given the needs they see in the Valley. Their backup plans are also reminders that marginalized communities also contain young people who want to find ways to give back. These students are very explicit about their wishes to improve their own lives and those of others, in ways both small and big. Economic precarity hovers over them. Tim doesn't have a stable place to live. Both students identify sports, working out, watching YouTube, and smoking weed as things they have turned to intermittently to find respite.

Yurok is their favorite class—the one they look forward to and are the most engaged and communicative in. They love Ms. Annie, who "teaches ways to make it stick, and it is competitive in a fun way," notes Vicky. Trasketball[14] and other games have made it fun to learn Yurok, and they describe the Yurok class as a drama-free space. When I ask if having Yurok in their schedules makes them more likely to come to school, Vicky and Tim both enthusiastically respond, "Definitely!" (Focus Group 11.1 2022).

In the face of challenges to well-being both on and off the high school campus, Tim and Vicky identify both Yurok language and other culturally sustaining classes as sources of strength and pride in who they are. They rely on that inner strength when faced with racist student-athletes and adults at other schools where they go to play sports. Clearly the road to well-being is complex and beyond what any one school can do—schools are, on the one hand, microcosms of the problems in society at large. On the other hand, schools are a realistic place to start the hard work of social change.

Conclusion

Teachers like Ms. Annie are engaging in locally relevant educational content while working to meet state standards and to help support students in a range of precarious circumstances. Such an ethics of care in education is both trauma-informed and culturally grounding. Such conscientious education supports young people like Tai, Delia, Vicky, and Tim in identifying school as a safe and healthy place to develop their own identities and map their futures.

HVHS is wealthy in its culturally sustaining curricula, even as its population faces numerous material challenges. Whereas some schools offer only Yurok language classes in an otherwise White-oriented curricula, for years KTJUSD has been innovating and placing thoughtfully developed and age-appropriate Indigenous curricula throughout the K–12 system. This culture-as-resource approach is visible in multiple curricular spaces and means that HVHS is ahead of its neighbors in the work of decolonizing its educational spaces. Educators elsewhere can and should learn from its culturally sustaining curricula and extend it to other districts.

PART III

Culture-Keepers and Advocates

CHAPTER 7

Thayallen Gensaw: Growing Up Yurok

Biosketch: Downriver Pride

Thayallen[1] Gensaw—the nephew of James Gensaw, the Yurok teacher at EHS and MHS—is a Yurok Tribal member. He is tall, with waist-length light brown hair, and on the foggy day of our interview he wears a #YurokTribe sweatshirt and downriver[2]-design necklace with a series of triangles pointing down. At the time we met in Ms. McQuillen's class at Del Norte High School in the spring of 2022, Thayallen was a senior in high school and a Yurok IV student, which is the highest level of Yurok offered. He feels a strong sense of Yurok identity through his family and upbringing. A mature analyst of life around him, Thayallen displayed a willingness to speak his truth that makes research a pleasure. I spoke to him early in the research process at DNHS, and his frank insights helped me to understand some of the school and community dynamics that others only alluded to.

We sat across a scuffed conference table in the conference room at DNHS in Crescent City, California,[3] and spoke for nearly two hours. At his request, Thayallen chose to use his real name rather than a pseudonym. In small communities, when people are talking about hard things, it is the respectful thing for researchers to deidentify speakers to afford people the maximum amount of privacy, especially when working with minors who may not be able to consider how their words will be visible in the future.[4] With Thayallen, we focused more on his experience of identity and solution-oriented opinions about what needs to be done to make things better. His analysis and degree of self-reflection were impressive, and it didn't feel quite right to "protect" him by anonymizing his interview without asking him. He had given permission for his name to be used early on, and I went back to him after editing the interview transcript and invited him to go over this draft chapter text with a guardian, edit as needed, and then decide about his name. He wanted to claim his words as his own. We also spoke in 2024 as the manuscript was in its final stages of preparation and he requested a few small updates to the text and affirmed the use of his name throughout. What follows is a snapshot of a young cultural rights activist.

"I'm not a White man": School and Community Climate

A senior at DNHS, Thayallen distinguishes between his Yurok life—fishing, ceremony, language study, and more—and his "colonialized life" where he participates in aspects of the White world, like school and sports. Thayallen introduces himself in terms of his Yurok identity: "I grew up between Crescent City and Klamath, doing a lot of cultural activities like going to ceremonies—Brush Dances and Jump Dances—and being on the river fishing with my dad, uncles, and cousins, stuff like that. I try to make being Yurok a big part of my identity because it is important to me. It really helps me push myself, and it motivates me and what I have interests in."

He goes on to explain how his physical appearance is interpreted by others:

> I've always tried to make it known that I am Yurok because some people don't realize I am. I'm light skinned. I don't have very dark skin, and growing up playing football and stuff, you know, I'd always have to tell them [peers], like, "Oh no, I'm Yurok, I'm not White." I think it's gotten better over the years as I've incorporated my culture a lot more into my appearance and my lifestyle. You know, I speak Yurok, I have long hair now. I make it known that I'm proud to be Yurok, so it [misidentification] doesn't happen as much anymore, but, like, meeting someone for the first time, they still don't see me as who I am. For a long time that kinda hurt, growing up being misidentified and stuff like that. I'm a Yurok man[5] and it has lots of importance in my life, so I don't want that to go over the heads of people.

Like Tim and Vicky in Chapter 6, Thayallen found additional ways to signal his Native identity to others because his physical features would sometimes result in his being misidentified.

Being recognized as Yurok governs Thayallen's public-facing physical presentation, but his peers were not always sensitive to his identity. Thayallen comments on how he has been treated at school: "As a Yurok, you can experience racism and stuff like that in schools. I have. I've been called names, but I never really cared all that much 'cause I'm not one to really be baited or get mad about someone not understanding me. I don't care about those people. I want to be known as who I am and not what these other people want to project onto me. I don't want to be identified as a White man. I'm not a White man."

Reflecting on his school, Thayallen notes that though it is bad, it could be worse. This level of resilience is again shared across the young people I spoke with at multiple schools.

> I wouldn't say it [DNHS] is very hostile. I've encountered some
> dumb people before, but usually it's, like, they think it's okay to just
> be rude to other people. I've never had someone beat me up 'cause
> I'm Native or anything like that. I feel very lucky. I'm not being
> singled out because there are tons of Natives here [at DNHS], and I
> know that they'll have my back, and I think other people know that.
> So even if they [other students] are being dumb or something like
> that, they know not to take it too far. I've never experienced, like,
> truly hard racism—just someone calling me "r–dskin" or something
> like that, especially back in middle school when kids are being dumb.

There is significant optimism evident here. Thayallen's differentiation between "hard racism," like getting beaten up for one's identity, and being the recipient of racial slurs like "r–dskin" is notable, as is his perception of a generally improving trajectory of peer behavior with advancing age. "It's gotten a lot better since high school, just people growing up and maturing and getting away from that edginess they had as a thirteen-year-old. Some people think it's cool to be rude to people, and as they grow up, they realize, 'Oh, that's probably going to have an effect on me later on in life, I should probably veer away from it.' But there's still people who do dumb stuff and are immature. I think they're starting to grow away from it as they grow older."

But by normalizing what many people would identify as a macroaggression as just part of life in a high school experience, Thayallen reveals the emotional armor he wears to get through his days. This armor—being strong in the face of discrimination because there are few other alternatives—is shared across nearly all BIPOC young people from many backgrounds who I have spoken with over years of research. While most often articulated by BIPOC students, the ability to not reveal being impacted by hurtful statements or actions was expressed by many types of students, including LGBTQ+ students and White students living in poverty or other forms of precariousness.

The emotional strength to withstand microaggressions is, on the one hand, indicative of a resilience that can serve young people well as they survive their own life experiences. On the other hand, such resilience requires some sort of self-protective measures—the armor—that may threaten long-term well-being. The way young people use emotional armor is variable, but it tends to manifest as either ignoring or justifying harmful behavior in some way. Or by creating an emotional disconnection from people and the broader demographic committing the harm to avoid damaging speech and actions. The fact that young people are resilient in the face of toxic school climates does not preclude the need for intervention.

Thayallen's hope that microaggressions will decrease as people mature is undercut by the fact that the community climate in Crescent City is often made hostile to Native and other BIPOC people by White adults: "When you're seen as White, you are just accepted in places like Crescent City. People still see this as, like, a hick town. The community as a whole hasn't stepped away from bigotry and all that. It is a lot better in Klamath just 'cause you're mostly surrounded by Natives. You're not going to experience that [discrimination] when it comes to your other fellow Natives and your Tribal members."

Given his observations of the racial climate in the two locations, it is no surprise that he prefers being in Klamath: "Usually, I feel more comfortable being Yurok in Klamath than I do here [in Crescent City]. I have the sense that I'm connected to my people there, whereas here, if I talk about something in my culture, not everyone's gonna understand. In Klamath, talking about Brush Dance or something, everyone knows what I'm talking about. Here, it's a lot more disconnected from all that. I've never really had issues with fellow Tribal members, whereas it [Native identity] has been a much bigger issue in my colonialized life, in school and things such as sports."

Thayallen's use of the phrase "my colonialized life" is striking. He identifies that he operates in two worlds. In Klamath, Thayallen, as a Gensaw—a widely visible Yurok surname—is recognized as Yurok. But in Crescent City, where most of his schooling has been, he operates in a settler-colonial world with different rules and values. There, his White-passing skin means he must assert his Native-ness through visual cues like long hair, clothing, and jewelry, or through activities like language use or other culturally associated behaviors. The Yurok Tribe's goal for young people to achieve "success in both worlds" summarizes the hope that youth can navigate both their decolonized Native identities and the colonized lives they experience in White-dominant spaces. It is a big aspiration and one that requires youth to code-switch across identities.

"Yurok every day": Language as Constant Cultural Practice

Thayallen's identity as a Native American descendant of boarding school survivors informs his relationship with language. The intergenerational trauma of mission and boarding schools affects not only individual families but also entire communities. Elders who would normally facilitate language transmission across generations are unable to do so because they themselves had their language, in some cases, literally beaten out of them at school. It is only as an adolescent that Thayallen has had the chance to be part of Yurok reclamation, but he was involved in numerous other cultural activities prior to high school:

> Language is one of the newer things for me in Yurok culture because, though I always grew up with ceremonies and fishing, I didn't start learning Yurok until, like, middle school-ish. I really started to hone in on language later [in high school], and that's why I'm trying really hard to get accustomed to it. Because with other cultural practices, like ceremonies and fishing, you can only do that part of the time in the year. You only have Brush Dances during the summertime, and you only have fishing season in late summer, early fall, and those things come a lot more naturally to me. I've always been comfortable going to ceremonies and staying up late and being with family. Or fishing, that's what I feel like I've been best at my whole life. That's the only time where I feel like I'm doing what I'm meant to do. I've always felt at home on the river and comfortable cooking fish the traditional way.

Seeing himself as part of the solution is one way that Thayallen resonates with the language reclamation process. "Language is one of the harder things to access today 'cause there are no more fluent speakers, and we only have so many resources. That's why I tried to make it a bigger part of my life because it should be more accessible than it is. There's so many people that aren't very interested in language because they think being Yurok is just, you know, going to ceremonies, whereas it should be more about being Yurok every day."

Being Yurok certainly can include going to ceremonies, but one of the characteristics of language is that it can be used daily in nearly any circumstance. But learning the language is not easy, as Thayallen admits.

> Language is kinda hard! It's a little bit easier once you've been around
> it for a few years. I've gotten a lot more accustomed to it and I understand things a lot more. But some of my peers, some of them haven't
> grown up in the environment that I did, being raised as Yurok, being
> a Yurok man. Some of them are kind of distant from that. Some of
> them aren't even Yurok at all, so they don't really have the same connection to it like I do. They might see Yurok as an easy class to pass,
> so they're not as passionate about it. Or they don't understand the
> cultural relevance that language has, the importance it has, and how
> endangered it actually is. They don't always realize how lucky they
> are to have Yurok 'cause they haven't had access to a lot of their other
> culture like I have.

I note the modesty with which Thayallen conveyed these points. He is in no way boasting about his own degree of cultural connectedness, but rather mourning the loss of that connection for his Native peers. He observes the special challenges for non-Native students in Yurok class who may not have the context or exposure to the language that eases Yurok learning for students like Thayallen.

Thayallen also reflects on his own Yurok language lineage, putting his enthusiasm in context, as his access to speakers has changed over time:

> I didn't really grow up learning language. There were speakers in my
> family, but my uncle James lived in Humboldt for a long time and
> other speakers didn't speak much. I heard words and phrases growing up but not much else. My grandparents and great-grandparents,
> they grew up around the time where they had language taken from
> them and they weren't super fluent in it. So, I never had a real elder
> speaker like that in my life. But now I have James [Gensaw], and I
> see that language speaking is in my family. My family is well known
> in the Yurok community. I want to represent my family well, as well

as contribute to our tribe's language revitalization efforts. There have been countless efforts to restore our cultural practices and our language, and I want to do what I can for the future generations to learn their ancestral way of life.

The composition of being a "good Yurok" for Thayallen includes participating in cultural reclamation. Thayallen's well-being as an individual is bound up in his community's culture surviving, and he wants to be part of it.

"Undam the Klamath": Political Participation as Yurok Cultural Practice

Cultural survival for Native American people is intrinsically bound to land and the water that is part of the landscape. While many young people I interview in far Northern California describe lives disconnected from politics, Thayallen is highly political. Coming from a fishing family, he had early exposure to water politics:

> Being a fisherman, environmental issues have always been a huge part of my life. I've always been protesting, you know, about water restoration and bringing the fish back and undamming Klamath— trying to really understand that this is who we are. We need to take care of ourselves. We need to take care of the land. Those values are hard to satisfy when you're not in the environment that gave you those values in the first place. I've been to a bunch of "Undam the Klamath" events[6]—going to protests about water restoration and stuff like that, and that branched off into me helping in American government too. I helped with Election Day in 2020, and then I helped with the recall election—I was a poll worker in both of those.

His upbringing, with a family involved in political action, helped Thayallen develop a political consciousness as a young person. This awareness of the intersection of his identity as both a Native American and someone subject to US politics, in combination with his family's support and encouragement for his political involvement, facilitates his participation.

Thayallen links his participation in "Undam the Klamath" protests to his identity as a fisherman, something that automatically predisposes him to care about the health of the river and the numbers of fish able to spawn each year. But his understanding of the identity complexity goes beyond that simple cause-and-effect significance. Thayallen recognizes that for people no longer connected to the natural world in the ways that created cultural practices in the first place, it can be harder to care about protecting it. Overcoming the barrier of getting people to care is the first objective of any political campaign for many communities. Naming it, as he does, is an important first step in building a social movement. Thayallen reflects that "the political values I have as a Native American man led me to help with American politics, to volunteer my time 'cause I know how important that is to make sure your voice is heard. And that all stemmed from being around protests my whole life, knowing what's right. One of the biggest protest moments I had was when they were building that pipeline in Oregon, and we went to the Oregon capitol and protested about the pipeline and so, I think, maybe they stopped the pipeline construction? That was really impactful to see everyone getting together and traveling and fighting for something."

In terms of politics, Thayallen's participation is part of his inheritance, as he grew up seeing family members stand up for their beliefs:

> My mom's side of the family has very strong opinions on the Amer
> ican political spectrum. She is the one that really got me into that.
> She did both elections with me as a poll worker, and we agree on lots
> of stuff. My stepmom's parents protested the G-O[7] road and went to
> jail for it. I'm willing to go to jail for protesting, to make sure that
> what I believe is right gets done, what is best for my people. And
> my stepmom, she and her family are also, like, big protestors for
> American rights. It's been a part of their lives since they were born,
> so they've always made sure that I understood the importance of it,
> whether or not I participated in it. Understanding it led me to being
> active in it.

Thayallen is quick to give credit for his political involvement to both sides of his family, who led through example by being highly involved in a range of issues, from undamming the Klamath River to oil pipelines to voting rights.

In this way, Thayallen and his family go beyond one-issue involvement and span their identities as both Yurok Tribal citizens—a sovereign people based on treaty rights—and US citizens. Given the generally low levels of voter turnout for US elections in Native American communities, this is particularly notable. Making connections between various layers of rights points to an intersectional political praxis, or combination of theory and practice, that is the gold standard for civic education. Thayallen has made this education for himself through his family.

However, being involved in politics also makes people vulnerable to the opinions of others. Thayallen recounts his experience working at the Fort Dick election polling place, just north of Crescent City. I quote him at length as he describes giving out the standard "I Voted" stickers in English, as well as bigger stickers that said it in Spanish, Yurok, Tolowa, and Hmong.

> The English ones were pretty small, maybe an inch long—the standard ones they send to polling places everywhere—and the other ones were a bigger circle, probably a different printer or something and only produced here. This was at the height of the pandemic [November 2020]. Tensions were very high. I would offer, "Would you like a sticker?" And people would say "Yes," and then I'd say, "What language?"
>
> Some people had a negative response. One person was like, "Why are the other language stickers bigger than the English one?" I was like, "These are just what were given to me." Other people were just rude about it. I remember one White lady that said, "This is America. We speak English!" I was sad, 'cause it's just a sticker! Some people would just say, "English, please," and they'd be nice about it. A lot of White people thought it was very cool to include other languages, and lots of Native people were very excited to see their languages. Hispanics often took the Spanish sticker.

Clearly, this excerpt shows that the sticker was more than just a sticker. *Keech-Yey-goh-che-nek* means "I voted" in Yurok. Owning that action in sticker form is also claiming a right to participation without assimilation. A sticker proclaiming voting—whether in Yurok, Tolowa, Spanish, or any other minority language—is an assertion of minority presence as political actors.

Since such non-assimilated political action implicitly threatens White majority-group control of US politics, it can be read as rebellious and as an act of claim-making. Minorities need not assimilate linguistically in order to vote, although many already have and some choose to do so. But when minorities assert their presence in hostile, White-dominated spaces, there tends to be backlash, as Thayallen experienced during his polling shift.

Thayallen also recounted an instance when a billboard in Yurok was put up in Crescent City, and some people got upset over it because they didn't understand it. While it is true that those who can't read it are excluded, having a diverse language landscape is a way to include those excluded by an English-only environment. Whether it's a billboard, a voting sticker, or a language elective class, language is political.

When I inquire if Thayallen's political involvement is shared by his friend group, he comments:

> My freshman year, everyone in this school protested for the teachers' payment 'cause there was a big deal about teachers not getting enough wages. So, everyone in the school kinda united for that 'cause we care about our teachers. However, that's a much more tame example of fighting for what we think is right because obviously teachers need to get paid more. Whereas, are you willing to fight for your beliefs as a person? What kind of person are you?
>
> Kids from Klamath might be involved in river issues, but otherwise I don't know anyone who's actually protested besides maybe the Black Lives Matter movement. They voiced their opinions on that, but none of them have really lived that life. They've [White kids] never really had to fight for something really being taken away from them. They haven't really had to fight for who they are. It's always just been accepted.

Thayallen's assessment of White nonparticipation is strongly linked to White privilege. White schoolmates do not protest the way he does because they are not fighting for their identity. They do not have to because the way White privilege operates in the United States means that White identity and its associated power sources are perceived as secure.

In contrast, Indigenous students have to protest the Klamath dams and oil pipelines because those things threaten the integrity of the natural world on which Native identity is built. It is both an existential threat—a dammed Klamath has cultural implications that can be hard for outsiders to grasp—and an immediate one. A dammed Klamath destroys salmon migration and spawning, and consequently destroys the food source that is the mainstay of Yurok and other far Northern Californian and Oregonian Native communities.

"Disconnectedness": Culture and Curricula

The Yurok language classes at DNHS are the primary spaces where Native perspectives are taught within the school setting. Yurok language at DNHS is conveyed through cultural stories and practices, rather than a repetitive language memorization approach. Given that most of the other classes at DNHS do not include Yurok or Native content more broadly, the language classes play a key role in raising awareness about Native Americans. Thayallen notes that Ms. McQuillen has shown videos on different issues like water rights, Native foods, Brush Dances, and songs as part of an effort to motivate student interest in Yurok language. However, for students without a Native upbringing, the cultural content can be harder to connect with.

DNHS has intermittently offered a Native American Studies class when a teacher was available, but it wasn't offered in 2021–2022 when I was spending time there. Thayallen notes that he never took it when it was offered because he perceived it as being geared toward White students who "didn't know much about Natives." This view, that the class was really an introductory class for non-Native students, was shared by nearly all other Native American–identified students I spoke with at DNHS. Like Thayallen, others appreciate that the course exists for those who need that type of introduction. But Thayallen wishes that there was a course intended more for those who already know the basics and want to go further in their knowledge of Native history and culture.

Regarding the Yurok language classes, Thayallen sees the ease of access to cultural knowledge through language as an opportunity for students from all backgrounds: "Anyone can understand the language, they just have to take the steps to learn it. And language can be the entryway into learning about your culture more or learning why things are the way they are. For the non-Native students in language [class], it is important to have them here; learning how they can help us and how they can be allies with us and support us. These people who live on Yurok land and Tolowa land, they should know these things. I think it's admirable that they even take it [Yurok] because they don't have to. They can take Spanish if they'd like."

Noting the broader impact of Yurok language for himself, Thayallen points out that interest in his own culture has made him more aware of other minority cultures around him: "There is a big Hmong population here; they also have ceremonies and stuff like that. I've tried to introduce myself to it and I see how other people peering into Native culture is also important—having the presence of different people felt in the schools is important. If I had a magic wand, I'd have different cultures of all types incorporated into history classes and other classes. I would make sure that everyone has at least an entry-level understanding of all the different communities here, and not just, 'Oh, they're Brown.'"

The wish for a more pluricultural education so that people have more understanding across cultures is part of Thayallen's recognition that it is easier to appreciate people from other backgrounds when people know something about each other. If the only thing people know about minority groups is "they're Brown," it makes it harder to foster healthy relationships. But where does the goal of pluricultural education fit with the current curriculum?

Thayallen reflects candidly on both his high school and elementary school stages of education, talking about the positive and negative ways that he experienced representation of Native American culture in educational curricula:

> With US history, you mostly learn about older history. When I took US history last year, the teacher started with the Yurok unit, and it was presented pretty well. The teacher talked about the indoctrination of Yurok people into boarding schools and the effect it had, and she worked her way up to modern stuff that I know about, like undamming the Klamath. I'm like, "I've been to those protests!" Those things have been a part of my life, and so I felt very happy that they got into there [the curriculum]. It had a big impact to see that things that are important to me are being taught. Including the culture of things that other people can really connect to is important to establish [Native] people more as *people* and not just something you learn about in school.

After this promising start to the US history class, Thayallen's history teacher then segued into the founding of the country and early United States government topics. From there, the class moved through some of the prominent social movements of the twentieth century, which Thayallen found impactful: "With the civil rights movements and Black history, I feel like that kinda stuff had a much more prominent effect on me. It had more meaning. Learning the history of other cultures and, like, what these people had to do to fight for who they are was more meaningful than studying other people coming in and establishing things that people in the future would have to fight."

The preference for studying diverse cultures rather than colonialism resonates with Thayallen's general appreciation for diverse content. It also links back to his earlier wish for more entry-level information about different groups to dispel simplistic knowledge of Brown "others." So much of standard US history curricula in US high schools contains a litany of colonial accomplishments, as if they were something one should be proud of and grateful for. Such an approach overlooks the fact that for Indigenous people, colonialism was an unqualified disaster. Events with standard textbook labels such as "westward expansion" were in fact appropriations of traditional Native American territory. The idea of appreciating learning about the struggles of other groups, rather than the force minority groups have to struggle against, resonates with the yearning for a decolonizing education.

Thayallen has siblings who attend Margaret Keating Elementary School in Klamath,[8] the main town on the Yurok Indian Reservation, where Yurok Language Program staff lead language classes with students. Cultural representation happens throughout the school day in formal and informal ways, and there is a Yurok house model on the school grounds. In contrast, Thayallen went to Bess Maxwell Elementary School in Crescent City, where there is very little Indigenous representation. There is no middle or high school in Klamath, so students have to bus to Crescent City after sixth grade regardless of their elementary experience:

> At a predominantly White school, they fall into teaching you about Columbus and all that other stuff. You know, I always grew up knowing Columbus was an Indian killer and a rapist and stuff like that, but that is not what they taught us in school, and I didn't like it. I'm glad that Columbus Day is slowly being shifted into Indigenous Peoples' Day. That makes me very happy. But growing up in Bess Maxwell, the students had more of a stereotypical view of what Natives were, just 'cause it's taught like that in school. They would talk about, like, the Plains Indians and Sacagawea, who lived hundreds of miles away from where we are, but never really taught about Yurok culture.

This critique of elementary educational curricula is widely shared among Native American students I spoke with across schools.[9] Columbus was the most cited negation of Indigenous perspectives. And the safer engagement with faraway "Indians" rather than bringing in content on local Tribes, which might bring up a whole slew of questions about colonization, is a disservice to young people.

Thayallen talks overtly about a feeling of disconnectedness. He distinguishes between his Yurok life—fishing, ceremony, language study, and more—and his "colonialized life" where he participates in aspects of the White world, like school and sports. In addition to language classes, Thayallen notes that there are other curricular spaces beyond Yurok where the class content makes school feel less colonizing. For example, reading Sherman Alexie's *The Absolutely True Diary of a Part-Time Indian* in English class helped him feel visible as a Native person in school. But the book generated controversy among White parents who were upset by some of the vulgar language and the candid discussion of a teenage boy's reality mixed with Native American life on a reservation. It came to a head at school board meetings in 2021.

Thayallen was frustrated that parents were ascribing so much weight to the language of the *one* book he had read during his entire high school experience that helped him feel less alienated by the curriculum. He also scoffed at the notion that the book was a bad influence on some of these parents' children, having spent years with them in school:

> My thinking is, like, do you know what your kid sees online every day? Do you know what they say every day? Like, I've heard your kid say the n-word before—you're not perfect, your kid is not perfect, and that isn't from the book. That book has a very good understanding of living two different lives. I felt connected to that book because I do live a colonialized life in school and in sports, and I have my own Native community back home at my house in Crescent City or in Klamath. I have this community that knows who I am. I never felt betrayed like the character in the book by their Tribe, but there was always this sense of disconnectedness between the two lives that I really do live.

Even as Thayallen strongly resonated with the book and felt himself visible in it in a way missing from the majority of his education, White parents took their grievance to the school board.

> They tried to get the book out of the school! The parents were complaining to the school board about it being on the curriculum. I'm not sure if their reasoning is for the language or some of the content

matter in that book—which is far tamer than whatever they have
access to on their phones—or if it's a more deeply rooted disgrace
for their child reading about Native communities and what it really
means to be Native in a White man's world. It is deeply upsetting that
they tried to get rid of a resource that can teach kids more about what
it's like to be in my life and in the lives of every Native person pretty
much in the world right now who's never really lived a full [Native]
cultural lifestyle. It's more hard to incorporate it into their colonialized life.

Ultimately, the parents were unsuccessful, and the book was not banned,
although *The Absolutely True Diary of a Part-Time Indian* has frequently
made the list of the top ten most banned books in the United States.[10]

Thayallen sees room for increased integration of Native American content in classes, not only in US history, but also in classes like oceanography,
where there is some mention of river cleanups, but not specifically about the
Klamath River: "There's room for the Klamath to be better incorporated [in
the curriculum], to connect it more to our own community. You don't even
have to be Yurok to support that. Everyone loves the Smith River 'cause of
how clean it is. We're [the Yurok Tribe] doing all these efforts to make sure the
Klamath River is restored and that we have water, and there's a good opportunity to introduce that into other classes through projects. Plus, introducing
literature from different cultures into the curriculum of any class would be
good." Educational administrators balance many competing priorities when
they hand directives down to teachers on what content should be included.
Standardized testing, state requirements, and community culture all contribute to what ends up on syllabi. Sharing the voices of BIPOC students describing the impact of accurate and meaningful cultural inclusion in their schools
is one goal of this book.

Coming of Age with Resilience and Well-Being

Many young people I spoke with across the four high schools were usually
able to identify at least one adult whom they felt safe talking to, which is an
indicator used to assess well-being in the *Healthy Kids Survey* that California
administers every several years. Adults may or may not be family members,
but young people who do not have a safe adult to turn to for help are at the

highest risk of dangerous behaviors. Nearly everyone I spoke with was able to identify healthy things they liked to do to feel good, whether they had much time or ability to do them. From sports to church to spending time in nature, self-care and coping behaviors are integral parts of building resilience that can help people achieve a baseline of well-being.

Thayallen likes to have stuff to do in town, recognizing that boredom can be dangerous. At school, sports keep him busy, and at various points he did football, soccer, baseball, and wrestling, and is now running track. In his words, "Those really just helped me stay on the right path." In a cultural sense, fishing is Thayallen's most important activity. "You know, sometimes when you do something and you're not good at it or you realize, 'Oh well, I'm not gonna be as good as this person at it,' it can be demoralizing. But fishing, I always felt comfortable, and, like, I knew what I was doing. It's second nature for me to go out on the river, throw my net out, catch fish, gut 'em, and cook 'em. Doing that always made me feel like I was grown up and had a calling in life." The sense of fishing as second nature emphasizes what is at stake for Thayallen when he protests water issues on the Klamath River, as the dams continue to greatly hinder salmon spawning, which translates into lower catches. He also recognizes that this source of cultural connection, which supports his own resilience, is not available to everyone. Many people don't know how to fish, don't have a boat, or don't know someone who can take them out fishing.

More available to the wider community, including his peers, are ceremonies, including Brush and Jump Dances that are held each summer. For Thayallen, ceremonies are a place where he can connect with relatives and feel part of the community while also helping someone, like a baby or someone who is sick (Gensaw 2022).[11] He feels obligated to go to them and support his community even if he is not dancing (Gensaw 2022). In addition to fishing and ceremonies, Thayallen mentions a few other things that he sees as part of his own resilience. The American Indian Movement flag in his room makes him happy and allows him to reflect on the struggles and strength of his community. He describes how he loves the smell of Angelica root, which Yurok and other Indigenous people use for prayer, and he keeps some in his backpack. He pulls out a small pouch for me to smell, and I fumble with its smooth leather ties. Thayallen opens it nimbly, sniffs, then passes it back to me, explaining: "Sometimes, if I'm having a hard time, just smelling Angelica gives me comfort. You know, just simple stuff like that can really help, just knowing that you are part of a community, being aware that you are important. If you feel lonely or something like that, I can look down at my necklace and realize, like, 'Oh, I'm Yurok, I have these people pulling for me. I have my culture, my way of life. It's always available to me.'"

The sense of strength that comes from being part of a community includes sharing context for intergenerational trauma: "Also being around other Yuroks who understand you and who may have felt things like generational trauma help. People in the Yurok community can relate to each other. Even just having good friends who will listen to you about Yurok troubles, like, I think that's important. For a long time, I didn't have anyone that would listen to me when I talk about how broken I am seeing people struggling in my community or struggling to really recover from things that they had no part of, like generational trauma. So, having that kind of resource as a friend can really help just to have people that will listen to you."

The feeling of being "broken" seeing people in his community struggle is something that can lead to a spiral of negative feelings. But Thayallen identifies the impact of friendships and relationships of trust, where he can talk about his feelings and be heard. Those relationships fortify him and help him cope with the sadness and helplessness that can come from witnessing the suffering of others.

I ask if people in his peer group or family talk openly about intergenerational trauma and Thayallen responds:

> I can see people struggling because they're poor, they're addicts, and stuff like that, and a big stigma around here is that because they can't get a job or something like that, they're lazy, you know, that they put themselves in that situation. Whereas really, some of them didn't. It's important to ask if people are struggling from their own faults, or if it's from having a lack of culture and not seeing a purpose in what they're doing.
>
> A lot of people don't grow up within a community of their people, so they don't have a connectedness. In contrast, I've grown up lucky and fortunate to be able to be a part of my culture and learn about it. I hear stories of creation and stuff like that and always have those resources available to me, and those give me my values and they give me purpose.

Thayallen is quick to recognize his own privilege in growing up culturally connected, and the negative impact on those who have not had that same cultural access. He also astutely recognizes the structural origins of some of the issues he sees around him, rather than ascribing them solely to personal failure, as some others do: "Some people may have not recovered from their grandmas and great-grandmas having it all taken away from them and never really getting it truly back. I know some people, they may not even realize that [their problems] could be related to generational trauma, like why they are depressed or anything like that. They should be able to find some purpose in their own culture, like, 'Oh, I'm good at basket weaving,' or 'I'm good at gathering,' and stuff like that. They may not have a reason to really try, whereas culture can give you that reason, that sense of purpose to help motivate them to do better."

Thayallen's own resilience is linked to his cultural connectedness because he has been lucky to grow up in a strongly rooted family that maintains Yurok cultural practices. He is also able to recognize the fact that colonization stole cultural connectedness from Indigenous people so that many people do not have the resources for resilience and well-being that he does. The insight that reconnecting people to cultural roots can define a healthy sense of self, including competencies that can boost self-esteem, is at the core of arguments for culturally connected wellness practices such as physical and mental health care. The benefits of cultural connectedness are also a reason to push for curricular decolonization in schools. In classrooms, the benefits of cultural grounding can be made available to the broadest group of young people in a given community.

Impact of the COVID-19 Pandemic

The COVID-19 pandemic provided a unique moment to reflect on the role of cultural practices in relation to well-being, namely because so many cultural gatherings were suspended over a prolonged period. Like his peers in other case study schools, Thayallen experienced the pandemic as a time of social and community deprivation. He had internet at home in Crescent City and was able to participate in synchronous remote classes, but it felt like a lost year since the learning wasn't the same. In addition, the lack of cultural activities during that time was acute for him:

> The pandemic was really hard for me just 'cause I'm so connected to
> my community and it was separated for a long time. You know, we
> couldn't have ceremonies. We couldn't have that good medicine run-
> ning through our community. We didn't have really anything going

on. The most I could do was fish. That was really my first experience having it [cultural practices and community] all stripped from me. I couldn't go to school and learn Yurok. I had to wait for Zoom classes, where it's not the same. I couldn't go to Brush Dances and see my family. I couldn't hear the songs of my elders and my community didn't have music. It wasn't really until then that I realized how impactful being Yurok really is on my life. I never knew the importance of culture and knowing who you are until I had it taken away from me, as I experienced it during the pandemic.

The cultural disconnection of the pandemic put the experience of his ancestors in context for Thayallen. While he recognizes how different the scenarios are, he explains that the feeling of having cultural practices taken away from him made him sympathize with what his forebearers must have experienced during colonization. "That was really the first experience that I got with not having my culture. I always grew up with Yurok beliefs and values, and those values were supported by my way of life: going fishing, going to the ceremonies, seeing people playing sticks, gambling, and stuff like that; stuff that we do as Yuroks. Having it all taken from you makes it hard to really support your beliefs and it demoralizes; it breaks you down, not having that support system of your culture to be there to help you do what is right. I truly sympathized with what my ancestors must have felt."

Here Thayallen makes a powerful comparative analysis of how the loss of cultural practices during the pandemic gave him empathy for what cultural suppression might have felt like for the generations before him who had been deliberately stripped of their Yurok identities. He also notes the demoralization that accompanies such cultural loss, a central aspect of the intergenerational trauma that has spurred so many vices on Native American reservations, including his own. The loss of a "support system" that can "help you do what is right" describes how cultural identity relates to well-being.

For Thayallen, the pandemic highlighted the vital role that his culture plays in his own wellness, and this has motivated him to work more to protect and expand access to Yurok culture. He explains how this awareness pushes him to want to better follow the steps of leaders trying to bring language and culture back to people, and:

To make sure that everyone knows who they are, and teach them their language, and teach them their culture. That's been a big reason of why I'm trying to pick up as much language as I can. Growing up I didn't have language classes, and now that I started to learn it, I realize what an absence it's been in my life. You know, maybe if I spoke Yurok more, if I had learned it when I was young, I wouldn't be misidentified [as non-Indigenous]. I think it is important, that sense of, "Oh, I'm Yurok and you're also Yurok, what if we spoke Yurok to each other?" You could feel more connected to your culture, especially at a young age. It could be solved much earlier on, that disconnectedness.

The idea that if he had been raised as a first-language Yurok speaker he wouldn't be misidentified shows the role of language as a powerful cultural marker. It also shows how language as a cultural attribute can help young people build a sense of belonging shored up by connectedness.

Conclusion

Thayallen and his peers are transitioning into adulthood at a time of profound unrest in the world. From intergenerational trauma caused by colonization to the COVID-19 pandemic to political violence both in the United States and globally, young people carry heavy burdens. Such challenges, both physical and emotional, test the resilience of young people to navigate their lives in healthy ways. Building well-being and the practices that support it can help young people to circumvent challenges and continue their life trajectories in positive directions.

Cultural connection can address many ailments at once. For Thayallen and other young people who are connected to Native cultures and hunger for even more connection, the perception of culture as a valid resource can have a significant impact on their own wellness. While there are numerous ways and spaces—both formal and informal—in which such cultural validation can take place, public schools are a potent one given their history as tools of culturecide. Convincing schools to be part of culturally sustaining work is hard, but the payoff in terms of boosting all-around student success is worth it. Integrating Native American culture into a range of courses in the K–12 system is one concrete way to support culturally meaningful teaching that in turn can support Native American student success in both worlds.

CHAPTER 8

Lozen Nez: Curricular Advocate

Introduction: Advocating for Native American Visibility

Lozen Nez has a grievance. She was enrolled in an AP US History (APUSH) class at McKinleyville High School in fall 2022 and still wasn't getting the content she was expecting. After enduring years of White-dominated social studies curricula at Dows Prairie Elementary, Morris Elementary, and McKinleyville Middle School—where Native Americans were mostly not talked about the way she thought they should be (if they were even talked about at all)—Lozen had hoped that in a class labeled "advanced," they would finally cover content left out of previous classes.

Born to a Yurok mother and a Navajo and Mescalero Apache father, and herself enrolled with the Yurok Tribe, Lozen tells me that she was raised with Indigenous values in a mostly White community. Though her family didn't go to all of the Yurok ceremonies, they participated sometimes, and Lozen describes herself as connected to her Native identity. She was enthusiastically enrolled in James Gensaw's Yurok language class at MHS and was also part of MHS's Native American Club, which meets at lunchtime and hosts different cultural events. Lozen wanted to see some of her own identity and the history that it is part of reflected in the APUSH curriculum. She was sorely disappointed.

What seems like a simple wish for accurate and visible curricula about Native Americans is in fact a deeply complicated one. It not only implicates the many branches of the US education system in ongoing culturecide, but also implicates systems of the US government at federal, state, and local levels that maintain White supremacy. In 2022, I completed a textbook analysis of the AP US history, non-AP US history, and civics textbooks in use in 2020–2022 in the four schools discussed in this book (Gellman 2024b). This chapter pairs curricula analyses with an interview with Lozen and her brother

Hosteen Nez,[1] in which Lozen discusses a grievance letter she sent to her school about the APUSH curricula. The responses to her letter tell a story about Indigenous invisibility, Native youth activism, and how addressing settler colonialism in the United States is deeply tied to addressing its presence in the schoolroom. As with Thayallen Gensaw, Lozen and Hosteen reviewed drafts of this chapter in consultation with their families and decided they wanted to be referred to by their real names.

"See the World from my Perspective"

Lozen is a hardworking and determined student. She rode out her sophomore year in the pandemic lockdown, attending school via Zoom from her home in McKinleyville, and eagerly looked forward to the in-person return in 2021. Her family was already familiar with the local high school; Lozen's older brother graduated from MHS in 2020. Since many Yurok language classes have a requirement to combine levels to fill seats, Lozen, a junior, was taking Yurok II alongside her younger brother, Hosteen, a freshman taking Yurok I. The three Nez siblings contribute to a small but vibrant Native American student population at MHS.

On a sunny spring day in 2022, Lozen, Hosteen, and I sit outside at a concrete and metal picnic table on the high school campus. Despite being outside in the breeze and at a distance from me, they keep their masks on, so I do too.[2] COVID-19 ravaged Native American communities with high death rates throughout the United States disproportionately (Foxworth et al. 2022), and far Northern California was no exception.

Because of the masks, I start off the interview asking about their COVID-19 experiences. They offer both political and personal reflections on what was so hard about COVID-19 over the last few years:

> *Lozen:* We did lose a few family members to COVID and we recently just lost another one. So, with that, it was also just a big eye-opener to see how this illness has been disproportionately affecting Indigenous communities and just people of color in general.
>
> *Hosteen:* It is kind of infuriating, too, with the anti-mask, anti-vax people. That's not helping nobody!
>
> *Lozen:* Yeah, you realize how *real* the pandemic is.

Hosteen: We lost, like, how many family members? And they wanna
   act like it doesn't exist!

The frustration Lozen and Hosteen show toward anti-mask and anti-vaccine
protestors is not only in reference to the national level. Humboldt County—
long a bastion of lawlessness—has low vaccine rates and mask-wearing was
spotty, even during peak COVID-19 spikes. This played out in public schools
like MHS across teachers, staff, and students. Many people heaved a sigh of
relief in March 2022 when schools switched to an optional mask policy. But
for students like Lozen and Hosteen, who have had multiple family members
die of the disease, the threat of COVID-19 still feels real.

Humboldt County, like much of the United States, has had many more
Indigenous people die of COVID-19 than those who are accounted for in
official statistics (Cimini 2021). Official numbers of Native Americans killed
by COVID-19 locally remain elusive (Cimini 2021), but it is clear that Native
American people were disproportionately affected (Meng 2023). While the
pandemic is not yet over for anyone, it feels particularly current for the most
vulnerable populations.

In addition to family death, Lozen and Hosteen also both describe a kind
of political restlessness during COVID-19 lockdown caused by watching bad
things happen and not being able to intervene:

Lozen: Because you're at home, you can't really do anything to help
   your community. Seeing all of the news articles, like, "These
   Indigenous peoples are being exploited," or "a pipeline is being
   built," or "violence in a certain area"—seeing all that and then
   having to be at home and not being able to do anything about
   it was very hard. And then, as I came back to school and saw
   those same problems, I was able to join a community where
   they were working to fix those problems or just address them.
   So being on campus is a lot more helpful.
Hosteen: I was very sad over the quarantine 'cause I missed my friends.
   I was kind of in a depressed state. And seeing all that stuff
   happening to us, like the Dakota Access Pipeline and its effects
   [on Native Americans] . . . And we couldn't really do much,
   especially with our age too. And, I mean, it's not like we have the
   money to do anything anyway, so we're just stuck here watching.
Lozen: Just like bystanders.

Lozen and Hosteen both signaled distress at their bystander status, wanting to be involved in fixing the problems rather than witnessing harm happen to other Indigenous people. They shared that the pandemic downtime turned into social movement research time for them:

> *Lozen:* Before COVID, we didn't know much about those protests going on. Like, now that we were at home and we had more time to research those things, we want to go too. But, like, locally, there aren't really any protests and stuff regarding Indigenous issues.[3]
>
> *Hosteen:* Actually being there, holding those flags and standing with your people out in the streets, that's where I wanna be, like, protesting about MM . . . what is it? MMIP [Missing and Murdered Indigenous People].[4]

Although both the siblings express frustration at the lack of ways to build a bridge between grievance and action nationally or locally, they are able to identify the micro-world of their school as a place where they might have more input.

I query in what ways they can make their voices heard on the issues they care about. Hosteen is mainly an observer for much of the conversation, but he chimes in occasionally and generally nods along, agreeing with his sister. Lozen describes:

> I usually just try to use my online platform for a lot of activism, but I also feel like a lot of my activism takes place here [at MHS]. 'Cause I do talk to my student counselor and my teachers about things that I feel like they should be talking about. Like, giving a land acknowledgment would be *something*, just a little representation, anything! But I also talk to my friends and I go to Native American Club and just anyplace where I feel like somebody actually might want to listen to what I have to say.
>
> This year, the only teacher that I've heard do a land acknowledgement was my art teacher. She did it twice, one at the beginning of the first semester and the other at the beginning of the second. And she does a lot of work too. She attends trainings and stuff, just, like, anything she can to help understand the Indigenous perspective and how we are affected by a lot of things that go on in America.

Lozen recognizes the effort of the educators who care alongside her, even as they are learning and unlearning in the process. Her plea for "just a little representation" is modest and plaintive. How hard would it be for the school to show up for her just a little? "In my art class, we were talking about doing a mural to acknowledge the ancestral Wiyot land and the local tribes like Yurok, Karuk, Hupa, and Tolowa. But it definitely depends on the teacher. 'Cause, like, out of all my history teachers, I only had one, in middle school, really acknowledge the land. Everybody else just didn't care or didn't seem to focus on it. They dismiss it."

I ask if there is anything she can do to encourage more people to do the kind of work her art teacher is doing to bring Indigenous content and awareness of issues to MHS. Lozen responds: "Something that I tried to do more is to go to those meetings and speak about things that you feel like should be talked about. And then a lot of times people agree with you or the people you were speaking to feel the same way, and so you feel heard. And then, if you don't feel heard in one place, you go to another place and discuss it with everybody or just, like, bring it to as many people as you can, so then they feel the need to also wanna participate. And then, just like that, you can spread the message of things you wanna fix or just address."

When I press for concrete examples of other things they want to fix at the school, the siblings quickly turn to curricula, pointing to Indigenous erasure in history classes as a central complaint:

Lozen: Recently, I had a history class who didn't teach anything about Natives. It was more so focused on, like, the glorification of war. It was AP US history, and I figured with that, you'd be really going into depth about US history! But we didn't touch on anything, really, and then the things we did touch on, they used terms like "Indians" and stuff like that, rather than the terms like "Indigenous" that we feel comfortable with. And so *not* learning about things that are, like, really big in Indigenous history—because Indigenous history is everyone's history— seemed wrong. Everyone should know . . .

Hosteen: . . . in order to learn from it! It just sucks coming here and seeing all this Whitewashed history . . .

Lozen: . . . You have no representation . . .

Hosteen: . . . And they don't wanna listen to you. It's, like, *we* have to be inclusive, but *they* don't wanna be inclusive.

This exchange over the US history curriculum shows how Indigenous exclusion makes them feel. Lozen had assumed that a US history class was an appropriate place to look at Indigenous history as well. Not only did that not happen, but the use of outdated, offensive terms for Native Americans further alienated her from the class.

The "Whitewashing," in Hosteen's words, underscores a rejection of Indigenous inclusivity. Even as students are asked to be inclusive in the social climate of the school, the curriculum, and some of the teachers, don't reflect that inclusivity. Hosteen's point is poignant—that BIPOC students are consistently asked to accommodate a White curriculum while districts, schools, and teachers are not being accommodating of BIPOC preferences for culturally sustaining curricula. Why should Native American students work to be inclusive of Whiteness when White-dominant spaces are not necessarily including *them*?

I ask if Lozen and Hosteen have given this feedback to the principal or to the school board or the district.

> *Lozen:* I do go to the equity meetings and I am on both the student-
> led Equity Team and the parent/teacher/administrator one,
> so, like, I do use that space to vocalize a lot of these things.
> The Student Equity Team right now is working on a racial
> incident reporting form. But, like, I think the first Equity Team
> meeting I went to, it was, like, staff and parents; we talked about
> decolonizing the curriculum and having more representation of
> Indigenous events and stuff.

When I press if the school and district administration is open to such innovation, Lozen acknowledges that "the principal, he wants all the diversity stuff, and he does whatever he can to help, so I feel like I am being heard by him. And Ms. Z,[5] I feel like she wants to help." There are some allies, but the process of changing entrenched curricula, and habits, is slow. Lozen wants people "to see the world from my perspective." In the following section, I show how Lozen makes her case.

The Grievance Letter and Its Aftermath

In March 2022, Lozen sent me a draft of a letter detailing her grievance about APUSH's curriculum, which she had not yet submitted to her school. I offered some basic professorial writing tips and grammar flags, as I frequently do on my college students' writing. Right around the time Lozen finalized her letter, a cover story in the *North Coast Journal*—the local free press—was published, calling for increased Indigenous curricula for young people.

The timing was opportune for Lozen's letter. She submitted it to *Redheaded Blackbelt: News, Nature, and Community Throughout the Emerald Triangle*, a widely read news and blog website that is regularly read by internet-connected and locally minded Humboldt residents. Her letter was published in May 2022, and I include the full, original letter in the section below (Nez 2022). I also examine some of the comments that were posted in response to Lozen's letter in the days immediately following its publication, which shed light on the community climate in which Lozen and Hosteen are coming of age:

Dear School Administrators,

I would like to draw attention to issues of harmful misrepresentation of Indigenous history in the high school curriculum. In the course of my high school education here at McKinleyville High, I have seen very little mention of accurate and inclusive United States history. Rather than fostering an inclusive academic environment that sets Indigenous students up for success in school, such misrepresentation leaves many of us feeling angry, offended, and excluded. The impact of this is that BIPOC students can feel discouraged and disconnected from their peers, families, and self-identity when the narratives of health and resilience that they have learned are contradicted by what is being taught by their teachers.

Indigenous history does not only affect Indigenous peoples, as it is a part of everyone's history, yet classes like AP US history and geography hardly mention it. Undoubtedly, the atrocities committed by US colonizers bring up guilty feelings, but avoiding talking about Indigenous genocide as a whole caters to White fragility and directly participates in the current whitewashing of history. Intergenerational trauma affects all sides; the roots of such traumas need to be talked about and could present an opportunity to resolve some of these traumas.

The rhetoric used to discuss what miniscule content on Indigeneity is being taught downplays the inhumanities endured by Native peoples; for example, words such as "Americanize" and "Christianize" are used rather than "colonize". The lack of accurate representations of Indigenous events in social studies classes has been apparent throughout the history of the US public education system. Topics within the curriculum largely revolve around and glorify war, as well as idolizing politicians and patriots who took part in the genocide of mine and others' ancestors. Although presidencies and government happenings are a large portion of class discussions, White behavior toward Indigenous people remains omitted.

One of the only times Native American people are mentioned is during the Andrew Jackson presidency, specifically the Indian Removal Act of 1830. There are mentions of us in Unit 2: 1607–1754 and Westward Expansion slides, and even then they are inaccurate and fragmentary notions. There is no mention of the residential schools, reservations, decimation in Indigenous populations, genocide, or the impacts on society. When talking about the Indian Removal Act, for example, only one of the many Trail of Tears were mentioned and with a sense of apathy as the number of Indigenous casualties was not important enough to be disclosed. The Indian Reorganization Act, Wounded Knee Massacre, and the Battle of the Little Bighorn are among the numerous other topics to not be taught. When Indigenous people are included, we're depicted stereotypically, as one, robbing countless other tribes of an identity. Though Indigenous people have been around on Turtle Island long before America was a concept, the lack of representation is and always will be disheartening.

I call on the Humboldt County Office of Education, Northern Humboldt Union High School District, and McKinleyville High School to please reflect on the way the curriculum stands now and how it can be made more accurate and inclusive. Students, teachers, and administrators all invest a lot of time and money into schools and education systems. Let's work together to improve what is being taught in schools. We need accurate textbooks or supplemental readings, cultural consultants, local history, and current day impacts on society. Creating an inclusive curriculum could promote a deeper sense of belonging in students if they could see themselves accurately reflected in their education. I recognize the issues and I want to help make an environment where everyone is included.

Sincerely,

Lozen Nez, 11th grade, MHS

After the letter was published, Lozen said in an email to me that even though she had also sent the letter to the district superintendent and copied the school board members, nobody had reached out to her directly for weeks. Only after a school board member contacted the superintendent about the letter did the superintendent write to her, saying he would reach out to her in the new school year. This was a frustrating response because many teachers prepare their educational materials over the summer, so waiting until the next school year to address her concerns basically proscribed little change for the year ahead. But Lozen knows this is an issue for the long run. Even if she won't reap the benefits of structural change around Native American representation in the curriculum, she hopes her younger brother might, along with future students.

As is standard with online content, in the first several days after the article was posted, comments appeared. Some of them are worth addressing, as they speak to the larger community climate around MHS. I approach the online comments as an opportunity for discourse analysis providing insight into community climate on the specific issue of curricular representation, while recognizing their polemics and limited scope.

There were a total of twenty-three comments by fourteen different users posted beneath Lozen's letter. One is an angry political rant that seems unrelated to her letter, so I do not address it; several comments are very supportive and similarly wish that they had the kind of content in school that Lozen is asking for; two users criticize the letter in various ways; and other comments are both supportive and critical. I include excerpts from select comments below to show the range of community reactions. All comments are reproduced verbatim, including grammatical errors.

The Comment Section

The first comments posted were congratulatory on the writing—"Excellent writing!" and "Very well-written for an 11th grader! Especially from McKinleyville ha ha!" Another was in solidarity with the message:

> Give them the facts, not the easy white-washed version. High schoolers are almost ready to step out into the world and we should be giving them as much relevant information as possible- no glazing over. As a kid I would have loved learning Indigenous history in school . . . They should teach both sides of history. History is not one sided.

One commenter also addressed the details of Lozen's letter directly and shows that the issue includes more than absence and misrepresentation for Native peoples:

> I made a formal complaint to the principal about the US History teacher after his comment to students to, "imagine yourself a Black slave." The response I got back from the principal this Spring was, "I'm not sure how to have a conversation with my employee counterpart about these complaints" . . . If the principal does not think that the history teacher's education is not a problem . . . then we as a community need to come together and make a formal complaint to Humboldt County Office of Education and support this youth who is sharing their narrative with lived experience at Northern Humboldt School District.

This commentator is taking issue with the teacher asking students to imagine themselves as slaves, given the objectification of Black people it entails. Yet when they took the concern up with the principal, they were met with admission of a lack of skill to navigate the situation as a delicate personnel matter. Their call to action is echoed in another comment, which starts off with a critique of writing the letter, but only because the commenter advocates for more extreme measures:

> I am not sure that the student writing a letter to the school board is the best course of action in this situation. I am astonished that her parents didn't march into the principal's office and throw a fit demanding that the teacher stop teaching lies, or be fired. I am not sure why they are using a textbook that portrays the "Indians" in the same manner as they were portrayed when I was in 2nd grade over 30 years ago.
>
>   If the teacher is choosing to teach lies "just because it says that in the book" then the teacher is making a wrong choice. Teacher, slam the book closed, apologize to the class that they just read some hate speech, and teach what really happened. Perhaps have your students write an essay on the difference between factual history and the textbook's version. Make it into a learning experience. Get all the students to write to the school board and the textbook manufacturer. The teacher could have fixed this on his or her own and made

it a learning experience, even if the school board decided to use
the book . . .

This comment rightly points out that teachers do have a significant amount
of agency within their classrooms, even if they are confined by school boards
and curriculum committees to use certain texts. However, the comment
does not engage with the fact that APUSH is a teach-to-the-test class. Such a
restriction will limit teachers in what innovations they bring in; this points to
the need for systemic change at the test level.

Another comment offers praise but then tries to reframe the problem by
jumping to an exoneration of Whiteness:

Well written and well said. Please don't make "white people" your
enemy, or stereotype us as one and the same. The global governments have maintained a focus of dividing the people through
mass media based on our racial, sexual and religious identities for
decades, and to this day retains a psychological monopoly of practi-
cally all peoples' sense of who and what "government" is and means.
White, brown, up and down . . . we're all being screwed.

A few heated responses appear below this comment: "They do not generalize
'white people', they are calling out the . . . whitewashing of history. You made
that jump yourself" and "You miss the whole point. She has not made 'white
people' her enemy, she would just like history to reflect the truth and that it
be taught that way."

In a similar genre of comments, which I coded in my notes with the heading "White defensiveness," two commenters focus on the allegation that if
Indigenous history were taught, it would have to include Indigenous violence
toward others.

Many indigenous tribes were terrible to each other and committed
atrocities just as bad as, or worse than "white people." You want to
focus on just "white atrocity" read American Holocaust. Real history
is brutal on every side. If anything, school curriculum omits more
native atrocities than colonial.

The polemic behind the comment above is disturbing in that it alleges
that schools are omitting Native atrocities, when in fact they are omitting

nearly everything concerning Native peoples and instead glorifying White domination.

Another commenter joins in this theme: "Be careful what you ask for. History has been highly sanitized. Some indigenous history is pretty brutal before the white man came riding over the hill. Do you want the good bad and the ugly?" Repeat commenters jump in to criticize this last comment: "Pretty sure the indigenous peoples are more aware of that than you are." The original commentator responds belligerently, "none that I've talked to," revealing the problematic "no one I know" trope that has long been discredited as a means of assessing social phenomena, yet retains its place in political discourse.

Similarly, a commenter who dismisses school as a viable space to address these issues is also problematic: "All history is slanted and abridged. There is simply too much to learn it all in school. Seek out your own info and expect the education system to feed you garbage only." With this mindset, not uncommon in the back-to-the-land, do-it-yourself, screw-the-system mentality of Humboldt County, the commenter essentially abandons the school system as a hopeless cause, which is the opposite of what Lozen is trying to do.

There is one comment I want to respond to, but I restrain myself. This person writes, "Without numbers it is impossible to tell if more or less focus on Indigenous history is needed. Can we get a percentage of material from specific classes that addresses these topics?" From my own history textbook analysis, I can say that Native American history appears as a minuscule part—perhaps 1 or 2 percent—of US history textbook content. Where present, Native Americans are mostly presented as a problem that White people solve through elimination and assimilation. I wrote an entire book about this kind of misrepresentation in US history textbooks from the 1950s through the 2020s (Gellman 2024b). So, we have the percentage, and we have data clearly showing the problems. What we need is the curricular reform.

"A very toxic masculinity kind of thing": MHS School Climate

Misrepresentative textbook content and educational media more broadly are not the only problems for BIPOC students in high school. When talking about diversity and inclusion issues in relation to school climate, the use of racial and ethnic slurs at MHS is very common, just like at EHS and DNHS. While access to White-passing identity allows some students a buffer from racist taunts or requires them to assert Native identity more forcefully to have it noticed, neither of these scenarios is the case for Lozen and Hosteen. They are black-haired and dark-skinned. When they say they are Yurok, people believe them at first glance, unlike White-passing counterparts who are compelled to deliver mini history lessons to explain how they can look White and be Native.

Lozen and Hosteen comment that at MHS, and throughout their K–12 schooling, slurs and insults were regularly directed at BIPOC students from the White population and at BIPOC students from other BIPOC students. Lozen describes that "a lot of times they have a colonized mindset, or they don't, like, wanna fix their way of thinking. Like they've inherited their parents' way of thinking, which may be harmful to, like, people now, I guess." Hosteen pipes up to share the perspective of a first-year student: "I mean, for me it's pretty toxic overall. I don't really have too many mellow friends, to be honest. Everybody is usually overhyped on things, or toxic, literally. I've been insulted before many times. I don't really like it too much here."

Both Lozen and Hosteen know there are social consequences for trying to intervene in the culture of insults. They relate:

> *Lozen:* Once people see you speak up, they look at you different. They'll be like, "Oh, well, she talks way too much," or like, "She cares about things that we don't value, so we can't associate with her." Over the course of my seventeen years of living, I've experienced a lot of racism and prejudice and stuff and so, like, even standing up for myself—I mean I'll do it, but at the cost of whatever emotionally, mentally.
>
> *Hosteen:* Yeah, it's a burden having to deal with all this stuff, at least it feels that way for me. 'Cause everybody wants to start fights for fun, and it just sucks 'cause they probably get enjoyment from it. A bunch of these kids, they do wrestling and they do a bunch of athletic stuff just to flex on other kids, act like they're stronger. Or they think they can win fights because of this, and it's just . . . very annoying. It's very toxic, a very toxic masculinity kind of thing.

Both Lozen and Hosteen say their family is there to support them. Lozen mentions feeling supported by Mr. Gensaw and the Yurok class, the Native American Club, her friends, and her academic counselor, who recognized

Lozen's concerns and helped her join the school's Equity Team to be involved in its meetings. The counselor, along with a few of her teachers, really cares about supporting Indigenous students and addressing harm in the school. But for the majority of students, Lozen says, "Anything that doesn't directly affect them, they don't care about," and Hosteen adds, "They're just so caught up in their own world."

Both Lozen and Hosteen have suggestions of how to address the toxicity at school, including: all-community assemblies; sending letters home specifically about diversity and behavioral expectations, including language guides, rather than having the information buried in a school handbook; and having parents or guardians involved. Lozen points out that family involvement is key "because you teach them or you talk to them at school, and then they go home and then they're just fed the same beliefs that you were trying to tell them not to believe!"

She also posits that confronting racist beliefs at the core of the behavior is important to stop some of the daily harassment. Interventions such as equity, diversity, and inclusion trainings are one such tool to break through to students who are operating with "colonized mindsets," regardless of their demographic. Yet MHS's attempt to hold these trainings flopped in 2021–2022, according to Lozen. Although the school was back to in-person instruction, that year's equity training was held on Zoom: "I feel like having somebody there in class to tell you about these things, and how they affect people would be a lot more beneficial. People did not take it seriously when it was on Zoom. Nobody was there to make eye contact with you, to make sure that you're listening, and to make sure that, you know, you're hearing what they're saying *and* understanding. And we [the students] were like, in class in-person for that, watching them [the trainers] over Zoom. It was very weird."

This was clearly a missed opportunity. The school was trying to bring important content to students, but students are used to tuning out of Zoom meetings. Even though there are admittedly more equity trainers outside of rural Humboldt County, spending the time and effort to find local, in-person trainers may be more effective for students who go glassy-eyed online. While schools everywhere have to decide what programming they return to in-person, flagging equity content as something that doesn't translate as impactfully over Zoom is significant. Given the importance of personal accountability for content like that of equity trainings to be effective, using online platforms to scale up access to equity work is not an automatic success.

Conclusion

Lozen dropped the APUSH class in January 2022 and switched to an independent study course on Apex.[6] The Apex class left out even more Indigenous content than the APUSH class did. But at least she didn't have to be around the APUSH teacher or spend as much time soaking in the White, militaristic history that the textbook showcased.

When I ask the siblings what they would change if they had a magic wand and could change anything in the community, school, or beyond, their answers were profound:

> *Lozen:* I would have everyone see the world from my perspective,
> or the Indigenous perspective, and see how what they say,
> even though it could be minuscule to them, is, like, huge for
> me. They could be, you know, disrespecting my entire ethnic
> background or my entire life! And so, the first thing I would
> change would be people's point of view, and how they view
> Indigenous peoples, or just POC in general.
>
> *Hosteen:* I'd add more diversity to this [school]; it's still very White.
> And, I'd say [like her], change their perspective! 'Cause they
> always say awful stuff, you know, they just be trying to get you
> to react.

To see the world from someone else's perspective is a clear way to break down judgment and misinformation about "others." This is what Lozen is asking for:

> *Lozen:* The way they generalize Indigenous people as a whole—
> you're robbing a sense of identity from hundreds of tribes. Like,
> if you just generalize with one depiction of an Indian—or an
> Indigenous person—like in the media, like, "all Indigenous
> people wear headdresses. . ." those things are very harmful . . .
>
> *Hosteen:* . . . or saying, like, "Indigenous people are lazy," or "they're
> alcoholics" . . .
>
> *Lozen:* . . . When those things in Indigenous communities are
> products of colonization! So, I feel like, when people view
> Indigenous people, they view us as lazy people, or drunks
> and alcoholics, and drug addicts and, you know, dropouts, or

they're stupid and those are all just products of colonization and
genocide and generational trauma.

Hosteen: And now we're just stuck in this hellscape out here. Not
enough water for the fish, the trees cut, capitalism, it's awful. It's
not how we lived.

Both siblings recognize the deep structural origins of inequality and are able to name the way that settler colonialism is a key element in the story of Indigenous survivance. The clash between Indigenous ways of life and settler colonial ones is enormous and plays out in numerous spheres: the ecology, including rivers and forests; media; and, central to this book, the formal education system. Pre-existing disparities between Native and non-Native communities, including in educational access and success, which were compounded by COVID-19, will take serious investment to address (Simon, Nelson et al. 2020, Foxworth, Evans et al. 2022).

We do not want the next generation to feel they are living in a "hellscape," but some of them, like Hosteen, do. There is an ethical obligation to intervene to promote youth well-being, particularly so for Native youth. "I feel like ignorance is not always bliss," Lozen tells me. And she's right. For Native American students, there is nothing blissful about others being ignorant of their existence.

CHAPTER 9

"Yurok Is What Got Me Through High School": California's State Seal of Biliteracy

Introduction: The Power of Credentialization

Maurice Alvarado and Danielle Schunneman were the first two students ever to obtain California's State Seal of Biliteracy (SSB) in Yurok. Both Yurok descendants, they graduated from EHS in 2019 and received the SSB after four years of studying the language and meeting all requirements (McGeary 2019). It is a first-in-the-world achievement, and symbolically significant to have official recognition of the Yurok language alongside other more commonly offered language electives.

SSB is one example of measuring the effectiveness of Yurok language teaching. Legislative and bureaucratic forms of support for Yurok language reclamation are few, but one pertinent example comes from state lawmakers. The California SSB went into effect in 2012 with the passage of Assembly Bill 815 and was later amended in 2017 (California Department of Education 2022). According to California Education Code sections 51460–51464, the SSB "recognizes high school graduates who have attained a high level of proficiency in speaking, reading, and writing one or more languages in addition to English" (California Department of Education 2022).

The state superintendent of public instruction can award the SSB to students who have completed four years of English and one additional language with good standing, or to those who pass examinations in reading, writing, and speaking the language that is in addition to English without the requisite years of formal instruction, as detailed in the legislation (California Department of Education 2022). This means that students who take all four years of Yurok and maintain As and Bs, as well as earn As and Bs in their English classes, can apply for and receive the SSB without testing for it. Students who complete only three years of Yurok prior to graduating high school can take an examination.

With Yurok eligible for SSB participation alongside other world language electives like Spanish, French, and German, the SSB operates as a formal inclusion mechanism for Indigenous languages in public high schools. The distinction of SSB, designated by a golden seal on student diplomas, is prestigious, and is an award graduates can put on their resumes. While recognizing that measuring teacher impact through standardized testing is problematic, in this chapter, I look to SSB as an indicator of the new place of Indigenous languages within formal education that contributes to the validation of Indigenous knowledge by White-dominated bureaucracies.

SSB as Identity Affirmation for Yurok Descendants

As of 2024, five students from EHS, three students from DNHS, and one student from MHS had achieved the Yurok SSB. Seven of these nine Yurok SSB achievers identify as Yurok, Yurok descendant, or descendants of another Native American tribe, and two of them are White. In 2022, when I interviewed Maurice Alvarado and Danielle Schunneman, each of them had been out of high school for several years and they were both trying to find their way in the world. I spoke with them to discuss the impact of taking Yurok on their identities and lives both in and after high school.

Even though we were living less than thirty minutes apart in spring 2022, COVID-19 caution, plus busy work schedules for all of us, made separate interviews via Zoom the most viable way to connect. Both EHS alumni were eager to talk. They both expressed pride in their accomplishment of being the first Yurok SSB students, but also disappointment in themselves for not continuing with the language after having put in so much effort. Neither of them had continued with Yurok language study in the three years since they graduated high school. To be fair, they graduated the summer before the world shut down due to the COVID-19 pandemic, but both expressed that they hadn't met their own expectations since graduating high school and earning the SSB.

When we spoke, Maurice and Danielle were working jobs to make ends meet in ways that they saw as temporary way stations to something else, with Maurice in food service and Danielle in childcare. They both attend community college part-time, but feel stretched thin. Nevertheless, they expressed that Yurok language study in high school had played a deeply meaningful role in their lives. They were interested in finding a way to continue with language, but didn't yet know what that was.

Maurice Alvarado, Blood Quantum, and the SSB

Maurice, who grew up in Eureka, struggles with his identity as a Native American descendant. His mother is White, and his father was an enrolled Yurok member who passed away in a boating accident in 2004 when Maurice was only three years old. Maurice has put in effort to define his own Native status, contacting the Yurok Tribe to get information about his great-great-grandmother's lineage—she was a tribal member—to calculate his blood quantum. Thus far, Maurice hasn't figured out how to enroll in the Yurok Tribe, even though his paternal line suggests that he should be able to. For people to be enrolled tribal members, they must meet a given tribe's requirements. For the Yurok Tribe, members must have one-eighth Native American blood in general, regardless of tribe, in addition to being a Yurok Tribal descendant (Yurok Tribe 1993, Yurok Tribe 1994).

The politics of blood quantum and Indigenous authenticity are rife and outside the scope of this book, but there is excellent discussion of it elsewhere (Garroutte 2003: 14–60; Ineese-Nash 2020; Kauanui 2008). Enrollment status notably carries significant financial benefits for some tribes. The Yurok Tribe does not distribute monetary payouts to enrolled members, but there are tribal benefits, such as traditional hunting and fishing rights, that come with enrollment status. Tribal members are distinct from Native descendants. The term "descendant" is used to indicate people who have some heritage from a particular tribe, but not at a sufficient threshold to meet a given tribe's enrollment requirements. Descendants generally receive no monetary benefits or other tribal privileges, although anyone with any Native American heritage in Humboldt and Del Norte Counties in California is eligible to receive free health care through United Indian Health Service (UIHS 2022).

The degree to which descendants are included in cultural practices varies widely based on specific family circumstances. Generally, in my work in far Northern California, descendants who are interested in continuing cultural practices tell me they are warmly included in culture work associated with a tribe, even though they know it will bring no financial benefit to them. While some of these young people talk about feeling like outsiders as nonmembers, others feel strongly that they have the ability to define who they are in the world regardless of official status.

Maurice is White-passing, and comments on how people's perceptions of him visually affect him: "Unless I am provoked to talk about it, no one in my day-to-day life identifies me as Native. They identify me as a Caucasian[1] male. Even going into Yurok I with James, neither he nor any students thought I was Native. From a young age, it never mattered to me who people thought I am. But I personally identify as Native American, as an American Indian, whether legal or nonlegal. I've never put Caucasian on forms, no matter what someone says. I've never understood why I couldn't get into the Tribe" (Alvarado 2022).

Maurice's identity as a White-passing person causes a cognitive dissonance between his own self-perception and how people perceive him and therefore relate to him. Blood quantum politics are confusing even for those who follow it closely, and for young people, it can easily come off as positively bewildering. But neither Maurice's misidentification as White, nor his exclusion from formal membership, has dissuaded him from investigating his Yurok heritage.

Maurice was automatically placed in Spanish II as a freshman at EHS because he had taken Spanish in eighth grade and done well. But when he got his class schedule just before the beginning of his freshman year, he requested to switch to Yurok and his request was granted. He knew that the Yurok language would be meaningful even before the class started. "For me it was a way to connect with my father and to connect spiritually with the Yurok culture" (Alvarado 2022). The yearning for that familial and heritage connection helped Maurice prioritize the class. And the mentorship he found there kept him coming back. Maurice shares that "a big thing that kept me staying in Yurok year after year was James Gensaw. He was someone I could look up to as a mini-father figure. I don't think I've ever told James anything of the sort, but I can see it clearly now several years later" (Alvarado 2022).

For Maurice, the biggest challenge for Yurok language learning was getting to the level where he could think in the language: "The inaccessibility of Yurok makes it really hard to keep improving. When I left James's classroom, I had no one else to even say hello to in Yurok, or anyone to talk to or connect with about it. That was the hardest thing. The only thing that helped was in between my periods, like during lunch, spending that time in James's room talking with him about language, like why a word sounds this way and not that way" (Alvarado 2022).

Trying to find a way to sustain his engagement in the Yurok language has been challenging since he graduated from EHS. But Maurice continues to try, and some of the pandemic innovations using online language learning have made it a bit easier.

> After high school, it was a blur to figure out if I was gonna go to college. I started working to be able to provide for myself. Right before COVID hit, I was going to start working on my Yurok again. Instead, I've accessed some of the language things he showed me, like the dictionary he gave me, and the UC Berkeley online courses. It was so awesome to be able to have iPhone games in Yurok and things like that! The ability to expand online was huge.
>
> At the moment, I'm working whatever shift I'm given [in fast food]. I've talked to James a little bit to try to get back into language. I'm trying to find a different job that can have a set schedule, because I can't commit to Yurok when my working schedule is so different each day and week. (Alvarado 2022)

Maurice knows about the online community classes of the Yurok Language Program, and he is interested in reengaging in language study. But his economic precarity and dependency on a contingent shift job prevent him from having the kind of set hours that could allow him to schedule in the language classes more easily. This situation leaves Maurice frustrated, because he feels both a responsibility and a calling to keep working on Yurok language transmission: "It has been a little bit of a personal dilemma in my head. Just trying to learn Yurok and expand it to be more than it is, is a big job. When I was leaving James's class, one of the things I was looking into was being a language tutor, if not a teacher. Then I could bring it to my family, who is more disconnected from their Native side since my father died" (Alvarado 2022).

Maurice retroactively wishes he would have investigated career paths involving the language more when he was in the class: "I should have asked James more questions about how to do it, how to become a teacher. James never knew I had that aspiration, so we didn't talk about it. But growing up as a kid who didn't have much family support, especially during the school week, teachers really had an impact on me. I think there is a lot more that kids get from teachers than from home life" (Alvarado 2022).

For his part, Mr. Gensaw, the Yurok teacher, recognized a hunger in Maurice to learn more about himself and tried to support him. He invited

Maurice to Yurok events, but Maurice didn't quite feel ready for a more active cultural participation role. Even when Mr. Gensaw invited him to dance in ceremony, he declined:

> Honestly, it seems really tiring, physically and spiritually. One thing that was conveyed by James in the class is that you need to be in a good space to even set foot in the dance circle. I always thought, "If I do not feel like I am mentally ready, I shouldn't go." I still don't believe that I'm right to participate. They'll dance for twelve hours, from sun rising to sun going down. You have to fast for seven or ten straight days or something; it is a rigorous process. But I did attend events, just not as a dancer. Being able to see all types of Native Americans was great, bringing health back to the earth [in the World Renewal Ceremony]. (Alvarado 2022)

When I ask Maurice about the wider academic impact that his enrollment in Yurok language classes had, his answer is a powerful testimonial to why culturally sustaining curricula are so important:

> Yurok was like 40 percent of the reason I went to school each morning. Whenever James had a substitute, I wouldn't even go to school. James brings such a lively environment and tries to make the best of every day. Once I would show up for Yurok, I'd stay for the rest of my classes too. I had, like, a 3.4 GPA at the end of high school. Yurok was one class where I never got lower than an A-minus. In a lot of other classes, I'd get a C, but I didn't care. I didn't need more than a 2.0 to graduate high school. But since Yurok is still a supplemental class, they could pull it if they wanted—if I was failing other classes. So, in order to stay in Yurok, I had to do well enough in my other classes. So Yurok is really what got me through high school. (Alvarado 2022)

If readers are looking for evidence that culturally sustaining curricula impact overall school success, here it is. Maurice describes how he would stay to attend other classes because he was already there for the Yurok class, and how he needed to do well enough in the other classes to be able to stay enrolled in Yurok.

Maurice sees how contingent this deeply meaningful class was on his early advocacy for himself: "Looking back on it now, if I did not send that email to my high school counselor [asking to switch from Spanish to Yurok]—from the Walgreens parking lot on Broadway in August before my freshman year—I would never have gotten into the class and not known James Gensaw. It all comes back to him. Honestly, looking back on it, meeting him was the most important thing I did. If I hadn't taken that first Yurok class, I wouldn't have wanted to keep growing at an educational level, to build a character, to build self-respect" (Alvarado 2022).

The impact of Mr. Gensaw on Maurice's sense of self was profound, and it is something that has stayed with him even years after graduating: "James fought for the things he believed in. It was more than teaching the language; he was teaching how to be a good human. A lot of kids took Yurok because it was the easy A. But even the kids who didn't want the Seal of Biliteracy, he was able to teach everybody something, even if it wasn't the thing they were there to be taught" (Alvarado 2022). Maurice's testimonial to the power of a caring educator, who was a large part of his motivation to come to school each day, holds deep lessons about the importance of making a teacher pipeline that is representative of a given student body. As a young man who lost his own father at a young age, he found a father figure in Mr. Gensaw. In turn, Mr. Gensaw was willing to teach the language, self-respect, and dignity as basic attributes of Yurok, and, more fundamentally, the human self.

Today, when I think about the need for culturally sustaining curricula for BIPOC youth, I think about Maurice's story. His description of what access to the Yurok class and having a Yurok educator meant at such a formative time in his life shines light on how to support youth in precarious circumstances. Yurok classes are essentially what got Maurice through high school. It seems unlikely, given what he describes, that he would have graduated without his Yurok classes motivating him to go to school and keep his grades up.

Also, Maurice's White-passing appearance and lack of tribal enrollment prevented him from being identified by his middle school educators as a Native American student. As a result, he was not flagged as a priority candidate for Yurok classes at the high school level. The email hastily sent to his high school guidance counselor from a parking lot in the weeks leading up to school set him on a very different course than what might have been had he stayed enrolled in Spanish, a language that did not hold the same degree of personal meaning for him. It was, in political science-speak, a critical juncture—a crossroads where a key decision was made.

The contingency in this story highlights the precarity of factors that influence youth identity formation. It points to the need to expand dialogue about education policy that prioritizes culturally sustaining curricula. Prioritizing such curricula in systematic ways is part of the work ahead for schools and districts. Confining access to culturally sustaining curricula to contingent moments of chance may inadvertently mean that such content bypasses students like Maurice, who need it most.

Danielle Schunneman and the SSB Responsibility

Like Maurice, Danielle took four years of Yurok at EHS and completed the SSB in Yurok just before graduating in 2019. When we spoke via Zoom on a Sunday afternoon, she had a rare day off. Most of her time is spent attending classes at College of the Redwoods, the local community college, and helping with her mother's home daycare business.

Danielle's Yurok lineage is on her mother's side, and her mother and maternal grandfather are both enrolled in the Hoopa Tribe. Danielle notes that:

> I'm seen as more Native by the color of my skin than my brother or sister. They could pass [as White]. My mom has a baby basket, and we went to Native American conferences and learned to make things. My sisters learned to weave baskets. My grandfather keeps trying to get us to go to dances. He is in the Hoopa Tribe, but he also has Yurok in him. He didn't learn the Yurok language, but my great-grandma was a speaker.
>
> My other great-grandma was adopted at young age. She didn't learn any Yurok because of that. She was so excited when I signed up for the Yurok class. My grandpa really wants me to teach him some of it. I'm kind of in between figuring out what I want to do, but have been thinking maybe I can be a Yurok language teacher or help out with that in some way. (Schunneman 2022)

Danielle has lots of partial ideas about what she wants to do professionally. "Maybe a dermatologist or a surgeon," but she also really likes Yurok language and culture and the idea of working with the language. She is still figuring it out, which is logical for a young person who graduated high school just before the COVID-19 pandemic struck. Danielle is also negotiating her Native identity in relation to tribal requirements. She notes that she is not currently enrolled in a tribe "but might be joining one soon" (Schunneman 2022). Given her Yurok and Hoopa heritage, she is exploring both options.

Though a sizable part of her family is White, Danielle's grandfather's identity as Hupa and Yurok is significant for her and her family. Because of this, access to the Yurok language in high school was deeply meaningful:

> I would not feel as connected to my family if I hadn't taken Yurok [at EHS]. I wouldn't have gone for the SSB. If I had done Spanish, I would have just thought, I've taken four years of that but it's not a big deal—other people can speak it. But with Yurok, it's like, you are one of the only people who can read it now. Because first language speakers have all died out, so you have to pick up the slack.
>
> Being one of the first people to do the State Seal of Biliteracy in Yurok felt like a big deal. I'm one of the only people who *can* do it, so I have to! It means a lot! There is more connection with the language for my family. Plus, I got to sing funny songs in class. I got a letter from a senator congratulating me when I passed the SSB! I put it on my resume. It felt special. (Schunneman 2022)

In offering advice for future Yurok students, Danielle encourages people to "stick with it! And make sure you practice your pronunciations!" She says the hardest part of language learning is the numbers, which are different for round objects, for animals, and for money.

The easiest part of Yurok, according to Danielle, was being present in class, because Mr. Gensaw made it a safe place for kids to be—and a fun one. Students *wanted* to attend:

> In Yurok I, James [Gensaw] did a lot of games to help memorize words. It helped relax a lot of the kids, instead of just reading out of a book and then writing a paper about what we read, like in some other classes. It was an easy start. Then as the years progressed, he added more papers, more projects that we had to do, and it wasn't an "easy" class anymore. He let us call him James in class and we'd hear stories about Yurok culture. That's why students liked him. Some kids were there for the easy A, but others really wanted to learn. One Native kid in there had a lot of trouble with authority. He only respected James and would act out in other classes or whenever James wasn't there. If there was a substitute, he'd slack off or get kicked out. But James could get through to him. I think he was a great teacher. (Schunneman 2022)

Danielle credits Mr. Gensaw for helping her get a foundation in the language, but when I ask what it means to her to be part of keeping the Yurok language alive, she looks away. "I don't really think about this stuff a lot. But it is a lot of weight, to know it" (Schunneman 2022). The weight is a responsibility to find ways to share what she knows, because so few people can help grow the speaker base. She doesn't quite see how language can fit into her work in the daycare, or in the nascent plans for next steps in her career, but she is grateful she took the classes.

The impact on Danielle from taking four years of Yurok was her wider awareness of local Native American culture and related political issues and sufficient Yurok language skills to pass the SSB. In some ways, it did just what a good high school class should. She learned important content and grew as a person. But the bonus, for a heritage-speaker like Danielle, is that it helped her feel more connected to the Native American part of her family. It affirmed that part of herself was worthy of deeper study, and that it was important enough to be taught in high school. Whatever she goes on to do in her life, that validation stays with her.

Conclusion

We filter our lives through our experiences. For Maurice and Danielle, being the first students to achieve the SSB in Yurok was a monumental experience. They are proud of this, and it buoys them as they sometimes feel off track. Such recognition affirms their visions of who they are in relation to their family lineages. They are still finding their way in the world, and economic necessity has kept them both in the workforce rather than pursuing full-time higher education. Neither Maurice nor Danielle has found regular ways to practice the Yurok language with other speakers since leaving EHS, although it continues to be meaningful in their personal lives. Their families don't speak the language, nor do most of the co-workers or friends they associate with on a daily basis. But as Yurok descendants, they both express being deeply fulfilled and moved by their language study and reaching the historic SSB benchmark. As they chart their next steps, they have the option to further the language if they so choose.

CHAPTER 10

Victoria Carlson: "We Have to Keep Our Language Alive"

Introduction: My Homage to Victoria

Victoria is dedicated.[1] I wanted her to write this book with me because she is one of the driving forces in Yurok language reclamation. She contributed tremendously to crafting the research questions undergirding this book and helped design the very same interview questions that I then posed to her. But as the Yurok Language Program Manager for the Yurok Tribe's Education Department, and a mother of four, Victoria is busy! She is constantly facilitating a language class on Zoom, writing grants to support the program, or giving someone a snack.

Victoria works between her home in Klamath, on the Yurok Indian Reservation, and one of the two Yurok Tribe Education Department offices in Crescent City and Klamath Glen. Some days she'll drive ninety minutes to Eureka for groceries after a full day of work, especially if the language program is putting on an event that includes food. She'll make work calls in the car as she weaves in and out of cell phone signal on the highway that snakes around mountains sacred to the Yurok and other tribes. So, Victoria didn't have time to help write the book, but she has been a stellar collaborator at each step of its development, including reviewing earlier versions of chapters pertaining to Yurok people and culture. This book is dedicated to her, as she was key to its existence in the first place.

When we finally sat down for a formal interview in May 2022, at the end of my semester as a visiting researcher at Cal Poly Humboldt, we had already stood in front of numerous Yurok classes and other community and tribal spaces together talking about this research.[2] Capping those talks with lunches together, we had also gotten to know each other personally, swapping tales of the antics of our children over meals. Parts of this chapter also developed through numerous Zoom conversations in fall 2022, when we followed up on points that needed fleshing out as the book took shape. The text in the reader's hands is one that has gone through iterative revisions and review processes by Victoria's family, in addition to the layers of formal permission-seeking and tribal reviews that happened both before and after the study itself. The result is a story of cultural reclamation that spans generations.

The Making of a Language Activist: Early Memories of the Yurok Language

For our in-person formal interview, Victoria and I meet in a Yurok Tribe conference room in Klamath. There is a boil-water notice from 2021 still taped above a sink, a reminder of the surrounding ecological fragility impacted by humans. We settle into plush chairs and I switch on the audio recorder. Victoria is a gifted storyteller. She says what needs to be said. I ask about how she first became aware of Yurok as a language:

> I remember the first time I heard the Yurok language. I was little, probably three or four years old. My mom, she never left me too much, but this one time I remember she left me with my great-great-auntie. We were in her house and she was sitting down to eat breakfast and came and got me to sit down to eat with her. She said something to me as I was about to sit down that had to be in Yurok, because it wasn't in English and I hadn't heard it before. I babbled something back, something made up, because I didn't understand her and couldn't speak the language. She laughed. At that time, I hadn't ever heard the language. I realized years later that she had been speaking to me in Yurok.

Looking back, Victoria can see some clear signs that she had an interest in language even as a young person, but that didn't find its full expression until she was an adult: "When I was in eighth grade at Hoopa Elementary, most things there were more oriented towards Hupa culture.[3] But there was a teacher at the elementary school who was taking Yurok language herself and she would teach us some words. For our eighth-grade graduation, me and my best friend decided we wanted to do a prayer in the Yurok language at the graduation ceremony. The school officials said okay and then we realized we had to go learn the language to do it!"

In typical Victoria fashion, she identified her goal, and even though it was hard, she made a functional plan to accomplish it. "We went to my grandma and recorded her saying the prayer, and then me and my best friend divided up the phrases and said the prayer at graduation. People liked it! I look back at that experience as an adult and think, we must have been a bit unique to want to add that to our graduation at that time! That is not what all the other kids were doing! We already had a love for the language, we just didn't know how to use it." Even though it put her outside the mainstream of her peers, Victoria's love of language was evident even as a child, and it persisted into adulthood.

While attending college in 2004, Victoria started working for the Yurok Language Program and didn't know what to expect at first:

> I had been very immersed in ceremony growing up, and my par-
> ents and grandparents made sure I knew the rules of how to live
> as a Yurok woman. I had attended language classes prior to when I
> started working for the Program and knew it was important, but it
> was once I was working for it that I realized just how important lan-
> guage was. Recognizing that the language was endangered was new
> to me. As a young person, I thought the language was flourishing,
> that there were hundreds of speakers! It was a big eye-opener to see
> that we can count the number of language speakers on our hands.
> There was this sudden urgency to document the language and help
> more people become speakers. I needed to do everything I could to
> help save the language!

Indigenous language reclamation is a survival strategy in the face of the impact of colonialism on intergenerational cultural loss. Victoria talks about language legacies in her own family:

> I grew up hearing my grandparents speaking the language, but I
> didn't get to learn from them both equally. My grandma was seventy-
> six when she passed away and my grandpa was ninety-four, so my
> time with her was not as much as with him. My grandfather, he was
> my master-speaker Yurok language teacher, with whom I spent the

most time conversing and who made the most impact on me. He told me one day when I was learning from him, "You know, Victoria, I've had so many learners come to me, and one after another, they start learning with me and when it starts to get hard, they drop off. I don't want you to give up when it starts to get hard. Don't give up! It's going to get hard, but don't give up!"

Her grandfather's admonition to not give up was deeply influential: "I'll always remember those words in my mind. Because it does get hard! To become an advanced or fluent speaker of the language is hard! It is not easy! And I see it in other learners—it gets hard and sometimes they want to give up. But when I see the next generation, I persevere. It is hard, but we have to keep going."

Whenever we talk about her language reclamation work, Victoria is quick to point out that she couldn't do what she does without the community of speakers, including her family members who labored to develop proficiency in Yurok as adults. Her mother had attended a boarding school as a child and so even though her parents—Victoria's grandparents—were fluent speakers, her mother had to relearn the language as an adult: "My mom was in the Yurok master-apprentice language program and was always asking questions. I couldn't wait until they were done so I could ask my language questions! My mom, my grandparents, my aunties—they have always played a vital role for me, and I wouldn't be who I am in my life if it wasn't for them. Those elders are all gone now and they're not able to see what we are doing to keep the language going, but they are still watching over us and smiling."

Victoria tears up here. She had recently lost another older member of her family, and the pain of a family member dying is mingled with the gratitude she constantly expresses for the community she is part of: "I wouldn't be able to do this work without Barbara, Brittany, James, and the community. If we don't do it as a whole, it won't be able to get transferred into the homes and other spaces where we all come together. It is really our language family that keeps it going. We are here to support each other. When we call it a family, it brings us together more. Some of our Yurok learners, maybe they are having a hard time learning and just knowing that they have our support makes a difference for them." Victoria embodies the kind of generous, supportive teacher that motivates others to do their best. Within her family and community, she is a cultural rights activist, even if she is too modest to describe herself as such.

"So they'll wanna teach their children": Why Language Continuity Matters

The importance of the Yurok language is intimately connected to Yurok cosmology. Victoria explains: "I grew up hearing that we weren't the first ones to speak the language, that the animals spoke the language before us and that's how far back it goes. When I teach my children the language, I teach them that when they speak, the animals will understand them because it's the language that they spoke before us. [My children] realize that they can do that, they have that ability to speak to the animals and the animals will understand them if it's in our language. And so that brings that connection of our language to the animals, to the land, when they speak to the environment, the trees, the river." Language not only is a tool of human communication, but connects nonhuman relations to each other as well.

Victoria reflects that one of the reasons it is important to speak Yurok today is that that's what they—both human and nonhuman relations—heard thousands and thousands of years ago. Without language, there is a rupture in communication across time, space, and communities. The absence of Yurok is "a missing piece that we have in our connection with our culture, with our land, and everything. You know, we still fish for our salmon, we still feed our elders, we still take care of our children, we still practice our ceremonies, but we don't speak our language in any of those places. And so, I think it's really critical that we bring that back because that's what our elders taught us."

In addition to the constant outward-facing work she is doing to bring language into the community, Victoria works hard in her own household to speak as much Yurok as possible to her children, and her husband is learning too: "I wouldn't be doing justice if I wasn't teaching my children the language. Teaching everybody in classes and everything is great, but if I don't implement it in my home and pass it to *my* children—making sure that I make it a number-one priority, not just in my workday but in my life with my children and my family—I wouldn't feel right in what I'm doing. I couldn't be Yurok Language Program Manager and not teach the people closest to me, who are around me all the time."

Such family-based language work is gratifying, as Victoria can see her language revitalization work play out right in her own home. "It's awesome to hear my kids correcting each other to use the language. One of my kids might say something like 'bread' in English and one of my other kids will say, 'No, that's not right, it's *pop-sew*.' Or one of 'em might say, 'Oh, get me some milk,' and then the other says, 'No, it's not milk, it's *muen-cherhl*.' So, it's that good feeling of language use. I never felt that way before and you don't see that a lot. Or at least I'm not in everybody's else's homes to hear it, but to see it in my home it makes me feel good."

There is a small but determined group of parents in the region who, like Victoria, are heritage-speakers who have become more proficient themselves as adults and are trying to raise a new generation of Yurok first-language speakers. This can be frustrating as children age and parents need to say more complex things to them that may exceed parental vocabulary, but it is also a motivator to keep learning with their children. For a language like Yurok, there are very few other people who can do this labor. Parents are a vital line of defense in language survival.

"School was set up to destroy our people": From Boarding Schools to Language Electives

Victoria focuses much of her time and energy on language dissemination, but she is acutely aware that language politics are at play behind her many impressive examples of educational media. I ask her to talk about the relationship between the Yurok language and decolonization:

> When I teach the students Yurok language, especially at the elementary school level, I always teach them about the boarding school experience. I talk about the experiences that the elders went through while attending Indian boarding schools. And they get really angry, you know? Like, school did this to our elders! I don't mean to make them angry, 'cause I don't want them to have this negative feeling on their shoulders about non-Indians or soldiers or even the school system. Because we know we have to use the school system to overcome certain things. But sometimes it [boarding schools] happened to their great-grandparents. I teach them that to decolonize, look at us today. Look at the school system—look how things have changed— where now we're coming into the schools to teach you Yurok!

Describing the transformation of schools from places of harm to places of culturally sustaining education is part of Victoria's work. She knows that in order for young people to achieve "success in both worlds" they need to know the truth about schools, and what is at stake in turning toward or away from schooling now.

> At one time the school system was set up to destroy our people and to take away their language and their culture and any Indigenous identity they had. And now we're using the schools—we're not using them, but it's a platform—to teach kids about the history, the true history, and to turn the table and say, "But now, look, we're here today, bringing in our tribal languages, bringing in our tribal basketries, bringing in people to teach about our fisheries." So, it's a different time now and kids need to continue to learn and to be involved in their education; to know that it's no longer an enemy of the Indigenous people. School is a place where they're able to learn their language and culture and they can have high goals in education.

In her reflections on the evolution of schooling for Native Americans, Victoria shows how much has changed and why it matters. Through age-appropriate content, Victoria explains the violence that boarding schools inflicted on Native American youth. In doing so, she helps illuminate for students the structural aspects of intergenerational trauma. Victoria uses the explanation of past schooling to highlight that schooling today is much more culturally welcoming and therefore something students should engage in and celebrate.

As she narrates the role of Yurok culture in her own life, Victoria is explicit in how her grounded identity fosters her own well-being: "Growing up, I always knew how imperative it was to maintain our culture, to know who we are as people and to never have any doubt. No one's gonna tell me 'You're not gonna be able to do something' because I know who I am. My identity gives me that sense of self-esteem, through my family, growing up, knowing who you are and what to believe and not believe, what's right and what's wrong, how to treat people and the environment. It leads me on my path, as a mother, as a wife, as a daughter, as a community member, as a language keeper, how to take care of one another."

This groundedness is a result of Victoria knowing her own past, being culturally connected in the present, and envisioning an Indigenous future with multiple benchmarks of success. "In a way, when you know what happened to your people, you're confident, you know what you've overcome, and you know that you can continue the culture and language even though they're not all here to teach you. We're here to teach them [students] that they not only should be involved in their culture and language and ceremonies and be a good member of the community and help one another, but also to go to school to learn as much as they can—to go to college!" For Victoria, her Yurok identity is the solid foundation on which she has developed both an individual and community-minded sense of self. She mobilizes her own well-being to help others do the same through her role as an educator. But it isn't always easy or straightforward, as the definition of success can vary so much across the Indigenous and White worlds in which she operates.

Speaking frankly about the tensions inherent in living in two worlds, Victoria comments on the distinct social hierarchies at play within Yurok and settler-colonial institutions:

> I never understood for the longest time—what's that paper that
> they're talking about putting on the wall from college? But you have
> to get that piece of paper! 'Cause my grandma said, "You gotta go to
> college and you gotta get educated, because that's the only way you're
> gonna be able to fight for our people. It's the only way that people
> are gonna think you're smart and listen to you in that other world."
> Because if you don't have that degree, it was kinda like, you won't be
> able to manage in the White world. If you don't have that bachelor's
> or that master's or that PhD, no one's gonna really listen to you there.

The emphasis on credentialization is something that is a struggle for many BIPOC communities, where structural racism has long barred people from achieving credentials at rates as high as their White counterparts. In addition, other ways of knowing and being are sometimes more valued. It is legitimate to think of higher education degrees as pieces of paper that symbolize monetary debt and time away from one's community, while still not inculcating skills needed to flourish in the community of origin. Yet as Victoria points out, not having the credentials sets people up for significant disadvantage in the White world.

Learning how to walk in both worlds is the Yurok Tribe's way of leaving as many doors open for people as possible. Victoria notes the need to balance these multiple truths: "It's important to keep that balance within your Indigenous ways and the White world. In this world we have to be civilized or feel like you have to talk a certain way, use these certain words, dress a certain way. That wasn't really what it was like a long time ago [pre-colonization], but we have to keep this balance. So that's just what I've tried to do, but it's not easy. I just hope that in our future generation, they are able to pick up where we left off, where I left, where I leave off." I consider the "both worlds" approach of Victoria's statement quite useful here. She wants her descendants, and those of her community, to achieve academic success in the White world as a way to have economic security and respect in that arena, while also furthering Yurok language and cultural continuity. By honoring the multiple cultural variations on well-being, Victoria illustrates the need for balance across multiple worlds in the pursuit of well-being.

Mainstreaming the Yurok Language

In order to support people more regularly speaking Yurok, it needs to be visible and available across the types of daily institutions people traverse. Victoria works constantly to expand language access and visibility throughout Yurok Tribal offices. Here she outlines some of the behind-the-scenes work that takes place to integrate Yurok language into multiple spaces: "Say I get a request to design a language lesson from the Tribal Court. As the language manager, I meet with the administrators of the tribal courts and we talk about 'What do you want your staff to learn?' I could say, 'This is what I want you to learn,' but I really meet with them one-on-one and we talk about what do you want your clients to learn and hear? What words would you want to learn to use in your workspace? We try to custom-make those classes specially for their staff and clients."

There has been keen interest in accessing the Yurok language from multiple departments of the Yurok Tribe. "We recently launched a language request process through Google Forms and I think we're up to almost 140 requests! I would say 90 percent of them come from tribal departments, from Head Start, fisheries, the Wildlife Department, housing, the Executive Office, Tribal Council, and so on. We get requests every day almost. People are really into wanting to name their divisions with Yurok names or name their programs Yurok names."

Some of the naming requests are challenging both linguistically and culturally because the concepts don't have direct equivalents, or the historical context is necessary to grasp the meaning of the term. This happened with a request from the Yurok Tribal Police Chief to translate the word "police" in Yurok: "The Yurok elders had an existing word for 'police'—*hley-go-meen 'oohl*. But that description translates into 'the grabbers of Indian people,' something that made sense in historical context because the police would come and grab people, including the kids to go boarding schools. To portray a more positive message about tribal police and how they serve their communities, language staff worked together to define police as *mey-ge-tohl-kwo-meen*—'the caretakers or protectors.' With every request we receive for translation, we have to think about what it means for us today as well as in the past."

Victoria also shares how she was asked to help create a Yurok name for the campaign to locate Missing and Murdered Indigenous Women and Girls. The Tribal Court wanted a culturally resonant name for the program, which is meant to raise awareness about and intervene in gender-based violence. But these were not terms or concepts commonly passed on in language reclamation communities, and so took extra attention.

> I met with them [Tribal Court] and I was like, "Well, what do you want to say with the name?" Because that's such a touchy topic. When you think of the Missing and Murdered Indigenous Women, it's so sad and then maybe you're mad 'cause it has happened or you're lonesome thinking about it. But we don't want to name it something sad, so we're like, "Well, what else could we say?"
>
> So we talked about it like this: When you see someone who has gone missing or maybe they're no longer here no more, the next time you see them you're gonna see them in a good way, meaning, it could be in a dream, it could be on the other side [after death], but whenever you see them next, it's gonna be in a good way. So they named it *skuy'soo kee kem ney-wo-chek*—"When I see you again, I'll see you in a good way."

The Yurok Tribal Council passed a resolution in December 2021 declaring a state of emergency in Yurok Country regarding Missing and Murdered Indigenous Women, later updated to Missing and Murdered Indigenous People. *Skuy'soo kee kem ney-wo-chek* is the title of the project that includes the creation of a database and reports on such people within the community, making visible both violence against them, as well as the hope to see them again "in a good way."

COVID-19 and Expanded Access to
Language Through Digital Spaces

The COVID-19 pandemic was generally terrible for Native tribes, with devastating loss of life compounded by preexisting medical conditions, food scarcity, and extreme isolation, among many other factors. Like Barbara McQuillen, Victoria notes that expanded technology skills and access has been a bright spot in an otherwise difficult time for the Yurok Language Program. As staff have pivoted to offering classes online, they also draw on a large collection of audio recordings and grammar books, which have been made digitally available.

Victoria and her colleagues are constantly liaising with teachers and schools as well as blasting out invitations for community language classes on social media. She summarizes current classes in 2022: "Before the pandemic we'd have a community language class in each area—Klamath, Weitchpec, and Arcata—in person, but since the pandemic we've moved it online. Once a week we teach a Yurok language community class online, and we've gotten so many more learners from out of the area who are tribal members but live further away, as far as Alaska, Pennsylvania, Texas, Kansas, Wyoming, Oregon, and Canada. They come back each week for an hour on Zoom."

In addition to weekly language classes, the Yurok Language Program also offers a once a week "immersion pod," for intermediate to advanced speakers. "They come together to have a safe environment to come and speak Yurok language. So, it's not really a classroom setting, it's more like you just show up. We do have an immersion facilitator—James [Gensaw]—and if it gets quiet or if people run out of things to talk about, we need to have that facilitator there to be able to say, 'Okay, what'd you do yesterday?' Then he asks everybody what they did yesterday or 'What are you gonna do tomorrow?' Those type of things keep the momentum going in the immersion pod."

In our conversation, Victoria points out that for the more advanced Yurok speakers, continuing to learn the language does not always have to revolve around highly structured lessons or other learning materials. Language advancement can take place in specially designated time like the immersion pods, where speakers can just talk and connect with one another. Not only does this immersion contribute to language practice, but it also fosters community among the speakers.

The drive to make Yurok as available as possible to Yurok staff is truly admirable. Victoria describes that:

We also hold Yurok language classes four days a week for Yurok Tribal employees. They're all online—virtual platforms—so if you work for the Tribe, you have the opportunity to attend language class four days a week from anywhere. It could be you're working from Weych-pues or Eureka, or up in Crescent City, and so to be able to bring people into language while far apart, that has never happened before so that's been pretty big.

We've also started creating Yurok language services for internal and external entities. Internally within the Yurok Tribe, we've made custom-designed classes for certain departments, like the TANF Department—the Client Services Department, they call it now. And then also tribal courts. We've helped design special classes, where the [Tribal] Court has actually paid the Language Program for their time to go in and teach their staff the language, hoping in turn that the staff would kind of trickle language down to clients; using common words and phrases that you can maybe use for conversation. That was how we started working with the employees, creating a Yurok-language-learning path for employees to converse.

Language teaching follows some basic principles across many languages— exposure to the sounds of the language, for example, but there are evolving strategies in Indigenous language revitalization, especially in small speaker communities, about how to focus limited available language energy and resources. Victoria explains:

Many years ago, we would focus on vocabulary, like, teaching words, just maybe nouns or something, but we are now transitioning to creating conversational speakers. You can't just go to a room and list out a bunch of birds or colors, so we're really trying to build a conversational learning path to be able to speak the language. It's been working out pretty well. In addition to daily and weekly classes, we have monthly workshops where we learn about the structure of the language from Andrew Garrett, UC Berkeley linguist and friend. We go over the grammar and talk about the structure of our language. It's a time where we work on transcription. It's definitely for intermediate and advanced learners, but we always encourage beginners to come and listen, so they're like the fly on the wall—they're just listening and seeing, you know, what's going on and picking up whatever they can.

In addition to these regular language exposure opportunities, there are also two Yurok Language Institutes per year that are four days each, where people come together to learn the language, with trainings and presentations for Yurok language teachers. There is also an annual language camp. "We've always received funding for just one camp a year and it's mostly directed towards our teacher candidates, depending on what grant we have. This year [2022] we have more of a community-wide grant, so we're gonna be able to hold a camp that's more focused on youth and families and community members. For the students who are learning Yurok in the schools, or for young people whose parents are attending the language classes online, they could come in person to engage with one another." The variety of in-person language learning contexts are complemented by a range of online learning courses that helps meet the needs of remote learners spread out across the United States and beyond.

The breadth of work undertaken by Victoria and the Language Program staff is remarkable, as is the depth of care they put into each opportunity for language learning and dissemination. The shift to online language learning is a monumental change, dramatically expanding access to Yurok: "We're the largest tribe in California and trying to reach them [Yurok Tribal members] or give them opportunity to have access to Yurok language is really important because we don't want them to lose the connection. So, ensuring that we're on our social media, providing access to Yurok language audio recordings, and making cultural connections is all just one way to continue our language."

Before the pandemic, Victoria would travel to teach classes in person, sometimes driving a few hours each way: "I taught an elders' class up there in Weych-pues and we had about a dozen elders or so there that would fluctuate. They loved learning the language! They didn't get to learn the language as kids—that was the gap generation, that era that didn't get to learn the language. Their parents didn't feel that their children would be safe if they spoke that language, like my grandparents with my mom, where they'd go in another room to speak the language." The interruption of intergenerational language transfer was something elders in the language classes acknowledged, and worked to overcome: "When I was teaching the elders the language, oh, they would feel so happy! They couldn't wait to be able to start speaking some words. So their grandchildren would hear them speak the language, they said! 'We just wanna know some words, then our grandchildren will remember us being able to speak the language!' They were all pretty knowledgeable elders of basketry and Indian law, which is not written, but it's something like the rules of our people and some things we have lost. The elders learned the language like it was like that missing link that would help them."

Enthusiasm for language learning among the elders was high, and had an emotional resonance as well as practical impact. "There was one elder who said, 'Do we get homework?' I'd give them homework and they would come back with their homework ready! I would say, 'Well, come back and say five animals.' It wasn't hard homework, but it was something that they felt like, 'I could do that and I'm gonna go home and work on my list and come back and say it!' Some of those elders have passed away since that class, but knowing that they were able to learn some Yurok and use the language in their homes, I think it made them feel really good."

Part of Victoria's job is to inspire others to use the language, which includes fielding requests for translation and word consultation on a near-daily basis. Though she doesn't label it as such, Victoria is articulating the implicit theory of change that guides the work of the Yurok Language Program. Boiled down, it amounts to teaching Yurok to everyone who wants to learn Yurok. By mainstreaming it, Yurok people will also have more access to and motivation for language revitalization.

This approach to language access has many strengths. Because of the Tribe's openness to sharing language with non-Tribal members, public schools have been a front-line space for language teaching of the next generation. While the Yurok high-school-level language classes tend to have a majority of heritage-speakers, especially at the higher levels, many non-heritage-speakers also take the classes and facilitate language revitalization both through their communicative abilities and by destigmatizing and mainstreaming Yurok language use: "Our work is to continue to make sure that we have language in the schools; that we have signage of the language in the communities and that people are seeing it there; that we have representation on the online platforms, making sure that we're into the new way of how people communicate today—on Facebook, on Instagram, on other social media platforms. But we're also just making sure we continue to have language books, language dictionaries, language grammar books. And we want to ensure that we are providing Yurok language access to Tribal members, or to community members." The willingness to teach community members should not be overlooked, as it is part of why the Yurok Language Program has been so successful in building a large base of beginning-level speakers in recent years.

The language program works to teach all people, community wide. We get a lot of learners who are not Yurok, but they live in the community or they work for the Tribe, and it makes them feel good to know the language or to have that cultural connection to the tribal people. A lot of non-tribal people will greet me in the language and I think it's great! I've heard stories that it's not like that for some tribes—some tribes don't agree to teach non-tribal members their language—but if we're able to use Yurok with non-tribal members in the community, it's still gonna benefit 'cause the children will hear it, the younger people will hear it, and it'll make them wanna speak it.

The openness to non-tribal members learning Yurok makes the public schools a straightforward place to insert language classes. Such an approach would not be feasible if language access was limited to heritage-speakers.

Intergenerational Education and
Learning to be a Yurok Woman

In April 2022, Victoria, James Gensaw, and I co-presented at the invitation of the Department of Politics and the Politics Club at Cal Poly Humboldt on decolonization and the Yurok language. Victoria's parents came to the event, and it was the first time I met them. Her mother, a beautiful woman with a face just like Victoria's, has a slender *111* tattooed on her chin.[4] Toward the end of the talk, her mother spoke up. She gave moving testimony as to how meaningful it is that her daughter is working to bring back the language that was taken from their community.

Victoria offered a part of her mother's story and how her mother shared Yurok values with her as a child, but she didn't want to include anything about her mother's story without asking permission first. During the drafting of this chapter based on my own recorded data, Victoria sat down with her mother one weekend in late 2022 to share the draft and talk through which parts of her mother's story it was okay to voice within her own narrative. The resulting text reflects their collective edits.

At the Cal Poly Humboldt talk, Victoria's mother described why she didn't get to learn the Yurok language as a child and how she was so moved that the next generation gets the opportunity to do so. Victoria stated that it was healing for elders to see the next generation learning Yurok. It helped fix something that the complex interplay of settler-colonial factors had broken. "My mom went to Indian boarding school. She had six brothers and sisters, so she felt kind of like a burden at that time. You know, it was so many children and during that time, my grandpa was the only one working. So, she felt it would be easier for her to go to boarding school. She wasn't forced to go; she made a choice."

For Victoria's mother, boarding school wasn't mandatory, but there were structural factors that showed it wasn't entirely free will either. It was a rational decision to take the best care of herself and her family as she could, something she continued to demonstrate throughout Victoria's life. Victoria recounts:

> My mom's a smart lady, and I listen to her quite a bit. She had me in 1979 when she was only one semester away from having her AA [Associate of Arts degree]. And then when she got pregnant with me, she just dropped school and was a homemaker and raised all her children. She was a homemaker all my life and she always encouraged me in school, made sure I passed all my classes and took classes that would benefit me in college and help me along the way.
>
> After I graduated from high school, she went back to college! She had to have been in her late forties and she was driving from Hoopa to CR[5] every day, taking eighteen units a semester. She got her LVN [licensed vocational nurse] license. To her, education was very important, and she always pushed that on us, like, making sure that I went to tutoring sessions if I was struggling with math.

In addition to success in her formal public education that her mother worked hard to ensure, Victoria also recounts the teachings she learned on Yurok ways of behaving.

> When we learned about our Yurok ways, it didn't feel like school. It was something that you almost learn by the mistakes that you make. So, if I do something . . . you're taught why you don't do that or ahead of time you're taught why not to do certain things or *to* do certain things, like respect your elders. Like when you see an elder you make sure to recognize them, you at least greet them. You *always* do that. You see an elder—you may not even know that elder—but you go over there and you say hello and you greet them because that's

just part of being Yurok. When you see an elder come in the room, you get them some "*pa'ah*," you get them some water no matter what. You don't *ask* them if they want water, you go *get* them water and you set it there and give it to them. Those are the type of learnings that are just taught through experience.

The learning-through-experience model conveys the everyday practice of Yurok relationships: "Those rules that we have in place mean a lot. They may seem like small little things, but if you see an elder come in and you're sitting, you jump up and you let 'em sit down! Even if there's a lot of other seats, if you got a good seat, you let 'em sit down. Those are just the type of things that you're taught."

These cultural rules define the parameters of social interaction in ways that delimit accepted behavior in a given community. Maintaining the rules also upholds the worldview that accompanies their practice. Elders are to be respected for the wisdom and labor of their long lives, with the hope that younger people may someday assume their places.

Gendered Roles in Yurok Life as Part of Well-Being

In Yurok worldview, defined social roles extend to gender. Gender roles in Indigenous communities have been under scrutiny for a long time, with tensions between those advocating for universal rights and those arguing for relative ones. Some Indigenous communities, most notably the Zapatistas[6] in Chiapas, Mexico, have found ways to reconcile feminism with Indigenous values by condemning gender-based violence and other forms of power-based oppression, while also allowing voluntary participation in customs that include gendered divisions of labor (Eber and Kovic 2003, Rus, Hernández Castillo et al. 2003, Jung 2008).

Victoria asserts that Yurok culture maintains gendered division of roles, but they are meaningful and feel equitable to their participants. It is a fundamental part of Yurok cosmology, and discussion about it doesn't really take place in the community. There has not been notable disagreement about gender roles when they are operating in line with Yurok customs:

I have four brothers, and all my life I heard "Because he's a boy, he can do that." It was something I never questioned, that is just the way I knew it was by Indian law. We just know that these are the roles that we live by. Everyone contributes for the benefit of their village, the families, the children, the men and women. Most important is to take care of not just your family, but everyone in your village.

There are females in the community who live by the roles that women hold in Yurok life, but they also balance it with the equity between men and women. We know how to live by Indigenous rules of men and women, and we also know how to balance fair relationships with men and women. I know this is a sensitive subject. I think that the rules for women—like, you can't touch the eel hooks, you can't touch the drums, you can't dance all your life like the men can. It can sound so negative. Even with my daughters, it can be confusing because when girls are little they can do things, they can touch the drum. But once they are of a certain age, they shouldn't. Basically, when they are able to understand that they can't do something and what the reason is for it, they shouldn't do it anymore.

The culturally held rules that govern gender can be difficult for both outsiders and insiders to understand sometimes, but they are encoded Yurok traditions.

There isn't always a good reason for why. That's just the way it is. It's not lucky if a woman touches the drum. It's not a negative thing, it's just, that's what keeps balance in the world. As men have roles to provide for their family: hunt and gather and fish and ensure that they have a warm home with a fire, preserving the food for their family. So, too, women have their roles. All those things are important. Keeping their family safe from any harm, that's what best describes a Yurok man to me. And when a woman knows how to make good *key-goh*—acorn soup—or cut up a deer, those things are also looked upon as very good.

Nowadays, there's a lot of women who like to hunt and fish and do those things that men do and it's acceptable. It's showing that she is independent and strong. It isn't so strict that women can't do those things. We maintain ceremonially appropriate roles of gender balance, but things may look different at home.

Victoria's description of Yurok gender roles may not easily square with standard notions of universal feminism. But she is describing the mutual and complementary labor of community members in ways that keep the world in balance in Yurok cosmology. Her observation that ceremonial spaces may be the most strictly maintained in gendered division of labor, even as such gender roles do not always play out at home, also allows for cultural change over time, including the right to renegotiate certain roles as needed.

One way that culturally based practices are passed down is through immersive experiences during ceremonies or the preparation for them. Victoria recounts: "Some of the things that I like to remember and to look back on is, like, when we were camping out at Sregon.[7] We were there for a month and we were trying to bring back the Brush Dance grounds 'cause it hadn't been there in quite a few years. So, my grandma—she's from Sregon—said, 'Alright, well, we're gonna go down to Sregon and we're gonna have a brush dance there,' and so it was like, 'Okay!'"

Victoria goes on to share a formative moment in her own experience of gender roles as a young person:

> You don't really know what you're in for until you're actually there. You're there for thirty days and you wake up before the sun comes up. You're taught to—as a girl—wake up before the sun comes up or else! You don't wanna be like the girl who wakes up after the sun comes up, even though it's super early! You just get in there and you wash your face, you wash your hands, and you start preparing breakfast.
>
> And then, the first ones we feed are the men because they're out there doing the work to clear the dance grounds. And then you feed the children after the men get up, and then after the children all eat and leave, the women are allowed to sit down and have their breakfast and stuff. But you're not sitting down very long before you have to get up and start washing all the dishes and pretty much getting everything all cleaned up, and then it's like a repetitive cycle. . . . Women have to do a lot of work and stuff, but that's okay.

Victoria comments that she doesn't feel bad that women eat last or have to work so hard, because it is part of the women's work. Doing that work is seen as an honorable way of upholding one's labor. It makes people feel good to contribute to the greater good—it made her feel good to support her community and participate in it. And it gave her the opportunity to experience a lifestyle that reminded her of the traditions of her ancestors. In this way, Victoria's well-being is bound up in culturally specific ways of being in the world, even as she recognizes the fluidity of those roles in contemporary times.

As we spoke more about her experiences camping in Sregon, Victoria reflects, "I think those kinds of experiences really impacted my life. Knowing who I am and grounding in my culture. Knowing what I wanna teach my children in the future" (Carlson 2022). The experience of the closest thing she can imagine to traditional village life is a reminder of both why Victoria works for language survival, and what is at stake if cultural practices are not continued. Her identity as a parent factors strongly into the cultural survival work she does, with each transmission of cultural knowledge something she knows is laying the groundwork for the next generation to be rooted in their Yurok identities. Such rootedness provides the core sense of self within community from which well-being can flourish.

Yurok Language Reclamation as Well-Being

Language reclamation contributes to well-being for heritage speakers. Victoria is clear in her own philosophy of the role language plays in building and maintaining healthy communities: "I think learning your Indigenous language is one part to building a community. It is just one piece that contributes to knowing who you are. I believe it takes a community; it takes Tribal people, it takes elders, it takes knowing about ceremony, knowing about the Indian laws, having knowledge of gathering with your people, fishing with one another, the process of smoking your fish all together, and then taking care of one another."

Victoria learned this philosophy of care from her elders:

Growing up, my grandparents always told me, told all of us, how important it is to take care of one another. That a leader is not someone who just has the buildup of regalia, you know, baskets and all that. Those are physical things. What my grandfather taught me was that a leader in the community, in the Tribal community, was someone who takes care of others.

If someone's cold, you help them. You help them to where you
might have to go get them wood so they'll have a warm house or you
might have to invite them into your house 'cause they're cold. You
don't just let people go cold, you don't let people go hungry, and you
always take care of one another. That's what a real leader meant to
my grandfather.

Like her reflections on gender, Victoria's statements on leadership and community espouse ideas at the heart of Yurok worldviews. Such values and
practices have been directly challenged by contemporary plagues of drug
and alcohol addiction, as well as mental health issues related to the pandemic and intergenerational trauma.

Well-being is intimately connected to cultural survival because cultural
identity grounds people in knowing who they are and what purpose they
have in life. Victoria is crystal clear on the implications of this for her own
work, and that of the language community she is trying to grow and nur-
ture: "I think that we need to reclaim our language and the spaces where
language is used. We are reclaiming our language in spaces where language
hasn't existed in quite some time and bringing it to new spaces where we want
to have language be heard. Resisting the use of English and instead using the
words that you know in Yurok is definitely hard, but that's what language
reclamation work is. Even if it's one word that you say in Yurok instead of
English, you're showing resistance to that [English and colonialism], you're
showing that our language is still alive."

For Victoria, keeping the Yurok language alive and flourishing is a path to
community well-being. She believes that:

The Yurok language thriving in our community and our families,
with our children, youth, and elders, is something that is invaluable.
The stories of our elders are vital to be carried on to the next generation. The language lies within ourselves and it is up to us to keep it
going, keep it alive. 'Cause the Yurok language is our true connection
to our ancestors, our environment, our river, our animals, and our
people. I truly believe without our language we wouldn't be able to
call ourselves *Oohl* [Indian people], *Pue-leek-lah* [downriver people],
and *pey-cheek-lah* [upriver people].[8] We would be lost without our
language.

The Yurok language itself offers the key to the use of terms like downriver and upriver: words that tribes and individuals use to identify and distinguish themselves. "Being lost," as Victoria describes, is something that can undermine well-being. In contrast, the continuation of stories, knowledge, and language is part of survivance in the face of settler colonialism. Yurok language supports this well-being.

Language is, of course, so much more than a means to the end goal of mutually intelligible communication. Language holds encoded worldviews, which are at stake as so many Indigenous and minority languages are repressed out of existence. Studying language for language's sake is a worthy goal because language carries so much cultural knowledge: "I also want us to know the deeper meanings of the language, to carry that on. Like, we have words—*sey-gap*—for years we taught it as 'coyote.' It's the word for coyote, but when you look into the deeper meaning of that word, it comes from the word *sey-po-lah* which is a 'meadow' or a 'prairie.' It means 'the one who is always in the meadow or the prairie, *sey-po-lah*.' So, keeping that deeper meaning of the language and making sure that we're teaching that and learning that is very important to me. Anyone can say, 'Oh, that's coyote,' but what does it really mean in the language?"

Getting to these deeper meanings takes hard work. But such work is vital for the integrity of the language itself:

> We do talk about—as language advocates, language learners, and language keepers—keeping the integrity of our language. So that's not an easy thing. It's an easy thing to say, but it's not an easy thing to do because it takes a lot of repetition and studying and listening to audio to try to sound as close to the speech of the elders or fluent speakers as we can—to the way they said it. Because if you say something just a little bit off, or you're not adding a certain emphasis, or your voice pitch is maybe not changing, then you're not saying the same word.
>
> We have to continue to talk about the integrity of our language and how we wanna keep those sounds that we don't have in English, that are in Yurok, and really not try to fit English into Yurok sounds. Like when we say *nek new* and it's not "neck now," like, in English the word "neck" and "now" and it's hard when people first start trying to say it. It's okay to make mistakes when you're first learning language, but just knowing that eventually you just keep practicing and you'll get it—*nek new*.

Victoria's example of the cultural meaning imbuing a vocabulary word resonates. I think of my own language-learning processes with Spanish, French,
Turkish, and others spread over a lifetime. The lightbulb moments of how
culture informs language and language shapes culture are part of the magic
of language learning.[9]

Learning any language takes practice and perseverance. Yurok in this
respect is no different. But because the speaker community is so small, the
stakes are extremely high. By approaching language and cultural reclamation
more broadly as tools for well-being, it may be easier to integrate them into
a range of community spaces and programs, alongside expanding their presence in formal education.

Conclusion

Victoria's life's work is to keep the Yurok language alive. For her, speaking the
language is living in well-being. Her own words about this close the chapter:

> Just like what our elders said, if we stop teaching our language, stop
> learning our language, then it'll just be gone, and it'll be something
> that has been lost within our culture and I can't accept that! I can't let
> that happen while I'm here on earth during this time, because I know
> the work and the time and the effort that our elders put into passing
> on our language, keeping our language alive. I have to continue that
> and ensure that it's in our Tribal community. We have to make sure
> that it's in our homes, we have to make sure that language is alive
> when we go out to the store, when we go to our ceremonies, when
> we see people in the community during events and activities.
>
> We need to keep making sure that we are speaking and hearing
> our language so that way our younger generation can hear it and
> know that they're the next ones in line to carry it on. And so, if they
> see community members and leaders speaking the language, work-
> ing hard to continue the language, then they'll wanna do that when
> they get older and teach their children someday.
>
> One day when we'll be able to all speak together, in these spaces
> where the language has gone dormant, it'll be—I could just picture
> us, laughing and speaking the language and conversing with one
> another and understanding one another and having that safe and

comfortable environment, like this is the way it was a long time ago! Bringing that back is a goal of mine as a language-keeper.

I'll hear my mom talk about, "Oh, I used to hear the elders, I used to hear mom and dad speak with other elders, speaking the language" and they were just laughing and they were just having a good time and being just immersed in the language. And she doesn't hear that anymore. So, I wanna be able to have that, to have those moments where me and my husband are speaking in the language and our kids can understand us and we're laughing. But not just for my family, but for all of our Tribal community, is really my inspiration.

PART IV

The Road to Well-Being

CHAPTER 11

Conclusion: Reimaging Education
for Well-Being

At HVHS, a Missing and Murdered Indigenous People flyer was squeezed next to others, edges rustling through windy hallways. Another flyer displayed the words "True Warriors Respect Women" printed in the school colors: red, white, and black. Sharing a staple was a flyer proclaiming "Don't be afraid to speak up! Know your rights as a teen" with smaller print telling teens to check for workplace safety and giving a number to call if they need help. Next to these flyers was an advertisement for Two Feathers' mental health programs and the high school's Rainbow Collective, a partnership with Two Feathers to make safe space for the 2SLGBTQAI+[1] community to gain support and celebrate queer community and joy. I marveled at the use of one strip of wall to hold so many messages about well-being all at once.

It isn't a coincidence this bulletin board is laden at a school. In many communities, schools are focal points of information and connection. The pressure on schools to become full-stop service centers addressing a range of insecurities from food to clothing to medical care is intense. For some of the administrators and staff I spoke with at multiple schools, it can be overwhelming. In addition to coat drives and evening and weekend meal packages to send home with students who would otherwise be hungry until the next school day, schools like HVHS have sought out grants to build wellness centers on campus. Recognizing the many barriers to obtaining health care for families living in poverty in remote locations, HVHS is trying to address both mental and physical health of students and their families right on its own campus. EHS is also creating a wellness center to shift some of the mental health care burden to professional staff from teachers and school success counselors who do not have clinical training, yet are on the front lines of wellness challenges.

Youth well-being depends on these often-fragile networks of care to get through childhood. School care networks have put so much effort into ameliorating the physical aspects of harm—what Ross, Hinton, et al. (2020) define as the objective domains of well-being. In light of the COVID-19 pandemic there is also increased attention to mental health on school campuses, alongside supports for learning accessibility. Yet two central issues—curricular misrepresentation and school climate—continue to be overlooked.

Curricula for Well-Being

Educational curricula have been much slower to change than legal and cultural norms in the United States, in part because of the massive bureaucratic and market infrastructure that produces and sustains them. The driving force of a capitalistic textbook publishing industry compounds the reluctance to disrupt myths of White glory. Changing what is actually taught in classrooms requires not only reframing old stories from multiple perspectives, but getting market forces to affirm it and school districts to approve and adopt it. Such change also requires supporting teachers—including in mainstream requirements like US history—to feel comfortable teaching perspectives that they themselves may not have learned until later adulthood. In the meantime, textbooks keep repeating the same worn, racist tropes (Yacovone 2022), with little evolution across the decades.

School curricula are difficult to improve because doing so requires painful confrontation with White supremacy. The lack of curricular innovation is not because there is a lack of information available to those who form, select, and implement curricula (Gellman 2024: 15, 93). There are many books that communicate the value of Native American people and other BIPOC populations; they just aren't the books selected by school districts to be taught. For example, instead of the thousand-page military glorification tomes frequently used as the core textbooks in US history courses, Roxanne Dunbar-Ortiz's *An Indigenous People's History of the United States* could be used to offer a critical, Native-centered accounting of historical events. Alternative texts abound, but implementing such change will require revisions to standardized testing and teacher education, not to mention the more subtle work of deconstructing assumptions about what curricula should be, and ultimately, who it is for.

School boards, superintendents, curriculum committees, principals, teachers, parents, and students themselves can all be part of this change. There are flickers of hope. In 2022, the Humboldt County Office of Education, which oversees three of the four schools included in this study, received a grant from the California Department of Education, alongside the San Diego County Office of Education, to develop a Native American Studies Model Curriculum. Dozens of listening sessions and community report-backs have been conducted in both counties, and new curricular materials are being crafted by Native American Learning Specialists (HCOE 2024). As someone who has sat in on a range of county-level meetings on this curriculum, I am hopeful in seeing community-level leaders recognize the myriad positive benefits of engaging in curricular revisions and including Native American Studies in multiple forms.

Such curricular work is labor-intensive and requires advocacy at every level of both political and educational systems. Nevertheless, it can be highly impactful, with curricular shifts having the potential to uplift the well-being of all students. Native students will benefit directly through identity-affirming content, and all students will benefit by being educated accurately on Native history and contemporary presence. Teachers will, too, benefit from increased accuracy of historical and cultural content, as will staff and the wider communities around the schools. Such a curricular shift is an investment in long-term structural wellness for society at large. With the layers of White supremacist doctrine peeled away, mutual recognition is more likely to take place. This is in line with tribal critical race theory's first tenet, that colonization is embedded in society and that we need to reckon with it.

School Climate as Community Climate

For many BIPOC youth, going to school each day can feel like a battle for survival. Whether from racialized bullying or other forms of negative messaging toward their communities of ancestral origin, students navigate difficult school climates constantly, in K–12 through college (Solorzano, Ceja et al. 2000, Maramba and Museus 2013, Nance 2015, Rivera 2022). As this book's title invokes, there is a double meaning in *learning to survive*. Students are both learning to survive the schooling experiences they are in, and they are also trying to survive in life as they transition to adulthood. For many BIPOC students, they are learning to survive both in and after school by achieving the "success in both worlds" that the Yurok Tribe advocates. Success within one's ethnic identity of origin and success within "colonized life," as Thayallen Gensaw put it, both matter. Learning for academic and life success allows Native American students to survive and overcome the structural barriers put in place by generations of settler-colonial policies and practices. Learning to survive takes place simultaneously within schools and in the lives students imagine for themselves afterward.

School climate is not determined in isolation solely by school personnel and students themselves. At its core, school climate is governed by the wider social and cultural norms of human interaction that students encounter through daily interactions with peers, but also from social media, news, religious organizations, pop culture, and family members, among many other variables. What is happening in school is usually happening at the grocery store, the mall, or the gas station. As I noted in Chapter 1, numerous variables, such as addiction, poverty, unemployment, illicit economies, domestic violence, mental health issues, homelessness, and many more, shape students' lived experience and the school climates they are in.

But, like changes in civic engagement among the citizenry at large (Nelsen 2021, Nelsen 2023), school climate can shift, even though the forces against such shifts may sometimes feel insurmountable. Basic social decency must prevail, but first, young people from many backgrounds have to agree on what those social norms and procedures are. At the very least, agreeing to not insult each other and to not inhibit each other's sovereignty would appear to be the lowest common denominator that can act as a starting point. When people are gracious and inclusive of each other, or conversely divisive and discriminatory, such norms become the social architecture of schools, governmental and non-governmental organizations, and other social spaces. Thus, it is difficult to facilitate culture change because culture is created through numerous intersecting layers of human life. Reducing racism and discrimination within school micro-climates implies the necessity of change in other social spaces. School climate change comes from societal climate change and vice versa. These are reciprocal processes, not linear ones. Being honest about the scale and scope of the work will allow us to approach it with a realistic sense of the distance we need to culturally travel.

It is worth remembering that although culture change is not easy, it does happen. For example, in my lifetime, national- and state-level reforms from same-sex marriage to the legalization of marijuana have taken place, but would have been unthinkable when I was a kid. Such change took place because of determined and ongoing collective action by people who identified a problem, conceived of a solution, and petitioned decision-makers until the solution became imperative to implement. Such a mobilization model is within reach for schools and community spaces too.

And yet, change is not unidirectional, only headed toward a progressive future. As this book went to press, the Trump administration's all-out assault on education is being rolled out. The Department of Education has been ordered to close via executive order, and all references to diversity, equity, and inclusion and other key concepts that address difference and how to engage it deliberately are being scrubbed from federal websites, mandates, and funding streams. Such a context makes it hard to imagine federal-level interest in Yurok well-being in this era, and yet this is where states, counties, and local school districts can benefit from the devolution of power back to states. HCOE, KTJUSD, and others are poised to showcase their innovation through culturally sustaining curricula. Local students will benefit, as will students in other places whose administrators and teachers are willing to learn from the model curricula. Even in the hardest moments, we can remember that survival itself is a form of resistance. Asserting one's ability to act and exert influence—what Elisabeth Jean Wood calls "the pleasure of agency" (2001: 272)—also fuels well-being.

At the same time, shifting school climate has more subtle benchmarks than federal administrative or legislative changes. Reducing discriminatory behavior in schools might look like the absence of insults—a hard metric to measure. But the absence of data is still data. The difference that it can make in the lives of Native American youth to *not* be called "r–dskin" in the hallway, as Thayallen was, to not be war-whooped and called "chief" as Mr. Gensaw's Native American club dancers were, is meaningful. The absence of insults means that Native American students can feel more welcome, connected, and invested in their own schooling. Such a sense of belonging has the potential to translate into stronger student success outcomes for young people, including a greater interest in envisioning further education for themselves beyond K–12.

All students should be able to move through school feeling proud of who they are, not demeaned for it. Some might say that addressing the curricular problems discussed in this book risks making White students feel guilty for a past in which they personally did not contribute violence toward BIPOC identities. Indeed, I have faced this argument with some school district–level personnel when sharing my research findings back to the communities. It is critical to resist this framing because it is an excuse for perpetuating White supremacy. If diminishing the pride often found in the experiences and identities of White students only occurs when they are finally told the truth about genocide, then perhaps we need to look at how that identity-based pride was built in in the first place. Persisting beyond "White fragility" (DiAngelo 2022) is an imperative for peaceful, intercultural coexistence. What's more, I am convinced young people are perfectly capable of learning from age-appropriate truth-telling, whether it is about Native American genocide, the Holocaust, or other forms of human rights violations. They don't need to be shown gory pictures to unpack the way that societal privilege operates. In fact, addressing structural violence helps explain the world as it is—the reasons for inequality and social ills become more evident when framed through historically accurate information about the structural contours of the past.

When we prevent curricular reform, what we are really saying is that White children deserve protection from stories about inequality because it might make them feel bad about their undeserved, phenotypical-based privilege. BIPOC children do not get the luxury of this protection. As Black children are taught from an early age how to handle interactions with police to avoid getting shot, so, too, are Native American children taught about the impact of boarding schools to explain intergenerational trauma. Why should White children be protected from the world as it is? Doing so reinforces asymmetries that play out in so many life arenas.

Curricular reform and school climate interventions are two ways that schools impact the identity-formation process of young people. Leaving things as the status quo—perpetuating harm against minority students through both formal curricula and school climate—continues cycles of assimilatory behavior mixed with self-doubt. We know that affirming self-esteem of young people contributes to a range of lifelong benefits, including school completion—which opens doors to college, careers, and financial stability—and contributes to pluriethnic flourishing, the basis for any functional democracy. Everybody deserves that. Supporting youth well-being in school is an investment in our shared future.

A Well-Being Toolkit

Everybody's child should have equal access to a basic toolkit for well-being, affirming who they are as a meaningful contributor to their community. When schools affirm the identity of their most vulnerable populations, it also sends messages about inclusiveness and the value of a diverse community. Addressing structural injustice is a multistep process that starts with settler-descendant residents having the tools to recognize that there is a problem in the first place. Next, facilitating structural change to address the root causes of violence—physical, emotional, societal, and more—is critical to promoting youth wellness.

There are concrete steps that can be taken to help young people thrive. At the structural level, changes that can promote youth well-being might include: intercultural competency training for all school personnel, including teachers as well as staff, from front office workers to bus drivers; curricular revision from the state and district level down to the classroom level; mandatory, compensated teacher trainings on up-to-date best practices for culturally sustaining pedagogy within their particular disciplines; school security practices that do not disproportionately profile or discipline BIPOC youth; partnerships between schools and community groups to enable guest speaker bureaus to bring local cultural expertise into classrooms; and partnerships to connect students and their families to resources for a range of insecurities.

Although it is true that it is a burden for schools to serve as a one-stop shop for families to access broader social services, the bottom line is that schools are the most common place to encounter the state in family life, and therefore school partnerships make sense when addressing issues like food, clothing, and housing insecurity. County or district mental health services, or nonprofit organizations like Humboldt County's Two Feathers, can work with schools to reach youth in need of their services. Some places, like rural Hoopa Valley High School, are piloting ways to bring wellness care, including mental and physical health care services, onto campus for students and for their families, recognizing that schools are the most regular point of contact for potential service providers and thus make families more likely to seek care.

Innovations like socio-emotional curricula and restorative justice techniques are part of setting school climate trends. And while the larger political climate will inevitably infiltrate school climate, modeling healthy interpersonal behaviors among staff, from district to school and across ranks, can show students how to navigate complex relationships. Even when people disagree with each other, it need not be done in personalized ways that tear people down. Calling people in, rather than calling them out, can set the foundation for evolving together while maintaining mutual dignity. It might feel small, but from little actions, relationships grow.

Everybody's Child

When I checked back in on Meri through our shared network in 2024, I heard she was no longer attending Del Norte High School but had instead enrolled in a high school equivalency program. She had a stable routine with full-time work and was doing well, able to support herself and contribute to her family economically. I hope she and the many other young people I spoke with over the course of researching this book are figuring out how to both survive and thrive.

Survivance is a lifelong process. I think about youth well-being constantly, like when I see teenagers in Boston, overflowing in their adult bodies but sucking lollipops and swinging on the swings in the playground where my child and his friend play. The teens type away on their glittery phones and post suggestive pictures to social media while kicking their legs in the wood chips. What messages are they projecting? What awaits them at home? Who lifts them up or shoots them down—sometimes literally—at school? I worry for Meri and other young people like her, but I am committed to staying hopeful and searching for solutions.

In summer 2022 I drove with my family out on Highway 96, a snake-like country road that runs from Willow Creek through the Hoopa Valley Indian Reservation and deep into the Californian mountains. We were heading over to I-5, up to Oregon to visit friends, and decided to take the scenic route. When we passed through Hoopa, I pointed the schools out to my kids. "They teach Yurok there, and that's where I do my interviews!" Distracted from their backseat snacking, they were mildly curious about where I had been disappearing to every so often all semester. In their minds—seven and ten years old at the time—"research" just equated to Mamá being away from them.

Highway 96 is spectacular in its isolation. There is no mistaking that nature is in charge. Whatever we humans might think about our own power to contain the wild, it isn't happening out past Happy Camp. The paved road has a skinny lane in each direction desperately kissing the side of the mountain, with broken asphalt trailing off the edges in places where earthquakes or landslides have destabilized the road. Perched hundreds of feet above surging river water, it is hard not to imagine my own death by car accident every time I pass another vehicle, especially big trucks.

The landscape is the kind of gorgeous that artists try to capture. Alders grow out of boulder cracks like magicians. A deer sprints out of the underbrush, vultures catch the currents in lazy sky circles. Oak trees tower and cast their shade, their acorns a main traditional foodstuff for local Native communities, who gather, soak, heat, and grind them into flour for use in staple foods. We see very few fellow humans on the drive.

And yet, in dozens of dusty roadside pull-offs along more than a hundred miles of rural road in and near Yurok, Hupa, and Karuk territories, people have staged an advocacy campaign. Red dresses and red-print shirts flap in the wind on plastic hangers suspended from tree branches. Handprints, made by someone's hands dipped in red paint and layered onto the fabric of the dresses and shirts, advertise pain. Rocks have been lined up to make a circle around the base of the trees, but we whiz past, with momentum toward a destination. After passing several of these protest shrines too quickly, I make my husband stop the car. We unspool from our seats, joints cracking, crumbs brushed.

The faces of disappeared Native women are printed on paper and covered with clear tape to protect them from the elements. Nevertheless, moisture has gotten in and seeped its inky tears. Their names, dates gone missing, a number to call if found, are listed below smiling snapshots, photos taken when they were still with people who loved them. "We Want Them Back!" proclaims one sign. "Bring back our daughters!" demands another. "Stop the Violence" insists a third, on posterboard duct-taped to a kindling-size stick stuck in the ground. It is homemade, grassroots, straightforward, and powerful. Naming what needs to be said. Plaintive.

The campaign to address the disproportionate number of Missing and Murdered Indigenous People in the United States and Canada has been gaining visibility in the 2010s and 2020s as the numbers keep climbing. A poster on an HVHS bulletin board in spring 2022 stated "5,712 Native women were reported missing or murdered in 2016. Now we've lost count." The MMIP campaign uses the slogan "Somebody's daughter" and the image of a red handprint over the mouth of a young woman as their logo. That image is

global, and I've seen it in country after country, from Indigenous rights con-
ferences in Massachusetts to Mexican International Women's Day marches. In
2023, strolling through an artisan market in Santiago, Chile, while on break
from a conference, I bought a photograph of a Chilean woman with the red
handprint over her mouth. The photographer attending his booth described
that she was protesting state violence against young activists and the silencing
of girls and women at the same time. I commented on how many places I've
seen it, and how much I wanted the campaign to work. We shared a knowing
silence; I handed over pesos. That photograph now sits on the bookshelf in
my faculty office in Boston, not letting me forget, demanding that I speak.

The roadside shrines use the red handprint too. The image is as powerful as it is distressing. The bloody connotation of the handprint leaves no
ambiguity about what happens when people have been disappeared. Girls
and women are being silenced. Murdered by domestic partners, or abducted,
raped, and killed by strangers, the lives of Native women have been cast as
expendable. Their own well-being is demolished by violence, while the well-
being of their communities is also shattered by the loss of a sister, a mother, a
daughter. The photos are a reminder that violence produces not just statistics.
They quantify trauma.

I count more than a dozen of these shrines as we continue on our family
road trip. Highway 96 is an interesting choice for their installation. It must be
in the running for one of the most desolate roads in California. But the inten-
tionality is evident. The highway spans Yurok, Hupa, and Karuk communities, and the people whose loved ones have disappeared drive those roads. So
do the perpetrators.

People involved in educational campaigns on MMIP are trying to raise
awareness, especially among young people. Art is a powerful communica-
tor on this issue.[1] From local press coverage to posters in storefronts, there
is a hope that increased knowledge about MMIP will decrease power-based
violence. Some young women who end up with their faces on the roadside
shrine posters previously attended local high schools. School bulletin boards,
as mentioned in Chapter 11, are also sites of awareness-raising.

My children initially groan when we pull the car over to visit the MMIP
shrines. They are White, they are privileged, and insulated from so many
harms. My daughter is taught to take no flak from anyone and to speak up if
her autonomy is compromised. I don't worry that she will become an MMIP
statistic. But I worry she will be complacent in the violence that happens when
societies ignore harms happening to those with the least resources. I worry

that my son will be another White male reveling in the self-congratulatory history that blinds him to its omissions. So I make us stop, insist on showing them, even though they don't want to see.

I remember my parents teaching my eight-year-old self about poverty, in their own kinesthetic way. They explained, as I looked out the window of our rattling Subaru crossing the border into Mexico for a childhood vacation, two life lessons. First, they taught me that a lack of resources is not something that people should be discriminated against for, and second, that we have an ethical obligation to alleviate suffering when we see it. The first lesson has catalyzed me to find structural ways to address well-being through my professional life, using my platform to address structural harm in the areas that I do research. The second haunts me, because I see suffering everywhere and I must work to narrow the ways in which I try to intervene. I can't fix everything, but I have to be part of fixing something. My parents' words helped make sense of the shacks we passed on that trip and the lifetime of hunger-swollen bellies and outstretched hands I have encountered in my worldly travels. The pain of it doesn't diminish, because I can't unsee or unknow once I see and know. But absorbing the facts of suffering, and finding ways to disrupt it, keep me from feeling paralyzed. Knowledge offers a path to intervention.

In the swirling dust of midday heat, I explain that we can't just be bystanders. They nod and look away. We squat to pee, swig from our water bottles, and stretch. I reread the posters to them, drill them on what they would do if anyone they knew was in danger. Who would they tell? How would they break the silence? I teach my college students this too. I reiterate, belabor. We have to speak up, make noise, demand what is right. Our children need to learn this. Everybody's children need to learn this. Who are we waiting for to do this work, if not ourselves?

APPENDICES

Research Proposal for Collaborative Study on Language, Identity, and Wellness: Yurok Language Access and Resilience

Overview

The proposed study is to look at the impact of Yurok language access on supporting wellness, with specific case studies at Del Norte High School and McKinleyville High School, to take place in 2021–2023. In addition, this study will draw on data from community Yurok classes and Yurok classes offered in Head Start and K–8 levels. Methods of data collection will include ethnography, interviews, focus groups, and surveys. The research design, including the research puzzle, case study selection, and types of questions included in the data collection, will be generated collaboratively with the Yurok Education Department.

Purpose of the Research

1. To advance understanding of the impact of Yurok language classes in relation to youth identity and behavior both during and after high school.

This proposal was generated in collaboration with, and approved by, the Yurok Education Department in July 2021. This is the final research proposal approved by the Yurok Tribal Council at December 2021.

2. To document the relationship between Yurok language access and wellness.
3. To further thinking about Yurok language as an intergenerational resiliency tool.
4. To connect culturally relevant teaching to broader issues of student success and well-being.

Research Puzzle

This study poses the question: how is Yurok language access connected to wellness?

Specifically, what is the role of Yurok language access as a tool for healing in mental health and recovery? The hypothesis is that Yurok language exposure positively reinforces the Native identities of students, and this kind of education-based identity support helps build resiliency. Resilience in turn may serve as a protective factor in mitigating youth risk. If this hypothesis bears out, it could then be argued that Yurok language access and cultural connection can potentially reduce harm and violence among those with this access. The larger implications of this study are connected to historical trauma, legacies of genocide and culturecide, and the future of pluriethnic coexistence.

While data collection will take place to test this argument, previous work on a related topic provides positive reinforcement. Mneesha Gellman worked with the Yurok Education Department in 2016–2021 on a project addressing the impact of Yurok language access at Eureka High School and Hoopa Valley High School on youth identity and participation. That study, which is comparative with high schools in southern Mexico, will be published in *Indigenous Language Politics: Cultural Survival in Mexico and the United States* (forthcoming 2023). The book argues that youth who have access to Indigenous languages in high school curricula are better able to resist culturecide—the killing of culture that persists as a tool of settler colonialism—and are also better able to conceptualize participating in meaningful ways in their communities. This next project extends the case studies to include the other two high schools where Yurok is taught, and also connects language directly to discussions of community resilience. This topic is of interest to many of the Yurok Education Department's stakeholders, including past, current, or potential funders.

Examples of Questions

For Yurok language students, teachers in interviews, focus groups, and surveys

Climate and Success

- How does existence of Yurok language class at school affect interest in coming to school? Staying in school? School climate? Community climate? Knowledge of Yurok culture and existence by non-Native students?
- What resources do you wish you had in school that you don't have?
- What do you want to do after high school? For those who say college, what do you want to do after college? Why?

Yurok Language Access Impact

- How has taking Yurok language classes affected relationships with friends? Family? Community?
- How has knowledge of Yurok language impacted interests in participating in Yurok community events? Dances? Youth council? Other examples?
- Can you give an example of something you've heard about in Yurok class that you have used in a particular moment in your life?
- What are the advantages and disadvantages to taking Yurok language classes?
- Have you taken Native American Studies or other classes that emphasize Native content in past, present, and future? How do you see cultures or identities lifted or silenced in school? Communities?
- Do you hear or learn language anywhere outside of high school class? Did you take Yurok in Head Start or K–8? Do you have family members who take community language classes? Do you ever use language outside school class?

Some of these questions can be used in modified form with school administrators and other adult community members

- How do you see yourself using Yurok language on a daily basis? Are there ways you practice Yurok now that you could imagine doing more of once the class is over? How can Yurok continue for you post-high school?
- Has the Yurok language class given you new ideas for what your career/future endeavors might be as an adult? Any new goals for your family and community?
- What new conversations or experiences have you had with your family since you began taking Yurok classes? Please describe.
- What tools has Yurok given you that you will take with you after high school?

Language and Wellness

- Could you describe a time when you used Yurok language or culture to help you through a hard time or difficult situation?
- Has Yurok language changed your sense of self-esteem, if at all? How does your inner strength or confidence connect to things you have learned in Yurok class, if at all?
- In your own experience, or that of your friends or family, can you describe how language connects to identity? To wellness? To mental health?
- What do youth do to keep themselves well? What do their families or peers do?
- What mental health resources or recovery resources do students have available to them? What resources do they wish they or their families had?
- What does it mean to be resilient? Successful? Healthy?
- How could you imagine using Yurok language later in life? In work? With family? Etc.

Intergenerational Resilience

- How have you been affected by hard things in your lives, or how have elders or other family members been affected? (*Leave this open to avoid retraumatizing—students who are comfortable speaking to this can, but state that they should only share what they feel comfortable sharing. Otherwise, this type of general information can be accessed by interviewing school counselors, language teachers, other adults in the community, and from media and literature.)*

QUESTIONS BELOW ARE FOR YUROK-IDENTIFIED
STUDENTS, OR STUDENTS FROM OTHER NATIVE
BACKGROUNDS, ADJUST AS NEEDED.

- Do you have anyone in your family who was a first language Yurok speaker?
- Is there anyone in your family that you are able to learn Yurok language from today?
- How do you think your language experience might be different from those who spoke Yurok as a first language?
- How do you think your experience of Yurok language might be different from those of your elders?
- Did anyone in your family attend boarding schools?
- If so, how has that experience affected your family?
- How do you see the connection between your family's past experiences of Yurok language and your own as a Yurok language student in 2022?
- How could you use the Yurok language and cultural knowledge shared in class to help yourself and family members continue to learn and stay strong and healthy in the future?

Informational Letter for Participants: Students, Parents, Guardians, and Community Members

Project Title: Speaking Wellness:
Connections between language access and
community resilience

Researcher: Dr. Mneesha Gellman, Associate Professor of Political Science, Emerson College, in collaboration with Yurok Education Department and Yurok Language Program staff

Introduction and Purpose

My name is Mneesha Gellman and I am an Associate Professor of Political Science at Emerson College, Boston. I research how individuals and communities generate resilience in the face of adversity. I am working with the Yurok Tribe Education Department and Yurok Language Program staff to research how access to learning the Yurok language impacts people's lives. I also look comparatively at the role of Spanish and other Indigenous languages. Information from this study will be used to develop academic materials such as articles, conference presentations, and books, and also could be used by the Yurok Tribe in grant applications and policy documents. The purpose of the research is to better understand what learning Yurok, Spanish, and other Indigenous languages means to people as they navigate identity, schooling, and life circumstances.

Project Summary

You are being asked to take part in this research study because of you or your child's connection to the study themes of language and wellness. Active participation can take three forms: surveys, focus groups, and interviews. Surveys do not ask for identifying information and take ten to fifteen minutes to complete during class time. There is no risk of identification because your name is not recorded in the survey.

Focus groups take 45–90 minutes and will be audio-recorded. Given that one is conversing with one's peers, there is a risk of loss of confidentiality because of peer-to-peer dialogue. After focus group conversations are transcribed, they will be coded to remove any identifying information before I use them further.

Interviews entail a 30–60 minute one-on-one conversation with me, and can have your or your child's name included or not, and be audio-recorded or not, depending on the preferences indicated on the consent forms. There is a risk of loss of privacy if you choose to participate with your name, but if you choose to participate anonymously, your comments will be deidentified. Risks for interviewees include a similar degree of discomfort someone might have discussing topics of language and wellness in their daily life. Although there may be no direct benefit to you for participating, you are contributing to knowledge that may be used both in academia and in education policy.

You can give your consent to participate, withhold it, or change your mind about participating at any time. Please read this entire form before you decide if you want to participate and then mark your corresponding preferences for participation on the permission form.

Privacy and Participation Procedures

If you choose to participate without revealing your name, I will not ask you for your last name at any point and it will not be included in the audio recording. I will assign to you a unique code that will allow me to match your answers in my notes, but any identifying information will be stored in a separate cabinet or electronic cloud from notes on your opinions. Any identifying information, including signed informed consent forms, will be kept in a binder that will be placed in a locked filing cabinet at Emerson College, or in a password-protected cloud, along with any notes that I type, or audio recordings.

In the surveys, focus groups, and interviews, depending on your own expertise, I may ask questions about language, identity, education, and adversity. You can opt not to respond to any question, as you choose. You are invited to participate in all aspects of the study, but you can select your preferences for participation on the informed consent form, for example, participating in one type but not the other, or not participating at all. These ways of participating will conclude your role in the study at this time. After the interview, I may contact you by email to follow up on points of clarification, but you are not obligated to respond.

Data Policies

In an effort to support data access and sovereignty, if granted permission, I will consider providing deidentified data (no names, locations, or other readily identifiable attributes) to approved researchers only through the Qualitative Data Repository (qdr.syr.edu), an online academic archive which securely preserves the data. Despite my best efforts to take out any personal information from the data, I cannot guarantee complete anonymity for data that might go into QDR.

Your participation in the project can happen whether you agree to this or not. You will be able to indicate separately (in Section 6 of the permission form) whether you want to have your deidentified data shared with other researchers in this way or not. I will only do interviews, focus groups, or surveys with people who have signed an informed consented form, and for minors, who have also returned signed consent forms from a parent or guardian. Your data may only go to QDR if you opt in on the permission form.

Risks, Benefits, and Rights

Your participation does not involve any risks other than what you would encounter in daily life in school or your community discussing the study themes. Your responses will only be used if you have granted permission, and you can choose to participate with or without revealing your name, as you prefer. You can also decide at the end of an interview to be quoted only anonymously in any published materials, even if you previously gave permission for your name to be retained in the data.

There may be no direct benefit to you by your participation in this research study. One potential indirect benefit may be the ability of the Yurok Tribe to advocate for Yurok language access with data documenting its impact, or for Spanish heritage organizations to similarly use data connected to Spanish access impact. There is no monetary compensation for participation.

Confidentiality

Participation in this research study may result in a loss of privacy, since persons other than myself might view the record of your participation. Unless required by law, only myself, the Emerson College Institutional Review Board, and representatives from the Office for Human Research Protections (DHHS) will have authority to review your full participation records. Yurok Tribe staff will have the right to review the Yurok data, however, any reviewers are required to maintain confidentiality regarding your individual identity unless you have given permission to be identified by name. Results from this project may be used for teaching, research, publications, presentations at professional meetings, or advocacy for language access. Deidentified data from those participants who have agreed to this will be shared with others studying related topics with secure access in the QDR research archive, as described above.

Please indicate on the informed consent forms if you prefer to be cited with your name or not, audio-recorded or not, and whether you agree to having your deidentified (names, locations, etc. removed) transcripts shared with other researchers after the end of the project.

Contacts

If you have questions about your rights as a research participant, you may contact the Emerson College Institutional Review Board (IRB), which is concerned with the protection of volunteers in research projects [email redacted].

You can also contact me directly: Mneesha Gellman
Address, Email, Phone: [redacted]

Thank you for considering participating in this research project.

Multilevel Permissions Form

Parent/Guardian/Student Permission Form

THIS FORM SHOULD BE FILLED OUT BY STUDENTS AND PARENTS/ GUARDIANS TOGETHER

I have read the attached informational letter for the study, "Speaking Wellness: Connections between language access and community resilience." I understand that any publication produced based on this research will honor the preferences marked below. All information will be kept in secure files maintained by the researcher during the course of the project. Any files shared with other researchers after the end of project, according to participants' permissions in Section 6, will not be publicly available, will be digitally encrypted and maintained by a professional academic data archive.

Indicate preferences below by marking one answer per section

1) **Survey participation:**

   ____ I AGREE to allow my child to fill out survey forms (will not collect names).

   ____ I DO NOT agree to allow my child to fill out survey forms.

2) **Focus groups:**

   ____ I AGREE to allow my child to participate in focus groups, which will be audio-recorded. Focus group participants will not be asked to give their names.

   ____ I DO NOT agree to allow my child to participate in focus groups.

3) **Individual interviews:**

   ____ I AGREE to allow my child to participate in individual interviews, which may be audio-recorded.

_____ I DO NOT agree to allow my child to participate in individual interviews.

4) If you agreed to an interview in section 3, please choose from below:

_____ I agree for my child's NAME TO BE USED with individual comments.

_____I agree for my child to participate WITHOUT THEIR NAME. I understand that if my child's individual comments are discussed, their identity will be protected with a code or pseudonym.

5) **Future participation:**

If you are open to the possibility of your child participating in this project in future years, please indicate how I may contact you:

Phone: _____

Email: _____

6) **Data sharing:**

_____ I AGREE to allow my child's deidentified data to be available to other approved researchers through the Qualitative Data Repository (QDR, qdr.syr.edu).

_____ I DO NOT agree to have my child's deidentified data available in QDR.

I understand that I may contact the researcher, Dr. Mneesha Gellman, at any point during the study to ask questions or raise concerns, via telephone, email, or mail: [redacted]. I also understand that my child's participation is voluntary and that I can decline or withdraw my child from the study at any point without penalty.

*BOTH STUDENT AND PARENT/GUARDIAN SIGNATURES ARE REQUIRED FOR PARTICIPATION

Student's Name (print)	Student Signature	Date

Parent or Guardian's Name (print)	Parent or Guardian's Signature	Date

Please return this form to the teacher that distributed it. Thank you!

Sources and Totals of Project Data

School	Class	# of enrolled students	# of returned student permission forms	# of students agreeing to any type of research participation	# of students who returned a "no participation" form	Total student interviews	Total number of focus groups	Total number of focus group participants	Total surveys completed	Total teacher/ adult community member interviews
EHS	Yurok III–IV	11	11	9	2	4	3	13	25	5
	AP Spanish	25	19	16	3	4	2	6		
	ELD Support	20	6	4	2	4	0	0		
MHS	Yurok I–II	32	16	12	4	3	3	19	19	1
	Yurok III–IV	7	5	5	0	1	1	7		
HVHS	Yurok II	15	8	7	1	2	1	2	14	3
	Yurok III–IV	8	4	4	0	2	0	0		
	Civics	14	4 (2 unique)	4 (2 unique)	2 (saw but uncollected)	0	0	0		

DNHS									
Yurok II/ III/IV	21	7	5	2	2	1	2	8	2
Spanish for Spanish--Speakers	23	12	5	7	4	0	0		
Interviews unaffiliated with schools									3
Totals	176	95	69	23	26	11	49	66	15

Note: The full study includes data on im/migrant youth of Latin American origin in California schools, but that data has been set aside for a subsequent publication, as it was too much data and too many variables for one book.

NOTES

Preface

1. A *shtetl* is the Yiddish term for a small village in Eastern Europe where Ashkenazi Jews lived before the Holocaust.

2. The Russian word *pogrom* refers to violent destruction or demolition, and is particularly used to describe violence toward Jews in Russia and Eastern Europe in the second half of the nineteenth century and through the first half of the twentieth century.

Chapter 1

1. A pseudonym.

2. Klamath is the main small town on the Yurok Indian Reservation in far Northern California and where the Tribe's headquarters are located. With a population that stays below a thousand residents, Klamath has an elementary school, casino, gas station, and a smattering of local businesses. The mouth of the Klamath River is adjacent to the town, where it meets the Pacific Ocean. Because the Reservation has a majority-Yurok population and is the location of many cultural projects, young people growing up in Klamath have access to Yurok culture in a way that is distinct from those growing up in White-majority towns.

3. Native American students have far lower achievement scores than their non–Native American counterparts on English, language arts, and math testing, and the vast majority of Native American students in Humboldt County do not meet college-readiness benchmarks upon graduation. See Simon, Theodora, Linea Nelson and Taylor Chambers (2020), *Failing Grade: The Status of Native American Education in Humboldt County*, American Civil Liberties Union of Northern California, https://www.aclunc.org/sites/default/files/ACLU%20Humboldt%20report%2010%2026%2020%20final%20web.pdf.

4. Many Yurok people I spoke with talked about themselves in relation to gendered divisions of roles and responsibilities within Yurok custom. Such gendered language is not meant to be exclusive, but rather reflects ways in which traditional Indigenous life has been transposed into the present day.

5. Two-spirit is a term used to refer to people who have some type of sexual or gender identity diversity that goes beyond a singular masculine or feminine identity. It is commonly used to define a range of Native American LGBTQIA+ people.

6. The original declaration in December 2021 used the language of Missing and Murdered Indigenous Women, as did the art installation I refer to in the epilogue. However, shortly after that, the language was updated to MMIP, which is what the Tribe continues to use.

Chapter 2

1. Although one of many variables, some concerning mental health indicators for youths coincided with the rise of smartphone-driven incessant access (Haidt 2024).

2. I hereafter refer to the organization as Two Feathers, and when citing from its website as TF-NAFS.

3. Humboldt State University (HSU) changed its name to California Polytechnic Institute, Humboldt, in 2022. I use the term HSU in direct quotes and otherwise refer to it hereafter as Cal Poly Humboldt, its local nickname.

4. Judge Abbi Abinanti is Chief Judge of the Yurok Court in Northern California and a leader in culturally based justice processes that are in line with Native American values. See: Makepeace, Anne (2017), "Tribal Justice," from https://www.makepeaceproductions.com/tribal justice/press/; Clarren, R. (2017, November 30), "Judge Abby Abinanti Is Fighting for Her Tribe—and for a Better Justice System," from https://www.thenation.com/article/archive/judge -abby-abinanti-is-fighting-for-her-tribe-and-for-a-better-justice-system/.

5. As of 2022, the Yurok Tribe's Enrollment Department counts 1,445 enrolled members ages zero to seventeen, with an additional ninety-nine enrolled eighteen-year-olds, but this does not differentiate between those who live in the region and those who do not.

6. Humboldt County has the highest percentage of youth with high ACES scores in the state, at 29 percent in 2022. See: Let's Get Healthy California. (2022), "Adverse childhood experiences have a lasting, harmful effect on health and wellbeing," from https://letsgethealthy.ca.gov /goals/healthy-beginnings/adverse-childhood-experiences/.

7. United Indian Health Services (UIHS) is the main health care provider for Native American people in Humboldt and Del Norte Counties in California. Often critiqued for having inadequate care and long waits to be seen in Humboldt County, which is chronically underserved for medical care in general, UIHS is inextricably bound up in the story of settler colonialism. Health care for Native Americans was transferred from the War Department to the Bureau of Indian Affairs (BIA) in 1849. In 1954, it was determined that the BIA was not meeting its mandate in health care provision, and two decades of different models of care preceded the official establishment in 1970 of UIHS, which was initially an Indian-led creation in 1960. Activism by the American Indian Movement (AIM) in the 1960s, the Civil Rights Movement, and many broken treaties, including the termination of California Indian Tribe status in 1963, all highlighted the need for Native American health autonomy, including culturally situated care, which UIHS is supposed to provide. UIHS (2022), "United Indian Health Service: Our History," from https:// unitedindianhealthservices.org/index.php/our-story/.

Chapter 3

1. The town motto "Eureka, I found it!" greeted visitors on a billboard at one of the entrances to town my entire childhood. Though meant to connote the gold rush, it also encapsulates the Doctrine of Discovery, whereby White people claim to have discovered a place that Native American people have already been living in.

2. There is not yet consensus on the best way to address gender neutrality in Spanish or Spanish-derived terms. Both Latinx and Latine have been taken up as gender-neutral terms to refer to people of Latin American origin in the United States, and I use Latinx here, as one of the more mainstream labels for this category of people, while recognizing its flaws. Surely the terminology will continue to evolve.

3. Pronounced "Jensaw."

4. Note that all names assigned to focus group participants are pseudonyms throughout this book, as the focus groups were intentionally designed to be anonymous.

5. At the Jump Dances and Brush Dances, there are families who help maintain the supply of food and drink for dancers and people attending the dances by running outdoor kitchens. These families tend to identify as culturally connected to their Native identities, as demonstrated by a willingness to expend resources and energy to maintain cultural practices. Many local tribal members, descendants, and families, across Yurok, Karuk, Hupa, and other local tribes, are involved in dances and dance camp labor.

6. EHS in general asks teachers to facilitate talking circles to foster student community. Based on teacher personality and trust with students, circles can be more or less impactful for students. Over the years of my research, I had the honor of sitting in several of Mr. Gensaw's talking circles in his classes. They are from the heart and provide real space for people to reflect and share how they are feeling. Students regularly commented that the circles were part of making the class feel like a safe space where they could share things with Mr. Gensaw and other classmates.

7. US history in all four case study schools is usually taught to eleventh graders.

8. Note that while "Hupa" refers to the language and ethnicity of the group, the "Hoopa" spelling is used in the Hoopa Tribe's official name, the geographic name of the Hoopa Valley, and the name of Hoopa Valley High School. The spelling differences are a product of colonization. The term for Hupa in the Hupa language is *Na:tinixwe*.

9. In fact, this book entered production shortly after the second Trump administration began in early 2025, so I do not address the wholesale dismantling of the Department of Education, coupled with the attacks on and defunding of diversity, equity, and inclusion work, which will surely impact the themes addressed herein.

Chapter 4

1. The subtitle of this section, "Where the horses have the right of way," is McKinleyville's town motto.

2. In 2019, the city of Arcata, after a public referendum, removed a statue of McKinley that was the centerpiece of that town's plaza from 1906 and throughout my childhood, as a way to distance itself from the racist and imperialist platform he embodied. See Ferrara, John Ross (2018, March 29), "7 Things You Probably Didn't Know About the Ol' McKinley Statue in Arcata's Plaza," from https://lostcoastoutpost.com/2018/mar/29/7-things-you-probably-didnt-know -about-ol-mckinley/ for more on the McKinley statue.

3. I collected data across the two Yurok classes: the combined Yurok III–IV level class and the Yurok I–II level class. Both classes had very high response rates and enthusiastic participation and made a robust contribution to the study. There was such robust participation in the research from students in MHS's two Yurok classes that I ended up getting a much more comprehensive view of the classes than in other schools that had lower participation rates across a larger number of classes. Such participation was in part encouraged by my long-standing relationship with Mr. Gensaw, who himself was invested in the research taking place. His enthusiasm for the study appeared to motivate students, who, as at EHS, generally adored him. Because of this, MHS has the second-highest participation rate after EHS.

4. Awok is the word that Yurok people put in front of the name of someone who has died.

5. Awok Kathleen Vigil retired from MHS at the end of academic year 2019–2020, and Mr. Gensaw began there in fall 2020. When Mr. Gensaw moved to teach Yurok at Del Norte High

School in fall 2022, a new teacher took over both his EHS and MHS classes, but had to drive about ninety minutes from Hoopa each day to do so.

6. "Coming up" is common slang for "growing up."

7. California's mission history has its own enormous literature that those interested can seek out: Jackson, Robert H. and Edward Castillo (1996), *Indians, Franciscans, and Spanish Colonization: The Impact of the Mission System on California Indians*, Albuquerque, University of New Mexico Press; Kryder-Reid, E. (2016), *California Mission Landscapes: Race, Memory, and the Politics of Heritage*. Minneapolis, University of Minnesota Press; Risling Baldy, Cutcha (2017), "The San Diego Mission and Kumeyaay Revolt: A (decolonized) mission report written by my nine year old daughter or don't try to tell me that fourth graders can't understand a more complex view of history," from https://www.cutcharislingbaldy.com/blog/the-san-diego -mission-and-kumeyaay-revolt-a-decolonized-mission-report-written-by-my-nine-year-old -daughter-or-dont-try-to-tell-me-that-fourth-graders-cant-understand-a-more-complex-view -of-history; Keenan, Harper B. (2019), "Selective Memory: California Mission History and the Problem of Historical Violence in Elementary School Textbooks," *Teachers College Record* 121: 1–28. In brief, the mission system was founded by Spanish Franciscan priests who came to California to convert Native American people to Christianity and forcibly train them for European colonial life. Native Americans were required to live in walled mission enclosures or separate rancheria settlements sponsored by missions, where they were taught Spanish, religion, and vocational skills such as construction, animal husbandry, and domestic labor. The missions are widely regarded by Indigenous people and others to have been systems of enslavement, yet a pro-mission history was taught as a mandatory unit in California's fourth grade until 2017, at which point it became an optional unit.

8. A traditional coming-of-age ceremony when a girl becomes a woman. The dance was suppressed for many years and has recently been revitalized as a rite of passage in the far Northern California region. See Risling Baldy, Cutcha (2018), *We Are Dancing for You: Native Feminisms and the Revitalization of Women's Coming-of-Age Ceremonies*, Seattle, University of Washington Press, for more information.

9. Mr. Gensaw has students in all his Yurok classes do a family tree project where they map their families, interview relatives if possible, and then present their findings to each other in class.

10. AP Spanish, as with any AP class, is weighted more heavily in student grade point average (GPA) calculations, so there is an incentive for college-bound students to take AP classes to get the additional GPA boost. There is no AP Yurok course offered.

11. It is worth noting that in many schools, this phenomenon extends to other marginalized student populations, such as those in special education.

12. All pseudonyms.

13. This book does not get into the politics of marijuana cultivation in relation to study themes, but like dams on the Klamath, water use and contamination for marijuana cultivation, both on and off reservation land, are pressing environmental issues in the area and for the Yurok Tribe. See Reed 2023 for more on settler cannabis. Note that California's legalization of marijuana has not solved water use issues, as legal grow sites continue to have as much demand for water as illegal ones, although contamination has somewhat improved with increased government oversight of the largest legal grows.

14. In spring 2022, some community members were protesting a very large-scale proposed legal grow on a mountain in Humboldt County and took steps that included trying to put a

measure on the ballot to limit the amount of marijuana grows that are allowable in a given space. Native American students described marijuana cultivation as an ongoing act of colonization of traditionally Native land and water.

15. Meetings for BIPOC students and their family members to gather and talk about school climate issues.

16. When I teach bystander interventions in my college-level human rights classes, for example, those are sometimes the activities that students remember most when we do end-of-semester reflections on what they have learned.

Chapter 5

1. Including incarcerated people in population numbers is highly political. Some state funds are distributed on a per capita basis, so towns with prisons get higher state revenues because of including incarcerated people as residents, while the communities that incarcerated people are from get lower revenues.

2. In spring 2022, I received permission from a number of Ms. McQuillen's twenty-one Yurok language students and their guardians to participate in interviews, focus groups, and surveys. Some of their insights appear in other chapters of this book.

3. All further quotes from Barbara McQuillen in this chapter are from this citation: McQuillen, Barbara (2022). Interview with author. #31CA #6DNHS. Yurok language teacher. Del Norte High School, Crescent City, California, 4/21/22. The rest of the quotes are not cited individually.

4. Teaching a tribal staff class four days a week, Ms. McQuillen offers the same lesson each day for a week, so employees can arrange their schedule to try to make at least one class, while others may choose to attend daily "for reinforcement." In spring 2022, there were six regulars coming to language class every day, but some days there would be as many as ten participants.

5. The town of Klamath is near the mouth of the Klamath River on the Yurok Indian Reservation, and Crescent City is the largest town thirty minutes north, off the reservation. Weitchpec is located near the northernmost part of the Yurok Indian Reservation, just under two hours from Klamath.

6. Nicole was one of the first people I interviewed for an earlier phase of this research in 2017 focused on the impact of Yurok language access on identity and participation, and her interview was part of the dataset for Gellman, Mneesha (2023), *Indigenous Language Politics in the Schoolroom: Cultural Survival in Mexico and the United States*, Philadelphia, University of Pennsylvania Press.

7. Chahpekw O'Ket-'oh (Stone Lagoon) Visitor Center is at Humboldt Lagoons State Park.

8. Last Chance Grade is a portion of Highway 101 clinging to the side of a mountain on the edge of the Pacific Ocean between Klamath and Crescent City where rockslides and mudslides have repeatedly washed over the highway, closing it and leading to ongoing construction that delays traffic in both directions.

Chapter 6

1. The phrase "how to be civilized" is from Tracy, Erica Eva. (2019), "Tribal Members Urge School District to Provide Transparency Around Funding," Hoopa Valley Tribal Administration, February 12, 2019, https://www.hoopa-nsn.gov/tribal-members-urge-school-district-to-provide-transparency-around-funding/.

2. Morek is the name of her family's ancestral village, and her first name, but at the time of research students used her second first name, Annie, calling her Ms. Annie.

3. Those who live to the south of the Hoopa Valley.

4. Such turnover is likely the result of the remote location as well as the conflictual politics of the district.

5. Dusty Rossman, Jim Roulsten, Jennifer Lane, and Craig Cornelson.

6. John Ray and Jennifer Glueck.

7. A pseudonym. Tai also presents as gender nonbinary and thus I use plural pronouns since they did not clarify their pronoun preference in the interview.

8. Ms. Natalie Scott née Carpenter (Hupa, Yurok, Karuk) is an HVHS teacher who teaches the Cultural Connections class, among others, helping students understand and experience local Native culture in context.

9. Some tribes in the far Northern California region give what is colloquially called "18 money," or sometimes "21 money," frequently tied to a percentage of casino revenues that are distributed to tribal members, meaning the payments enrolled members receive upon reaching age 18 or 21. The Yurok Tribe does not distribute per capita money in this way, but some other California tribes do.

10. A pseudonym.

11. This is a colloquial expression that indicates going out of the Hoopa Valley, frequently to larger coastal towns.

12. I spent time in 2018, 2020, and 2022 doing research at HVHS and EHS.

13. Refereeing, by the paid referees at high school matches.

14. A game played with a wadded-up ball made from old papers and a garbage can—basketball from trash—that students play as they say words in Yurok.

Chapter 7

1. Pronounced "Thayuhlen," with emphasis on *Thay* (thāy- uhlən).

2. The word Yurok means "down river [people]" in the language of the Karuk, the Native American Tribe that traditionally lived, and continues to live, up the Klamath River from Yurok territory. The downriver design is a common symbol used in Yurok artistry to identify people or things as Yurok.

3. All interview quotes in this chapter if not cited otherwise are from Gensaw, Thayallen (2022), Interview with author, #2 CA #1DNHS, Yurok III-IV student, Del Norte High School, Crescent City, California, 3/18/22.

4. My default assumption was always to deidentify student data, only switching to their real names when students and guardians gave permission to use their real names after reviewing a draft of the chapter they featured in.

5. In this book, I briefly address the traditional Yurok gender binary and put it in conversation with expansive conversations about gender identity happening in other spaces. This speaker is strongly rooted in a traditional Yurok conception of masculinity, and I respect that while also recognizing its limitations.

6. "Undam the Klamath" protests and strategy meetings have been a regular part of life for many people in Humboldt, Del Norte, and Trinity Counties who are affected by water shortages and fish kills based on the presence of the dams, which facilitate water supplies to farmers north of the Yurok Indian Reservation. For more, see: Bring the Salmon Home: Undam the

Klamath (2023), "The Path to Removal." Retrieved 3/22/23 from https://bringthesalmonhome.org/understanding-dam-removal/#how.

7. The Gasquet-Orleans (G-O) road was designed by the US Forest Service to facilitate resource extraction, including mining and timber harvesting, in the Six Rivers National Forest. The proposed road passed through land sacred to the Karuk, Tolowa, and Yurok Tribes, and was challenged in multiple courts, including in the US Supreme Court, where tribes ultimately lost and road construction began. The G-O road was stopped, partially constructed, when Congress passed the 1984 California Wilderness Act. See Maher, Anne (2018, June 1), "Saga of the G-O Road, 30 Years Later" from https://www.yournec.org/GO-Road-30yr-anniv.

8. Like Hoopa Valley High School, Margaret Keating is a public school on an Indian reservation that is administered by a regional district that is generally not staffed by Native American people, and as such, discord between Native American values and White school district plans frequently occurs, as it did in the 2000s and 2010s, resulting in lawsuits and settlements to address discrimination against Native American students.

9. I document such misrepresentation at the high school level in another book (Gellman 2024b).

10. See, for example, "Top 10 and Frequently Challenged Books Archive," American Library Association, https://www.ala.org/bbooks/frequentlychallengedbooks/top10/archive.

11. Yurok, Hupa, and Karuk Tribes in the Klamath/Trinity watershed hold Brush Dances (*mey-lee* in Yurok) as a curing or healing ceremony for a sick child. Yurok, Hupa, Karuk, and Tolowa Tribes also hold Jump Dances, which are world renewal ceremonies.

Chapter 8

1. All quotes from Lozen and Hosteen Nez in this chapter come from our interview, cited here and in the bibliography instead of following each quote: Nez, Lozen and Hosteen Nez (2022), Interview with author, #15CA #4MHS, Yurok I–II students, McKinleyville High School, McKinleyville, California. 4/6/22.

2. While I was masked all the time in indoor meetings even if students chose not to be, I generally unmasked for outside meetings if students did. If student masks stayed on, I made sure mine did as well.

3. To be clear, there are multiple active and vocal politicized Indigenous communities in the region, but they may not be easy to find information about, especially during COVID-19 and if young people didn't know where to look or have access to people that could direct them.

4. The Yurok Tribal Council passed a resolution in December 2021 declaring a state of emergency about Missing and Murdered Indigenous Women, and media attention has finally brought a little more visibility to this issue that has long been overlooked in Humboldt County. Casarez, Iridian (2021), "Yurok Tribes Declares Emergency in Response to Missing and Murdered Indigenous Women," from https://www.northcoastjournal.com/NewsBlog/archives/2021/12/17/yurok-tribes-declares-emergency-in-response-to-missing-and-murdered-indigenous-women.

5. Deidentified intentionally—a teacher at MHS.

6. Apex Learning Virtual School is an accredited, private online school for sixth through twelfth graders that offers a range of curricula and pairs students with teachers who provide support virtually.

Chapter 9

1. I avoid the term Caucasian in line with Mukhopadhyay, Carol C. (2008), Getting Rid of the Word "Caucasian," *Everyday Antiracism: Getting Real About Race in School*, Ed. Mica Pollock, New York, The New Press: 12–16, but repeat here verbatim the interviewee's quote.

Chapter 10

1. Victoria is one of the most humble people I know. She was reluctant to even include this chapter in the book because in Yurok culture, bringing attention to oneself is not considered appropriate. She constantly questions her own right to speak on behalf of the Yurok language, and yet, from an outsider's perspective, she is doing the critical work to promote its revitalization. To that end, Victoria wants to make clear that she is not in this work alone. She extends tremendous gratitude and appreciation for the many people who continue to work to restore the Yurok language, including but not limited to Elders 'aa-wok Jimmie James, 'aa-wok Aileen Figueroa, 'aa-wok Georgina Trull, 'aa-wok Archie Thompson, 'aa-wok Jessie Exline-VanPelt, and many other L1 Yurok speakers as well as Carole Lewis, Kay Inong, Seafha Ramos, Chelsea Reed, Annelia Hillman, Annie O'Rourke, Brittany Vigil-Burbank, Barbara McQuillen, James Gensaw, and Victoria's family, including her parents, husband, and children.

2. All of Victoria's quotes are from our interview: Carlson, Victoria (2022), Interview with author, #41CA #6 community, Yurok Language Program Manager, Klamath, California, 5/18/22.

3. Hoopa Elementary School sits across the parking lot from Hoopa Valley High School, and both are located on the Hoopa Valley Indian Reservation. Students from many backgrounds attend both schools, although the vast majority—upward of 85 percent in the 2010s—identify as Native American. The Yurok Reservation is just to the north of the Hoopa Valley Reservation and there is a long history of coexistence between the tribes. Victoria's experience of growing up Yurok in Hoopa is one shared by many Yurok people.

4. The 111 tattoo was traditionally a coming-of-age marker for Indigenous women for many western tribes, but during colonization it was banned. The practice has been making a resurgence among younger Native women who are willing to be visibly identified as Native, and there are only a handful of elders still living who had the tattoo ritually imparted in their youth.

5. College of the Redwoods is the community college south of Eureka, and more than a ninety-minute drive each way from her mother's house in Hoopa.

6. The Zapatista Army of National Liberation (Ejército Zapatista de Liberación Nacional; EZLN) is a notable case of Indigenous women denouncing patriarchy and redefining what Indigenous feminism can look like.

7. Sregon is a Yurok village located on the upper Klamath River below Weitchpec, traditionally associated with Yurok medicine people.

8. *Pey-cheek* means upriver, *pue-leek* means downriver, *lah* means people. So *pey-cheek-lah* refers to the upriver Karuk people, *pue-leek* refers to downriver Yurok people, and *ner'-er-nerh* refers to coastal Yurok people.

9. For me, *ama de casa* (meaning "owner/holder of keys"), the Spanish term for "housewife," was one language moment where the cultural weight of gender norms in Latin America was so important for understanding the Spanish term.

Chapter 11

1. The "2S" addition to LGBTQAI+ acknowledges people who identify as "two spirit," referring to the culturally situated third gender found in some Native American cultures, where

people identify as more than solely masculine or feminine and may take on identities of a sex beyond their biological one.

Epilogue

1. See Skye, Elizabeth (2022), Unbottling an Epidemic: Missing + Murdered Indigenous Women + Girls: Jane Doe Edition, https://www.sovereign-bodies.org/_files/ugd/6b33f7_c2393 cebdd9f46b5b0865b7cc7e7d823.pdf, Sovereign Bodies Institute, for another example of an art-based MMIP awareness campaign.

BIBLIOGRAPHY

ACLUNorCal (2015). "Eureka City Schools Officials Settle Lawsuit with National Center for Youth Law, ACLU." From https://www.aclunc.org/news/eureka-city-schools-officials-settle-lawsuit-national-center-youth-law-aclu. 1/29/2015.

Adams, David Wallace (1995). *Education for Extinction: American Indians and the Boarding School Experience, 1875–1928*. Lawrence, University Press of Kansas.

Alexander, Sage (2023). "Coastal Commission tosses appeals for Nordic Aquafarm's fish farm." *Times Standard*. https://www.times-standard.com/2023/12/15/coastal-commission-tosses-appeals-for-nordic-aquafarms-fish-farm/. 12/15/23.

Alvarado, Maurice (2022). Interview with author. #23CA #2community. Via Zoom video call. 4/12/22.

Anderson, Robert (2018). Interview with author. #63CA 3HVHS. History and Civics teacher. Hoopa Valley High School, California. 1/17/18.

Anonymous (2018). Interview with author. #26CA #14 EHS. Eureka High School, Eureka, California. 1/11/18.

Anonymous (2022a). Interview with author. #1CA #1HVHS. Yurok III–IV student. Hoopa Valley High School, Hoopa, California. 3/16/22.

Anonymous (2022b). Interview with author. #38CA #7HVHS. Yurok II student. Hoopa Valley High School, Hoopa, California. 5/9/22.

Au, Wayne. (2015). "High-Stakes Testing: A Tool for White Supremacy for Over 100 Years." *What's Race Got to Do with It?: How Current School Reform Policy Maintains Racial and Economic Inequality*. Ed. B. Picower and E. Mayorga. New York, Peter Lang: 21–43.

Austin, Gregory, Thomas Hanson, Nisha Bala, and Cindy Zheng (2023). Student Engagement and Well-Being in California, 2019–21: Results of the Eighteenth Biennial State California Healthy Kids Survey, Grades 7, 9, and 11. California Department of Education. https://data.calschls.org/resources/18th_Biennial_State_1921.pdf.

Berryman, Mere, Suzanne SooHoo, and Ann Nevin, eds. (2013). *Culturally Responsive Methodologies*. UK, Emerald.

Bowen, Serenity (2022). Interview with author. #36CA #5 community. Via telephone. 4/26/22.

Brayboy, Bryan McKinley Jones (2005). "Toward a Tribal Critical Race Theory in Education." *Urban Review* 37: 425–446.

Brayboy, Bryan McKinley Jones (2013). "Tribal Critical Race Theory: An Origin Story and Future Directions". In *Handbook of Critical Race Theory in Education*. M. Lynn and A. D. Dixson, eds. New York, Routledge: 88–100.

Brayboy, Bryan McKinley Jones, Heather R. Gough, Beth Leonard, Roy F. Roehl II, and Jessica A. Solyom (2012). "Reclaiming Scholarship: Critical Indigenous Research Methodologies." *Qualitative Research: An Introduction to Methods and Design*. Ed. S. D. Lapan, M. T. Quartaroli, and F. J. Riemer. San Francisco, CA, John Wiley & Sons, Inc./Jossey-Bass.

Bring the Salmon Home: Undam the Klamath (2023). "The Path to Removal." Retrieved 3/22/23 from https://bringthesalmonhome.org/understanding-dam-removal/#how.

Brodkin, Karen (1998). *How Jews Became White Folks and What That Says About Race in America*. New Jersey, Rutgers University Press.

Burgos-Debray, Elisabeth, ed. (1983). *I, Rigoberta Menchú: An Indian Woman in Guatemala*. London, Verso.

CADOE (2024). Culturally Sustaining Pedagogy. California Department of Education https://www.cde.ca.gov/ci/pl/culturallysustainingped.asp.

Cahill, Cathleen (2011). "Tales of Subversion: How Native Peoples and Some Whites Sabotaged Federal Efforts to Kill a Culture." *North Coast Journal*. https://www.northcoast-journal.com/humboldt/tales-of-subversion/Content?oid=2132281. July 14, 2011.

California Department of Education (2022). "State Seal of Biliteracy." From https://www.cde.ca.gov/sp/el/er/sealofbiliteracy.asp.

Carlson, Victoria (2022). Interview with author. #41CA #6 community, Yurok Language Program Manager. Klamath, California. 5/18/22.

Casarez, Iridian (2020). "'A Curriculum That Empowers': Virtual Roundtable Focuses on Need for Better Education Outcomes for Native Youth." *North Coast Journal*. https://www.northcoastjournal.com/humboldt/a-curriculum-that-empowers/Content?oid=19179142. December 10, 2020.

Casarez, Iridian (2021). "Yurok Tribes Declares Emergency in Response to Missing and Murdered Indigenous Women." *North Coast Journal*. https://www.northcoast journal.com/NewsBlog/archives/2021/12/17/yurok-tribes-declares-emergency-in-response-to-missing-and-murdered-indigenous-women. December 17, 2021

Cimini, Kate (2021). "'We're Born Indian and We Die White': California Indigenous Fear COVID Deaths Undercounted." *CalMatters*. https://calmatters.org/california-divide/2021/03/california-indigenous-fear-covid-deaths-undercounted/. 3/2/2021.

Cintli Rodriguez, Roberto (2009). "'Greco-Roman Knowledge Only' in Arizona Schools: Indigenous Wisdom Outlawed Once Again." In *Rethinking Multicultural Education: Teaching for Racial and Cultural Justice*. Ed. Wayne Au. Milwaukee, WI, Rethinking Schools: 99–102.

Clarren, Rebecca (2017, November 30). "Judge Abby Abinanti Is Fighting for Her Tribe—and for a Better Justice System." From https://www.thenation.com/article/archive/judge-abby-abinanti-is-fighting-for-her-tribe-and-for-a-better-justice-system/.

Cubit (2022). "Hupa Demographics Summary." From https://www.california-demo graphics.com/hoopa-demographics.

Demmert, J., William, G., and John C. Towner (2003). A Review of the Research Litera-ture on the Influences of Culturally Based Education on the Academic Performance of Native American Students, Northwest Regional Educational Laboratory.

DiAngelo, Robin (2022). *White Fragility: Why Understanding Racism Can Be So Hard for White People (Adapted for Young Adults)*. Boston, Beacon Press.

Duran, Eduardo (2006). *Healing the Soul Wound: Counseling with American Indians and Other Native Peoples*. New York, Teachers College Press.

Easthouse, Keith. (2003). "Destination Humboldt Bay: The Liquid Natural Gas Debate Heats Up." *Northcoast Journal*. https://www.northcoastjournal.com/110603 /cover1106.html.

Eber, Christine. and Christine Kovic, eds. (2003). *Women in Chiapas: Making History in Times of Struggle and Hope*. New York, Routledge.

EdData (2022). "Eureka High School: Demographics. Education Data Partnership." From http://www.ed-data.org/school/Humboldt/Eureka-City-Schools/Eureka-Senior -High.

EdData (2022). Eureka Senior High School. From https://www.ed-data.org/school /Humboldt/Eureka-City-Schools/Eureka-Senior-High. Accessed 8/6/2024. Educa-tion Data Partnership.

EdData (2022). "Hoopa Valley High School: Demographics. Education Data Partnership." From https://www.ed-data.org/school/Humboldt/Klamath--Trinity-Joint-Unified /Hoopa-Valley-High.

EdData (2022). "McKinleyville High School: Demographics. Education Data Partner-ship." From http://www.ed-data.org/school/Humboldt/Northern-Humboldt-Union -High/McKinleyville-High.

EdData (2024). "Del Norte High School: Demographics. Education Data Partnership." From https://www.ed-data.org/school/Del-Norte/Del-Norte-County-Unified/Del -Norte-High.

Engster, Daniel (2020). "A Public Ethics of Care for Policy Implementation." *American Journal of Political Science* 64(3): 621–633.

Faingold, Eduardo D. (2018). *Language Rights and the Law in the United States and Its Territories*. Lanham, Lexington Books.

Fenelon, James V. (1998). *Culturicide, Resistance, and Survival of the Lakota (Sioux Nation)*. New York, Garland Publishing.

Fensterwald, John (2021, October 8). "California Becomes First State to Require Ethnic Studies in High School." From https://edsource.org/2021/california-becomes-first -state-to-require-ethnic-studies-in-high-school/662219.

Ferrara, John Ross (2018, March 29). "7 Things You Probably Didn't Know About the Ol' McKinley Statue in Arcata's Plaza." *Lost Coast Outpost*. https://lostcoastoutpost.com /2018/mar/29/7-things-you-probably-didnt-know-about-ol-mckinley/.

Focus Group 1.1 (2022). Focus group with author. #1CA #1EHS. Yurok III–IV students. Eureka High School, Eureka, California. 3/8/22.

Focus Group 3.3 (2022). Focus group with author. #3CA #3EHS. Yurok III–IV students. Eureka High School, Eureka, California. 3/15/22.

Focus Group 4.1 (2022). Focus group facilitated by teacher. #4CA #1MHS, Yurok III–IV students. McKinleyville High School, McKinleyville, California. 3/15/22.

Focus Group 6.2 (2022). Focus group with author. #6CA #2MHS. Yurok I–II students. McKinleyville High School, McKinleyville, California. 3/30/22.

Focus Group 10.1 (2022). Focus group with author. #10CA #1DNHS, Yurok III–IV students. 4/4/22. Del Norte High School. Crescent City, California. 4/4/22.

Focus Group 11.1 (2022). Focus group with author. #11CA #1HVHS. Yurok II students. Hoopa Valley High School, Hoopa, California. 5/9/22.

Foxworth, Raymond, Laura E. Evans, Gabriel R. Sanchez, Cheryl Ellenwood, and Carmela M. Roybal (2022). "'I Hope to Hell Nothing Goes Back to The Way It Was Before': COVID-19, Marginalization, and Native Nations." *Perspectives on Politics* 20(2): 439–456.

Fujii, Lee Ann (2010). "Shades of Truth and Lies: Interpreting Testimonies of War and Violence." *Journal of Peace Research* 47(2): 231–241.

Garrett, Andrew (2014). "Basic Yurok." From https://escholarship.org/content/qt2vw 609w4/qt2vw609w4.pdf.

Garroutte, Eva Marie (2003). *Real Indians: Identity and the Survival of Native America.* Berkely, University of California Press.

Gellman, Mneesha (2021). "Collaborative Methodology with Indigenous Communities: A Framework for Addressing Power Inequalities." *PS: Political Science and Politics* 54(3): 535–538.

Gellman, Mneesha (2022a). "Collaboration as Decolonization? Methodology as a Framework for Research with Indigenous Peoples." *Qualitative and Multi-Method Research* 20(2): 8–13.

Gellman, Mneesha (2022b). "Unsettling Settler-Colonialism in Words and Land: A Case Study of Far Northern California." *International Journal of Critical Indigenous Studies* 15(1): 22–40.

Gellman, Mneesha (2023). *Indigenous Language Politics in the Schoolroom: Cultural Survival in Mexico and the United States.* Philadelphia, University of Pennsylvania Press.

Gellman, Mneesha (2024a). Considering Collaboration as Part of Your Research Design. *Doing Good Qualitative Research.* J. Cyr and S. W. Goodman. Oxford, Oxford University Press: 156–165.

Gellman, Mneesha (2024b). *Misrepresentation and Silence in United States History Textbooks: The Politics of Historical Oblivion.* Switzerland, Palgrave Macmillan.

Gellman, Mneesha, and Mandi Vuinovich. (2008). "From *Sulha* to *Salaam*: Connecting local knowledge with international negotiations for lasting peace in Palestine/Israel." *Conflict Resolution Quarterly* 26(2): 127–148.

Gensaw, James (2019). Personal communication with author. Yurok language teacher. Eureka High School, Eureka, California. 11/18/19.

Gensaw, James (2022). Personal communication with author. Eureka High School, Eureka, California. 3/15/22.

Gensaw, Thayallen (2022). Interview with author. #2 CA #1DNHS. Yurok III-IV student. Del Norte High School, Crescent City, California. 3/18/22.

Gone, Joseph P. (2013). "Redressing First Nations Historical trauma: Theorizing Mechanisms for Indigenous Culture as Mental Health Treatment." *Transcultural Psychiatry* 50(5): 683–706.

Greenson, Thadeus. (2020). "'Crawling in the Right Direction': A look at the state of the local cannabis industry from bookending perspectives." *North Coast Journal*. https://www.northcoastjournal.com/humboldt/crawling-in-the-right-direction /Content?oid=16848658. 3/18/20.

Haidt, Jonathan (2024). *The Anxious Generation: How the Great Rewiring of Childhood Is Causing an Epidemic of Mental Illness*. New York, Penguin.

HCOE (2024). The Native American Studies Model Curriculum. https://my.hcoe.net /native-american-studies-model-curriculum/, Humboldt County Office of Education.

hooks, bell (1994). *Teaching to Transgress: Education as the Practice of Freedom*. New York, Routledge.

Hornberger, Nancy H. (2008). *Can Schools Save Indigenous Languages? Policy and Practice on Four Continents*. New York, Palgrave Macmillan.

Ineese-Nash, Nicole (2020). "Is Resistance Enough? Reflections of Identity, Politics, and Relations in the 'In-Between' Spaces of Indigeneity and Settlerhood." *AlterNative: An International Journal of Indigenous Peoples* 16(1): 10–17.

Jackson, Robert H., and Edward Castillo (1996). *Indians, Franciscans, and Spanish Colonization: The Impact of the Mission System on California Indians*. Albuquerque: University of New Mexico Press.

Jacob, Michelle M. (2013). *Yakama Rising: Indigenous Cultural Revitalization, Activism, and Healing*. Tuscon, University of Arizona Press.

Joshi, Ella, Sy Doan, and Matthew G. Springer (2018). "Student-Teacher Race Congruence: New Evidence and Insight from Tennessee." *AERA Open* 4(4): 1–25.

Jung, Courtney (2008). *The Moral Force of Indigenous Politics: Critical Liberalism and the Zapatistas*. Cambridge, Cambridge University Press.

Kauanui, J. Kehaulani (2008). *Hawaiian blood: Colonialism and the politics of sovereignty and indigeneity*. Durham, NC, Duke University Press.

Keenan, Harper B. (2019). "Selective Memory: California Mission History and the Problem of Historical Violence in Elementary School Textbooks." *Teachers College Record* 121: 1–28.

Kirmayer, Laurence J., Joseph P. Gone, and Joshua Moses (2014). "Rethinking Historical Trauma." *Transcultural Psychiatry*. 51(3): 299–319.

Kryder-Reid, Elizabeth (2016). *California Mission Landscapes: Race, Memory, and the Politics of Heritage*. Minneapolis, University of Minnesota Press.

KTIEP (n.d.). *Native American Curriculum Catalog*. Hoopa, California, Klamath-Trinity Indian Education Program.

KTJUSD. (2022). "Program Overview." From https://www.ktjusd.k12.ca.us/apps/pages /index.jsp?uREC_ID=551291&type=d.

Ladson-Billings, Gloria (2021). *Critical Race Theory in Education: A Scholar's Journey*. New York, Teachers College Press.

Lara-Cooper, Kishan, Everett Colegrove, Tescha Gensaw, Charlene Juan, and Gabel Ammon (2022). "'In the Telling and in the Listening, Humanity Meets': Youth Testimonials of Resilience from Yesterday and Today." *The Routledge International Handbook of Indigenous Resilience*. Ed. Hilary N. Weaver. New York, Routledge: 222–237.

Lara-Cooper, Kishan, and Walter J. Lara Sr., eds. (2019). *Ka'm-t'em: A Journey Toward Healing*. Pechanga, CA, Great Oak Press.

Lee, Emma and Jennifer Evans, eds. (2021). *Indigenous Women's Voices: 20 Years on from Linda Tuhiwai Smith's Decolonizing Methodologies*. London, Bloomsbury Academic.

Let's Get Healthy California (2022). "Adverse Childhood Experiences Have a Lasting, Harmful Effect on Health and Wellbeing." From https://letsgethealthy.ca.gov/goals /healthy-beginnings/adverse-childhood-experiences/.

Lindsay, Constance A., and Cassandra M. Hart (2017). "Exposure to Same-Race Teachers and Student Disciplinary Outcomes for Black Students in North Carolina." *Educational Evaluation and Policy Analysis* 39(3): 485–510.

Love, Bettina L. (2019). *We Want to Do More than Survive: Abolitionist Teaching and the Pursuit of Educational Freedom*. Boston, Beacon Press.

Lowry, Chag (2014). "History and Hope." From https://www.youtube.com/watch?v= 4FSiiuMAfFo.

Lowry, Chag, and Rahsan Ekedal (2019). *Soldiers Unknown*. Pechanga, CA, Great Oak Press.

Mack, Kristen, and John Palfrey. (2020). "Capitalizing Black and White: Grammatical Justice and Equity." https://www.macfound.org/press/perspectives/capitalizing -black-and-white-grammatical-justice-and-equity. 8/6/20.

Madley, Benjamin (2016). "Understanding Genocide in California under United States Rule, 1846–1873." *Western Historical Quarterly* 47(4): 449–461.

Madley, Benjamin (2019). "California's First Mass Incarceration System: Franciscan Missions, California Indians, and Penal Servitude, 1769–1836." *Pacific Historical Review* 88(1): 14–47.

Maher, Anne (2018, June 1). "Saga of the G-O Road, 30 Years Later." From https://www .yournec.org/GO-Road-30yr-anniv.

Makepeace, Anne (2017). "Tribal Justice." From https://www.makepeaceproductions .com/tribaljustice/press/.

Maramba, Dina C., and Samuel D. Museus (2013). "Examining the Effects of Campus Climate, Ethnic Group Cohesion, and Cross-Cultural Interaction on Filipino American Students' Sense of Belonging in College." *Journal of College Student Retention: Research, Theory & Practice* 14(4): 495–522.

Margolis, Rebecca (2023). *Yiddish Lives On: Strategies of Language Transmission*. Montreal, McGill-Queen's University Press.

McCarty, Teresa L., Mary Eunice Romero-Little, Larissa Warhol, and Ofelia Zepeda (2009). "Indigenous Youth as Language Policy Makers." *Journal of Language, Identity, and Education* 8(5): 291–306.

McGeary, Stephanie (2019). "Eureka High Students to Receive First California Seal of Biliteracy in Yurok Language Tonight." Lost Coast Outpost. https://lostcoastoutpost .com/2019/may/14/eureka-high-students-receive-first-california-seal/. 5/14/2019.

McKinleyville Chamber of Commerce (2022). "Pony Express Days." From https:// mckinleyvillechamber.com/member-services/pony-express-days2022/.

McQuillen, Barbara (2017). Interview with author. #12CA. Language teacher and staff member of Yurok Tribe's Education Department. Del Norte High School, Crescent City and Klamath, California. 7/24/17.

McQuillen, Barbara (2022). Interview with author. #31CA #6DNHS. Yurok language teacher. Del Norte High School, Crescent City, California. 4/21/22.

Meek, Barbra A. (2010). *We Are Our Language: An Ethnography of Language Revitalization in a Northern Athabascan Community*. Tuscon, University of Arizona Press.

Meng, Qingmin (2023). "A Locational Analytics Approach to COVID-19 Discrimination and Inequality Against Minorities Across the United States." *Social Science & Medicine* 318(115618): 1–8. https://doi.org/10.1016/j.socscimed.2022.115618.

Miranda, Deborah A. (2012). *Bad Indians: A Tribal Memoir*. Berkeley, Heyday.

Montes, Verónica, and María Dolores Paris Pombo (2019). "Ethics of Care, Emotional Work, and Collective Action of Solidarity: The Patronas in Mexico." *Gender, Place & Culture* 26(4): 559–580.

Moore, David D., and Don Coyhis (2020). "The Psychologist and Allied Behavioral Health Facilitators Retrained as Humanistic Firestarters." In *Radical Psychology: Multicultural and Social Justice Decolonization Initiatives*. Ed. S. O. Gelberg, M. A. Poteet, D. D. Moore, and D. Coyhis. Lanham, Lexington Books: 61–88.

Moorehead Jr., Virgil (2022). Interview with author. Executive Director. Two Feather Family Services, McKinleyville, California. 4/20/22.

Mukhopadhyay, Carol C. (2008). Getting Ride of the Word "Caucasian." *Everyday Antiracism: Getting Real About Race in School*. Ed. M. Pollock. New York, New Press: 12–16.

Nance, Jason P. (2015). "Over-Disciplining Students, Racial Bias, and the School-to-Prison Pipeline." *University of Richmond Law Review* 50: 1063–1074.

Nelsen, Matthew D. (2021). "Cultivating Youth Engagement: Race & the Behavioral Effects of Critical Pedagogy." *Political Behavior* 43(2): 751–784.

Nelsen, Matthew D. (2023). *The Color of Civics: Civic Education for a Multiracial Democracy*, Oxford University Press.

Nez, Lozen (2022). "11th Grader Writes Letter to Local School Admin Asking for Indigenous History to Be More Accurately Represented." https://kymkemp.com/2022 /05/11/11th-grader-writes-letter-to-local-school-admin-asking-for-indigenous -history-to-be-more-accurately-represented. 5/11/2022, Redheaded Blackbelt.

Nez, Lozen, and Hosteen Nez (2022). Interview with author. #15CA #4MHS. Yurok I–II students. McKinleyville High School, McKinleyville, California. 4/6/22.

Norton, Jack (1979). *Genocide of Northwestern California: When Our Worlds Cried*. San Francisco, Indian Historian Press.

O'Rourke, Morek Annie (2022). Interview with author. #32CA #4HVHS. Yurok language teacher. Hoopa Valley High School, Hoopa, California. 4/22/22.

Olson, Tim (2022). Interview with author. #11CA #4EHS. Eureka High School, Eureka, California. 4/1/22.

Olthuis, Marja-Liisa, Suvi Kivelä, and Tove Skutnabb-Kangas (2013). *Revitalising Indigenous Languages: How to Recreate a Lost Generation*. Bristol, Multilingual Matters.

Ongtooguk, Paul, and Claudia S. Dybdahl (2008). "Teaching Facts, Not Myths, About Native Americans." *Everyday Antiracism: Getting Real About Race in School*. Ed. M. Pollock. New York, New Press: 204–208.

Overall, Michael (2022). "Cherokee Nation Opens $20 Million Immersion Facility Where English Becomes a Foreign Language." From https://www.nativeoklahoma .us/cherokee-nation-opens-20-million-immersion-facility-where-english-becomes -a-foreign-language/. 11/11/2022.

Pachirat, Timothy (2018). *Among Wolves: Ethnography and the Immersive Study of Power*. New York, Routledge.

Paglayan, Augustina (2022). "Education or Indoctrination? The Violent Origins of Public School Systems in an Era of State-Building." *American Political Science Review* 116(4): 1242–1257.

Paris, Django (2020). "Culturally Sustaining Pedagogies in the Project of Black and Indigenous Solidarities on Turtle Island." *Education in Movement Spaces*. Ed. A. Eagle Shield, D. Paris, R. Paris, and T. San Pedro. New York, Routledge: 23–29.

Paris, Django, and H. Samy Alim (2014). "What Are We Seeking to Sustain Through Culturally Sustaining Pedagogy? A Loving Critique Forward." *Harvard Educational Review* 84(1): 85–100.

Pollock, Mica, ed. (2008). *Everyday Antiracism: Getting Real About Race in School*. New York, New Press.

Powers, Kristin M. (2006). "An Exploratory Study of Cultural Identity and Culture-Based Educational Programs for Urban American Indian students." *Urban Education* 41(1): 20–49.

Prose, Francine (2023). "Ron DeSantis' Academic Restrictions Show He Hopes to Change History by Censoring It." *Guardian*. https://www.theguardian.com/books /2023/feb/09/ron-desantis-florida-education-censorship. 9/9/23.

Prussing, Erica (2007). "Reconfiguring the Empty Center: Drinking, Sobriety, and Identity in Native American Women's Narratives." *Culture, Medicine and Psychiatry* 31(4): 499–526.

Race Counts (2024). McKinleyville. https://www.racecounts.org/city/mckinleyville/.

Reay, Diane (2017). *Miseducation: Inequality, Education, and the Working Class*. Bristol, Policy Press.

Redding, Christopher (2019). "A Teacher Like Me: A Review of the Effect of Student–Teacher Racial/Ethnic Matching on Teacher Perceptions of Students and Student Academic and Behavioral Outcomes." *Review of Educational Research* 89(4): 499–535.

Reed, Kaitlin (2023). *Settler Cannabis: From Gold Rush to Green Rush in Indigenous Northern California*. Seattle, University of Washington Press.

Risling Baldy, Cutcha (2017). "The San Diego Mission and Kumeyaay Revolt: A (Decolonized) Mission Report Written by My Nine Year Old Daughter or Don't Try to Tell Me That Fourth Graders Can't Understand a More Complex View of History." From https://www.cutcharislingbaldy.com/blog/the-san-diego-mission-and-kumeyaay-revolt-a-decolonized-mission-report-written-by-my-nine-year-old-daughter-or-dont-try-to-tell-me-that-fourth-graders-cant-understand-a-more-complex-view-of-history.

Risling Baldy, Cutcha (2018). *We Are Dancing for You: Native Feminisms and the Revitalization of Women's Coming-of-Age Ceremonies*. Seattle, University of Washington Press.

Rivera, Rafael (2022). Interview with author. 4#CA #2EHS. Spanish and English Language Development Support Teacher. Eureka High School, Eureka, California. 3/28/22.

Ross, David, Rachel Hinton, Meheret Melles-Brewer, Danielle Engel, Willibald Zeck, Lucy Fagan, Joanna Herat, Gogontlejang Phaladi, David Imbago-Jácome, Pauline Anyona, Alicia Sanchez, Nazneen Damji, Fatiha Terki, Valentina Baltag, George Patton, Avi Silverman, Helga Fogstad, Anshu Banerjee, and Anshu Mohan (2020). "Adolescent Well-Being: A Definition and Conceptual Framework." *Journal of Adolescent Health* 67(4): 472–476. Available at: https://www.ncbi.nlm.nih.gov/pmc/articles/PMC7423586/.

Rus, Jan, Rosalva Aída Hernández Castillo, and Shannan L. Mattiace (2003). *Mayan Lives, Mayan Utopias: The Indigenous Peoples of Chiapas and the Zapatista Rebellion*. Lanham, Rowman & Littlefield.

Sabzalian, Lailani (2019). *Indigenous Children's Survivance in Public Schools*. New York, Routledge.

Savage, J. A. (2022). "Aquafarm Ecology: Energy and Water In, Water and GHG Out, Fish on the Go." *North Coast Journal*. https://www.northcoastjournal.com/humboldt/aquafarm-ecology-energy-and-water-in-water-and-ghg-out-fish-on-the-go/Content?oid=22925743. 3/3/22.

Save California Salmon (2020). "Advocacy and Water Protection in Native California Curriculum." From https://savecaliforniasalmonteachersre.godaddysites.com/our-curricula.

Schunneman, Danielle (2022). Interview with author. #20CA #1community. Via Zoom video call. 4/10/22.

Scott, James C. (1990). *Domination and the Arts of Resistance: Hidden Transcripts*. New Haven, Yale University Press.

Simon, Theodora, Linea Nelson and Taylor Chambers (2020). *Failing Grade: The Status of Native American Education in Humboldt County*. https://www.aclunc.org/sites

/default/files/ACLU%20Humboldt%20report%2010%2026%2020%20final%20web
.pdf, American Civil Liberties Union of Northern California.

Sirleaf, Matiangai (2023). "Rendering Whiteness Visible." *American Journal of International Law* 117(3): 484–487.

Skye, Elizabeth (2022). Unbottling an Epidemic: Missing + Murdered Indigenous Women + Girls: Jane Doe Edition. https://www.sovereign-bodies.org/_files/ugd/6b33f7_c2393cebdd9f46b5b0865b7cc7e7d823.pdf, Sovereign Bodies Institute.

Slack, Jeremy (2019). *Deported to Death: How Drug Violence Is Changing Migration on the US–Mexico Border.* Oakland, University of California Press.

Solorzano, Daniel, Miguel Ceja, and Tara Yosso (2000). "Critical Race Theory, Racial Microaggressions, and Campus Racial Climate: The Experiences of African American College Students." *Journal of Negro Education* 69(1/2): 60–73.

Sovereign Bodies Institute (2021). To' kee skuy' soo ney-wo-chek'—I Will See You Again in a Good Way." Year 2 Progress Report, Missing and Murdered Women, Girls, and Two Spirit People of Northern California. https://www.sovereign-bodies.org/_files/ugd/6b33f7_d7e4c0de2a434f6e9d4b1608a0648495.pdf.

Stephen, Lynn (2013). *We Are the Face of Oaxaca: Testimony and Social Movements.* Durham, Duke University Press.

Supahan, Sarah E. (n.d.). *Points of View vs. Historical Bias: Recognizing Bias in Texts About Native Americans.* Hoopa, CA. Klamath-Trinity Joint Unified School District's Indian Education Program.

TF-NAFS. (2022). "Two Feathers: Native American Family Services." From https://twofeathers-nafs.org/.

Thomason, Andy (2023). "Florida's State Colleges Say They'll Ban Promotion of Critical Race Theory." From https://www.chronicle.com/article/floridas-state-colleges-say-theyll-stop-promoting-critical-race-theory. 1/18/23.

Tracy, Erica Eva (2019). "Tribal Members Urge School District to Provide Transparency Around Funding." From https://www.hoopa-nsn.gov/tribal-members-urge-school-district-to-provide-transparency-around-funding/. 2/12/2019.

Tuhiwai Smith, Linda (2012). *Decolonizing Methodologies: Research and Indigenous Peoples.* London, Zed Books.

Tula, María Teresa, and Lynn Stephen (1994). *Hear My Testimony: María Teresa Tula, Human Rights Activist of El Salvador.* Boston, South End Press.

UIHS (2022). "United Indian Health Service: Our History." From https://unitedindianhealthservices.org/index.php/our-story/.

United States Census Bureau (2024). Crescent City, California. https://data.census.gov/profile/Crescent_City_CCD,_Del_Norte_County,_California?g=060XX00US0601590620. Accessed 8/7/2024.

United States Census Bureau (2 024). Eureka, California. https://data.census.gov/profile/Eureka_city,_California?g=160XX00US0623042#income-and-poverty Accessed 8/5/2024.

United States Census Bureau (2024). McKinleyville, California. https://data.census.gov /profile/McKinleyville_CDP,_California?g=160XX00US0644910, Accessed 8/7/2024.

Valenzuela, Angela (1999). *Subtractive Schooling : U. S.–Mexican Youth and the Politics of Caring*. Albany, State University of New York Press.

Vizenor, Gerald, ed. (2009). *Survivance: Narratives of Native Presence*. Lincoln, University of Nebraska Press.

Vizenor, Gerald (2010). *Native Liberty: Natural Reason and Cultural Survivance*. Lincoln, University of Nebraska Press.

Walls, Melissa L., Dane Hautala, and Jenna Hurley (2014). "'Rebuilding our community': Hearing Silenced Voices on Aboriginal Youth Suicide." *Transcultural Psychiatry* 51(1): 47–72.

Walls, Melissa L., and Les B. Whitbeck (2012). "The Intergenerational Effects of Relocation Policies on Indigenous Families." *Journal of Family Issues* 33(9): 1272–1293.

Whitbeck, Les B., Mellissa L. Walls, Kurt D. Johnson, Allan D. Morrisseau, and Cindy M. McDougall (2009). "Depressed Affect and Historical Loss Among North American Indigenous adolescents." *American Indian and Alaskan Native Mental Health Research* 16(3): 16–41.

Wilson, Shawn (2008). *Research Is Ceremony: Indigenous Research Methods*. Halifax, Fernwood Publishing.

Wilson, Stan, and Barbara Schellhammer (2021). *Indigegogy: An Invitation to Learning in a Relational Way*. Germany, wgb Academic.

Wipf, Carly (2022). "'Long Overdue': Student Advocates Push for Indigenous Curriculum Countywide." *North Coast Journal*: 12–15. https://www.northcoastjournal.com /news/long-overdue-23404605. 4/28/22.

Wood, Elisabeth J. (2001). "The Emotional Benefits of Insurgency in El Salvador." In *Passionate Politics: Emotions and Social Movements*. J. Goodwin, J. M. Jasper and F. Polletta, Eds. Chicago, University of Chicago Press: 267–281.

Wyman, Leisy Thornton (2012). *Youth Culture, Language Endangerment and Linguistic Survivance*. Bristol, Multilingual Matters.

Yacovone, Donald (2022). *Teaching White Supremacy: America's Democratic Ordeal and the Forging of Our National Identity*. New York, Pantheon.

Yosso, Tara J. (2005). "Whose Culture Has Capital? A Critical Race Theory Discussion of Community Cultural Wealth." *Race, Ethnicity, and Education* 8(1): 69–91.

Yurok Tribe (1993). The Yurok Tribe Constitution, Article II Membership. https://yurok .tribal.codes/Constitution/II.

Yurok Tribe (1994). Tribal Code. Chapter 4.05, Enrollment and Membership. https:// yurok.tribal.codes/YTC/4.05.110, October 6, 2022.

Yurok Tribe (2022). "Yurok Language Program." From https://www.yuroklanguage .com/.

INDEX

ACKNOWLEDGMENTS

This book would not exist without the ongoing partnership of the Yurok Tribe. I am grateful for the time and energy of staff in the Yurok Tribe's Education Department and Yurok Language Program in helping to envision this project. I am humbled to help steward these testimonials. In particular, I owe tremendous thanks to language-keepers Victoria Carlson, James Gensaw, Barbara McQuillen, Morek Annie O'Rourke, and Carole Lewis for opening their Yurok classrooms to me over the years. The work you are doing is inspirational and intergenerational.

To Office of the Tribal Attorney Annie Perry and her colleagues, I am so grateful for your careful review at each step of this project—your feedback has been an invaluable learning tool on this and other related manuscripts. Similarly, feedback and process with Thayallen Gensaw and Lozen Nez has been insightful. May your words reach those who need to hear them. My thanks to Jim McQuillen for his willingness to take on this work together in the first place. Any errors persist despite my best intentions for accuracy as well as iterative stakeholder consultations.

I offer my enormous gratitude to the study participants, both those whose words are featured in this book, either named or anonymously, as well as the many participants whose stories are not included here. In order to look at the issue of well-being through a social science lens, I had to triangulate data—confirm information from multiple angles—and also hit saturation, meaning to get enough data that the findings were overwhelmingly confirmed by repeat data. This means there are many interviewees and focus group participants who won't see their stories on these pages, since there was simply too much data to include in one book. Nevertheless, their words contribute to the arc of the story told here, which would not have been possible without them.

I thank the teachers and administrators at the schools and districts that participated in this research. I took their time and energy through emails, phone calls, and meetings, and gave back an analysis that includes significant critique. It isn't always easy to hear that things are broken, but being willing to listen is the first step toward problem-solving. And to the teachers and administrators working to disrupt educational trauma and make more culturally sustaining curricula and pedagogical practices, thank you for your labor. It is legacy work.

To the many colleagues in far Northern California and beyond whose works are cited in this book's bibliography, thank you for your own analyses of Native American well-being from various angles, especially Kishan Lara-Cooper, Walter J. Lara Sr., Kayla Begay, Kaitlin Reed, Michelle Jacob, Leanne Betasamosake Simpson, Cutcha Risling Baldy, Leilani Sabzalian, and many more. Your printed thoughts have informed my own, and I hope will continue to be widely read and taken up into action. Gratitude for what you do.

To my colleagues at Emerson College, thank you for helping to co-create social justice–oriented, scholarly and creative spaces in which to explore the world of ideas. We see the seeds of possibility in the students that we inspire and are inspired by. My special thanks to Cara Moyer-Duncan for being my dear colleague at the Emerson Prison Initiative. Although it is with a different population than this book, Cara is a thought partner in well-being and education politics day in and day out. The whole Emerson Prison Initiative team helps me keep faith in the world of equity in education that we are trying to build.

I also thank the Huret family for the faculty award that allowed me to relocate to far Northern California for spring 2022, when the majority of the fieldwork for this book was carried out, as well as the Leibniz Institute for Educational Media/Georg Eckert Institute, which extended my leave time with a fellowship in Germany and allowed me to write a companion book to this one. I appreciate Emerson College, and my faculty and administrators therein, who made it possible for me to be committed to fieldwork and writing during those semesters.

When I decided to propose this book to University of Pennsylvania Press, it was because Jenny Tan was such a phenomenal thought partner on my previous book that I wanted to work with her again. Her careful engagement with prose and structure was a gift. I also thank my research assistant, Emerson College MA '24 Abigail Lange, for her meticulous and dedicated labor on every aspect of book production, from tracking down hard-to-find articles to copy editing and indexing. Jocelyn Peikes provided final copy editing and submission compliance assistance. Thanks also to Kiernan Rok, a high school vice principal interested in supporting culturally sustaining curricula, for reading the whole manuscript and providing excellent nudges to communicate things better.

I want to acknowledge my family, both bio and chosen, as a source of my own inner fire. My parents taught me to care for others and the earth as a baseline way of being in the world. My father's fierce work ethic and my mother's appreciation for creativity and self-care are my inheritance, which I work to balance in myself. To my *compadre* and *comadre* Bryan and Lisa, you have taken me in and helped me reground time and again, the gift of a lifetime. The difficult work of my own identity formation and quest for well-being in a broken world is one you have all helped me navigate.

To friends and colleagues in Boston and far Northern California, thank you for the many potlucks, child-care swaps, and power walks that help create and sustain a sense of community. In a world that is bent on isolating and dividing us, we come together to support each other's well-being. Friendship matters, and I am grateful for yours.

I have been late to my own party in recognizing the role of my religious minority status as a Jew at play in my interest in Indigenous and minority politics. The tumultuous politics of violence in Israel/Palestine across the lifespan of this book brought it to the forefront. I appreciate my Jewish community both in Boston/Brookline and California. You help me hold space to investigate how one can live a culturally grounded and spiritually infused life while not turning away from pain inflicted in the name of that identity. As my Jewish family reckons with our own identity politics, my scholarship and advocacy continue to be places where I explore how to be part of healing rather than hurting.

My children Matolah and Chayton both tire of my work governing their lives, and yet I think secretly they appreciate the way that politics infuses our family . . . or at least they will someday! Thank you, *mis queridos*, for going along with my plans even when they are in opposition to your own desires. In the bigger picture, may it feel like a net positive. To my husband Joshua, thank you for sharing the commitment to right livelihood. It isn't always easy, but aligning our work with our principles for justice is a core value that sparked our love, and it continues.

Silence renders invisibility. May this offering give voice and be part of structural change to support the well-being of all. Idealism is not naivete, but the persistence of hope.